Portals

Portals

Opening Doorways to Other Realities through the Senses

Lynne Hume

Oxford • New York

First published in 2007 by
Berg
Editorial offices:
1st Floor, Angel Court, 81 St Clements Street, Oxford, OX4 1AW, UK
175 Fifth Avenue, New York, NY 10010, USA

Berg is the imprint of Oxford International Publishers Ltd.

Library of Congress Cataloging in Publication Data
Hume, Lynne.
   Portals : opening doorways to other realities through the senses / Lynne
Hume.
      p. cm.
   Includes bibliographical references (p.   ) and index.
      ISBN-13: 978-1-84520-144-9 (cloth : alk. paper)
      ISBN-10: 1-84520-144-2 (cloth : alk. paper)
      ISBN-13: 978-1-84520-145-6 (pbk. : alk. paper)
      ISBN-10: 1-84520-145-0 (pbk. : alk. paper)
   1. Consciousness. 2. Senses and sensation. 3. Altered states of
consciousness. I. Title.

   BF311.H77 2007
   154.4—dc22
                                                                        2006027512

British Library Cataloguing-in-Publication Data
A catalogue record for this book is available from the British Library.

ISBN-13 978 184520 144 9 (Cloth)
ISBN-10 1 84520 144 2 (Cloth)

ISBN-13 978 184520 145 6 (Paper)
ISBN-10 1 84520 145 0 (Paper)

Typeset by JS Typesetting, Porthcawl, Mid Glamorgan
Printed in the United Kingdom by Biddles Ltd, King's Lynn

www.bergpublishers.com

To my son, Steve

How would you like to live in Looking-glass House, Kitty? I wonder if they'd give you milk in there?

Perhaps Looking-glass milk isn't good to drink – but oh, Kitty! Now we come to the passage. You can just see a little *peep* of the passage in Looking-glass House, if you leave the door of our drawing-room wide open: and it's very like our passage as far as you can see, only you know it may be quite different on beyond.

Oh, Kitty, how nice it would be if we could only get through into Looking-glass House! I'm sure it's got, oh! Such beautiful things in it!

Let's pretend there's a way of getting into it, somehow, Kitty.

Let's pretend the glass has gone all soft like gauze, so that we can get through.

Why, it's turning into a sort of mist now, I declare! It'll be easy enough to get through...

Lewis Carroll, *Through the Looking-Glass*

Contents

Acknowledgements

I wish to thank David Howes for helpful comments on early drafts, the editorial staff at Berg, and the work of the writers cited in this book who paved the way, enabling me to arrive at this point.

−1−

Entrances and Exits

Each of us lives within ... the prison of his own brain. Projecting from it are millions of fragile sensory nerve fibers, in groups uniquely adapted to sample the energetic states of the world around us: heat, light, force, and chemical composition. That is all we ever know of it directly; all else is logical inference. The senses are the portals to the mind.

Biocca, The Cyborg's Dilemma

Philosophers, visionaries and writers throughout history have written and discussed the notion of separate realities that can be accessed by moving beyond the physical body via some sort of doorway or passage. This idea has permeated children's stories as well. Lewis Carroll's 'looking glass' enabled readers to move, along with Alice in Wonderland, into a world that was similar, but strangely different in many ways to their own. Wonderland was a place where anything could happen: rabbits could speak, Cheshire cats could appear simply as a smile and fish were footmen.[1] If the reader persists in following the arguments in this book to its conclusion, Lewis Carroll's fictional world may not seem as bizarre as it once did. As I want to articulate, the everyday reality that we perceive through our senses can be altered dramatically by 'working' the senses using a variety of somatic stimuli, creating a paradigm shift in perception. Not only is this possible, but certain practices have been used the world over to bring about this shift in perception, which, as I point out using examples from vastly different cultures and historical epochs, include a kind of set of sensory syntactics to what we might call the spiritual encounter.

In my research into altered states of consciousness over several years, I have found not only that the notion of moving through some sort of portal or doorway to access another type of reality is widespread, but that there are certain techniques employed to do so. These techniques are used universally by shamans, monks, religious specialists and lay people, and involve different physical senses. Sometimes only one of the senses is involved (for example, visual concentration on a particular object) and sometimes a combination of senses is used. With the aid of the senses, and devices such as mandalas, voice and/or musical instruments, body movements and decoration, physical pain, and olfactory and tactile stimuli, it is possible to move from what we call mundane, or ordinary reality, into alternate reality.[2] This can be done with or without the use of entheogenic or psychedelic substances (drugs). All these techniques will be investigated and discussed under the general framework of sensorial anthropology, using a multidisciplinary approach.

The sub-field of sensorial anthropology has emerged in recent years to acknowledge the fact that most people in contemporary Western cultures have focused almost exclusively on the visual and the verbal, neglecting the importance of other senses. Yet one perceives the world through all the senses. The recent anthropological focus on the senses developed from an emergent interest in bodily modes of knowing and exploring how the possibilities of awareness contained within the senses were used by different cultures. Bodily modes of knowing become intimately connected to methods of healing in Nepal, for example, where Robert Desjarlais (1992) did fieldwork. Desjarlais studied the relationship between culture and emotional distress among the Yolmo Sherpa, a Tibetan Buddhist people living in north-central Nepal. Becoming an apprentice to a healer, he discovered that shamanic rites work principally to change how a patient feels, and shows the cultural forces that influence, make sense of and heal severe pain and other forms of malaise. Desjarlais calls for a more sentient anthropology and points to the profound role of aesthetic sensibilities in everyday life that could well be pursued more earnestly by fieldworkers. His own cultural background, he writes, did not precondition him for trance experiences, in spite of the fact that, unlike other anthropologists, he could let himself go enough to be able to enter a trance state – one that paralleled the descent of the gods into the body of his shaman teacher, Meme (Desjarlais 1992: 5):

> Taking the role of shamanic initiate, I would sit in a semi lotus position to the right of my 'guru' and attempt to follow the curing chants. In time, Meme would begin to feel the presence of the divine, his body oscillating in fits and tremors, and my body, following the rhythm of his actions, would similarly 'shake'. Tracked by the driving, insistent beat of the shaman's drum, my body would fill with energy. Music resonated within me, building to a crescendo, charging my body and the room with impacted meaning. Waves of tremors coursed through my limbs. Sparks flew, colors expanded, the room came alive with voices, fire, laughter, darkness.

After several months of learning how to use his body in a way that was conducive to acculturation (by picking up on sounds, smells, ways of talking, walking, sensing), his trance experiences slowly began to be more comparable to those that his guru experienced. The more experience he gained of trance, the more controlled, centred and steady were the visions he had. His own fieldwork in Tibet made him realize that it is possible to expand one's 'field of awareness', and that a 'less cognate, more sensate treatment' now seems needed by anthropologists who wish to really understand certain aspects of culture (Desjarlais 1992: 27).

The 'sensuous awakening' (Stoller 1997: xii) that has occurred within certain sectors of anthropology is providing us with more juicy, vibrant, sensual and exciting ethnographical accounts that take us into the field to experience the smells and feelings of what it is to actually 'be there' or to imagine other historical epochs in all their tasteful and distasteful glory. As a case in point, Stoller (1997: 48) writes of his experience in Nigeria:

> The acrid smell of burning resins wafts through Adamu Jenitongo's compound, preparing it for the *holle* (spirits). It is late afternoon in Tillaberi, and the sounds of a Songhay spirit possession ceremony crackle through the dusty air: the high pitched 'cries' of the monochord violin, the resonant clacks of bamboo drumsticks striking gourd drums, the melodious contours of the praise-singer's 'old words', the patter of dancing feet on dune sand.
>
> It is a white hot day in June 1987, and the mix of sounds and smells brings the spirits to Adamu Jenitongo's egg-shaped dunetop compound. Four mudbrick houses shimmer in the languorous heat. From under a thatched canopy at the compound entrance, the orchestra continues to play spirit music. [...] Drawn by pungent smells, pulsing sounds and dazzling dance, they visit it day and night.

One cannot help but be impressed with writing that transports us from sterile academic offices into the pulsing everyday life of Africa. Stoller's own terrifying bodily experience in Nigeria, where he became paralysed through the effects of sorcery, makes us aware of how our bodies and our senses are our greatest research tools for attuning us to other cultural realities. A more sensuous scholarship, suggests Stoller (1997: xvii), is one that accepts 'the complexities, tastes, structures, and smells' of the world.

These sensual complexities are what David Abram (1997: 1) came to acknowledge during his stay in Bali. One evening, as he stepped out of his hut in the rice paddies of eastern Bali, under a 'black sky rippling with stars', he encountered a 'whirling world', the sensation of falling through space and the realization that there was much to be learnt from listening to the land, to non-human creatures and becoming aware of ecological clues. He came to appreciate the world of insects and the importance of altering the common field of perception to include the perceptions of other creatures that inhabit the same world as humans, but experience it from a completely different universe. He discovered that the natural world that most Europeans regard as merely a pleasant backdrop to more pressing everyday concerns, consists of 'deeply mysterious powers and entities with whom the shaman enters into a rapport' (Abram 1997: 9). There are 'multiple nonhuman sensibilities that animate the landscape' including plants, animals, insects, forests, winds, and so on, and if humans can learn to propel their awareness laterally, outward into the landscape, as do the shamans, they can achieve an intimacy with non-human nature that can take them back to what has been lost – ancestral reciprocity with the animate earth.

What Westerners label 'spirits', suggests Abram, are primarily those modes of intelligence or awareness that do not possess a human form. Some intelligences lurk in non-human nature: the ability of a spider to spin a complex web, the organizational capabilities of ants, the nightlife of fireflies; and if one observes these natural, non-human existences, it leaves one open to 'a world all alive, awake, and aware' (Abram 1997: 19). Close observation of insects heightened Abram's own awareness of the 'countless worlds within worlds that spin in the depths of this world that we commonly inhabit', and during his sojourn in Bali he learned that his body could, with practice, enter sensorially into those dimensions (p. 19). He began to see and hear in ways that he had not experienced before: the subtle ways a breeze may flutter a single leaf on a whole tree, the precise rhythm of the crickets and the taste of a special power in a particular field at a specific time of day, when the shadows of the trees fall in a certain way, the smells on the grasses wafting in the wind and other natural facets to which he slowly became increasingly susceptible, all of which contributed to his appreciation of the interconnectedness of the human community and the natural landscape. We are, he says, human only in contact and conviviality with what is not human (Abram 1997: 22), and our senses are the media through which we can appreciate all this.

The senses can also be employed through archival research, as Constance Classen demonstrates. In *The Color of Angels*, her history of the senses from the Middle Ages to the rise of modernism, she evokes the rich sensory symbolism of a far-from-sanitized Europe of the Middle Ages. As well as uncovering the gender politics behind cultural constructs such as the 'dominating male gaze' and the 'nurturing female touch' (Classen 1998: 6), she discusses how the Renaissance women's sensibilities were linked with intuition, emotion and sensuality. The senses of smell, taste and touch were considered to be associated with the earthy female domain, and of lesser importance than the masculine senses of sight and hearing, which were accorded a more important role and linked with the more valuable attributes of culture and reason. Such unbalanced dichotomies in Western perspectives persisted into the modern era, with its masculine, rationalist model of the world and its disdain for anything connected with emotions and feelings.

Classen talks of the medieval obsession with the witch's supernatural sense of smell, 'her seductive/destructive touch, her evil eye, her gluttonous appetite, and her poisonous speech', all as 'evidence' of female sensory powers (1998: 6); and of the 'stench of hell' (p. 48), the 'fragrance of stigmata' (p. 52) and the 'sweet scents of heaven' (p. 46). Such evocative calling forth of a sensuous Europe, as well as the practical, everyday smells of the Middle Ages, with its lack of plumbing, its disguising of bodily odours with heavy perfume and its absence of hygiene, is lost in scholarship that is less concerned with the senses.

Many scholars are also referring to the documentary films (particularly *Les Maîtres fous*) of Jean Rouch that graphically and shockingly portrayed Hauka spirit possession. In *Les Maîtres fous*, possessed Africans are seen chomping sickeningly on boiled dog meat, drinking warm blood from a freshly slaughtered animal and frothing at the mouth. In a grotesque parody of white colonials, this dramatic display of spirit possession is, as Paul Stoller says, an 'incontestably embodied phenomenon' (1997: 65). External forces are enticed into willing bodies through the medium of culturally prescribed methods, using sights, sounds, smells and tastes through music, poetry, songs, perfumes, dance and bloody flesh. However, much more underlies the staging of this ritual performance of mimicry in the Hauka cult. It is itself a parody of the madness of colonial power through the equally powerful medium of mimicry; the Hauka empower themselves by demonstrating the insane behaviour and mannerisms of those caught up in a colonial regime which aims to undermine Hauka power and sensibilities, while engaging in what the colonials themselves would regard as a special kind of madness. Dressed in pith helmets and play-acting the swaggering antics of the white men, members of the Hauka movement informally undermine the power of the colonials by mimicking particular individuals and creating a ridiculous parody of the entire colonial government. The trance possession during these mimetic performances, along with frothing at the mouth, involves bulging eyes, contorted limb movements and the inability to feel pain, and the spirits possessing them, in many cases, are those of foreigners who entered the Hauka pantheon as violent spirits (Taussig 1993: 240).

While perhaps not quite as visceral as the Hauka spirit possession, other cultures employ equally provocative sensual material that has been, in the past, less than adequately conveyed or analysed in anthropological texts.

Anthropology of the senses, as explicated in David Howes' edited volume, *The Varieties of Sensory Experience* (1991), highlights the ways in which bodily senses influence social organization, conceptions of self and cosmos, the regulation of the emotions and other forms of cultural expression. It clearly demonstrates the textual and visual biases of the Western episteme, and the neglect of other sensory modalities, such as taste, touch and sound. The pluri-sensorial nature of the Shipibo-Conibo Indians of eastern Peru is given by Howes as one example of a culture that incorporates multiple ways of accessing knowledge. During a Shipibo-Conibo healing ritual a shaman is said to perceive, while in a hallucinogenic trance, pulsating designs that float downwards to the shaman's lips. On reaching his lips, the shaman then sings the designs into songs, and at the moment of coming into contact with his patient, the songs once again turn into designs that penetrate the patient's body, at which time the healing takes place. These design-songs also have an olfactory dimension, as their power is said to reside in their 'fragrance'. Indeed, the Shipibo-Conibo term *quiquin*, which means both 'aesthetic' and 'appropriate', is used to refer to pleasant auditory and olfactory as well as visual sensations.[3] Thus, not only are all the senses employed and acknowledged, but they become part of the transformation process that allows healing to take place.

In this book I investigate how all the senses are employed to enable people to move beyond the physical body into what has been described as other realms of existence, union with the divine or deeper levels of consciousness; the experiences people describe in these 'other realms', and their subsequent interpretations of the experiences are also discussed. The practical techniques used to take people through the portals, and the cosmological, symbolic and practical implications of portalling are also addressed, and questions are raised, such as: how is knowledge that is putatively derived from journeys through portals used to validate a culture's ideology and epistemology? I explore a range of spiritual practices in order to tease out and reflect upon the fundamental techniques that employ the senses in order to open 'the doors of perception' (Huxley 1971). My purpose is to delve into the phenomena in such a way as to highlight the commonalities of techniques, in spite of the vastly different contexts and frameworks within which they are employed, and to acknowledge that there are different ways of gaining knowledge in addition to intellect and reason.

In an article entitled 'Mirrors, Portals, and Multiple Realities', George MacDonald et al. discuss the cross-culturally common mystical experience called portalling – moving from one reality to another via a tunnel, door, aperture, hole or the like (MacDonald et al. 1989). An American movie screened in 2000 entitled *Being John Malkovich* highlighted the idea of using a doorway to enter a tunnel that led to someone else's consciousness and popularized the experience to a large public audience.

The notion of getting through an obstacle, or having a passage open up to permit entry to another, more sacred dimension, permeates myths, legends, religious writings and personal narrations throughout history. From many accounts, life in the physical, mundane world is connected to other planes of existence, but the passage from one to the other requires opening some sort of portal. Expressions such as 'gate', 'way', 'door', 'ladder', 'bridge', have been employed in religious discourse and texts to indicate that movement is indeed possible. Exceptionally holy people can provide the means of access. To Christians, Jesus Christ is 'the way, the truth, and the light', and one enters the Kingdom of Heaven through him. In the Acts of John 95:26–27, Jesus Christ is quoted by John as saying:

95:26 I am a door to you
       who knock on me. Amen.
95:27 I am a way to you
       the traveller. Amen.

In the Baha'i faith, the young man in Persia who announced, in 1844, the imminent appearance of the Messenger of God, was called the Báb, which means 'the Gate'. In some mystery religions, keys to closed doors form a symbolic part of esoteric knowledge (Butler 1970: 17, 31). And in Hinduism, Ganesh, often shown as sitting above a doorway, is the guardian of the threshold, armed with a hatchet to prevent the passage of miscreants (Eck 1985: 28).

In order to arrive at one's destination, the spiritual journeyer may have to surmount obstacles such as guarded doorways, walls of fire, curtains of mist, and face many ordeals. Access is always difficult and passing through thresholds is not without danger, a danger that is acknowledged in myths by the presence of monsters, spiders, dragons or other frightening apparitions that guard passages from one place to another. The bridge may be narrower than a hair, the cave lined with teeth, the passage a maze and the monsters numerous. Only the most stalwart adventurer transverses the many obstacles and seductive challenges encountered to reach the final goal. Having penetrated the impasse, however, the person may then feel oneness with the universe, meet an illuminated or enlightened being, or gain knowledge that is unattainable on the earthly plane.

Sometimes, by focusing on a visual device, such as a mandala, a mirror or pool of water, or a repetitive sound, such as drumming or rattling, or by donning a mask, one can achieve a sense of passing from one state of consciousness to another. A portal may or may not be acknowledged as the point through which one enters and leaves. Caves are both physical and imaginal entrances to other realms and figure prominently in the beliefs and practices of early humans. Anyone who has entered a silent, deep-set cave, crawled along a narrow passageway within a mountain or floated through waterways from the entrance of a cave, cannot help but be struck by a feeling of awe or the sensation of the numinous. In the next section I discuss the significance of caves; then I move on to some explanations for rock art that incorporate notions of transformation, and then to a discussion of trance, followed by the importance of the emotions.

Caves as Portals

Neoplatonist philosopher Porphyry (*c.*234–305) said that prior to the advent of temples, religious rites took place in caves (Walker 1983: 155). Many pagan mystery cults, such as those at Eleusis in Greece, both prior to and during the early Christian era, celebrated their most sacred rites in caves or underground chambers. Indeed, followers of the Mithra mystery cult in the first four centuries CE in Rome considered the cave so essential to proper worship that if the site of a temple had no natural cave, an artificial one was dug (Walker 1983: 155).

Many myths incorporate a descent into the underworld through a cave; and, like the mouths of rivers, caves were likened to the vagina of the Earth Mother. Cybele's cavern-shrines were also called marriage chambers, and Cybele's castrated priests claimed that none of their brotherhood ever died, but instead went 'down into the cavern' to be united with their goddess (Walker 1983: 155). Many holy hermitages were first established in caves, and some Hindu holy places were caves whose entrances were painted red to represent the Great Mother's yoni (vagina). The combination of Mother Goddess, yoni, cave, and their links with birth, death and rebirth are to be found in myths universally. The Earth Mother is both giver and taker of life, and the female body is viewed as both creation and destruction.

To penetrate a cave or a labyrinth was the equivalent of a mystical return to the womb of the Mother. The correlation of passageways to other worlds and a terrible mother figure emphasizes the connection between this world, the other world, birth and death, and a devouring Mother Earth illustrated in some myths by the *vagina dentata* (toothed vagina). In Malekula (Vanuatu), a terrifying female figure called Le-hev-hev guards the entrance to the cave of the dead. In order to pass by her, a labyrinthine design that is half obliterated is found on the ground in front of the cave. If the dead person can complete the design (knowledge that becomes known through a process of initiation in this world) they are allowed to pass through; if not, Le-hev-hev devours them (Deacon 1934).[4]

Rock Art

The decorated caves of the Palaeolithic era indicate that caves were magical or sacred places, entrances to other worlds and places of transformation. Indeed, it is now also suggested that they were sources of regenerative power, and that entering certain caves, such as those in western France, was like making a journey into another world. While early explanations of rock art suggested magical purposes to cave hunting scenes and other motifs, more recent research proposes that rock art actually depicted the mental imagery and somatic hallucinations experienced in trance (Lewis-Williams and Dowson 1993; Whitley 1998; Patterson 1998; Lewis-Williams 2002).

Images found in some Franco-Cantabrian Upper Palaeolithic cave art were most likely closely associated with various shamanic practices (Lewis-Williams and Clottes 1998: 13) and were probably a location for vision quests. Lewis-Williams and Clottes (p. 16) argue that caves were regarded as 'topographical equivalents to the psychic experience of the vortex and a nether world' by human beings living during the Upper Palaeolithic in western Europe. The surfaces of the caves were a 'thin membrane' between living humans on the outside and the beings and spirit-animals behind the cave wall surfaces. Cave art, they propose, enabled 'interaction between universal neuropsychological experiences and topographically situated caves.' The cave surfaces themselves became the portals, and the paintings and engravings reflected experiences in altered states of consciousness. The flickering of firelight on the uneven surfaces of cave walls would have provided a third-dimensional effect and moving shadows would have increased the vividness of the images.

Carol Patterson's investigation of petroglyph designs at a Willow Creek site in north-eastern California seems to confirm Lewis-Williams and Dowson's theory that certain designs most probably played a role in the process of achieving altered states of consciousness in prehistoric shamanic practices (Patterson 1998: 38). Patterson points out that visual images appear during the first stages of a trance state (this will be further articulated in chapter 2).

Patterson demonstrates from both archaeological and ethnographic evidence that shamanic practices of Northern Paiute culture in northern California and the

Great Basin have changed little over thousands of years. The main objective is to 'seek power', and the traditional method is to 'seek power through a dream or vision while spending time in a cave and fasting' (Patterson 1998: 38). Patterson interviewed present-day practising shamans, who confirmed that there are several caves in the Paiute territory where shamanistic power is still sought. They supplied her with interpretations of the designs and stated that they had experienced visual phenomena that resemble the glyphs recorded on the cave walls. Designs such as circles and wavy lines (like those described by Lewis-Williams and Dowson) were highly significant to the shamans interviewed by Patterson. They told her that circles represent power and dreaming, and indicate entrance and exit holes for the spirit of the rock, and that the wavy lines are the spirits coming (Patterson 1998: 46). A seeker has to undergo the ordeal of staying the night in a cave in spite of fear and hearing 'terrible noises' (p. 43). In order to bring about access to power and the spiritual realm, the shaman enters a trance state or altered state of consciousness (ASC). The engravings found at Willow Creek show strong similarities with those found in Europe (p. 38).

While investigating a number of caves in Europe, Lewis-Williams and Dowson (1988) found that images at the entrances to the caves differed from those found on the internal chamber walls, and that, characteristically, the engraved lintels over doorways suggested a significant threshold for passing through. Their findings led them to think that mental images that were created during altered states of consciousness may have common forms historically and culturally. Patterson shares this view.

Yet another example from a different part of the world, South Africa, offers similar findings. With regard to the South African San rock art, the San saw the rock surface as a veil between this world and the spirit world (Lewis-Williams and Dowson 1993). Many images could be interpreted as depicting entrance and exit through cracks and steps in the rock surface. Blundell writes that since the San regarded the rock surface as a veil between this world and a supernatural one, it is highly probable that a San shaman experienced these images during trance. He or she then construed the dark, invisible area and the outer arc as an 'opening through the veil' (Blundell 1998: 9).

Descent and Ascent

An ancient Indian legend of underworld descent is to be found in the Katha Upanishad, where a young Brahman descends to the abode of the god of death, and brings back to the land of the living knowledge of the fire-sacrifice and meditative disciplines by which one can win release from the cycle of death and rebirth (Zaleski 1987: 24). According to prophetic and devotional traditions, the Prophet Muhammad was miraculously transported from Mecca to Jerusalem one night in the company of the angel Gabriel. In several versions, his magical flight is described as mounting a 'ladder' to the sky. Lao Tzu, the legendary founder of Chinese Taoism, is said to have left his body inert and lifeless in order to go 'for a stroll to the origin of things'. In some Taoist sects, an essential mark of the holy man is the ability to take flight and wander freely through enchanted islands, sacred mountains or celestial spheres (Zaleski 1987: 24).

The monk of Wenlock, whose vision was narrated by St Boniface in the early eighth century, reported that his departure from the body was like the lifting of a veil (Zaleski 1987: 48). Carol Zaleski's comparison of medieval and modern vision and otherworld journey narratives offers a variety of pathways that lead to spiritual transportation, some of which describe either a dark path into an underworld or a bright and delightful path into the heavens (p. 56). The stories show remarkable structural similarities. First, a separated spirit looking down on its physical body, hovering just overhead, watches the scene of crisis in a mood of detachment; then comes the tunnel motif, the presence of a guide, the revision of one's life, meeting others who have died, and so on. The most striking difference between medieval and modern accounts of otherworld journeys, however, is the prominence in the former of obstacles and tests, purificatory torments and doom, reflecting Catholic teachings on purgatory and penance, whereas in the latter there is an indication of inevitable progress, with some sort of pedagogical message. This suggests that, although experiences may be very similar, their interpretation is a reflection of cultural and/or religious expectations.

While 'visions' have been reported in all religions, they are often of a spontaneous nature. However, some religious specialists, particularly shamans, often undergo training so that such experiences can occur at will. Richard Noll points out that mental imagery cultivation (the repeated induction of enhanced mental imagery, or imaging) is important in the training of shamans, with the goal of developing a 'strong eye', or an 'inner eye', in order to see things that cannot normally be seen (Noll 1985: 443). During training, novice shamans are taught not only to cultivate mental images, but to enhance the vividness and controllability of an image. Mental imagery cultivation as a tool to move an individual into a transcendent experience is employed in the Western esoteric tradition as well. This is a *visual portal* and will be pursued in later chapters; but it is just one technique among many. What seems to be essential to the majority of experiences of movement through portals is to experience an altered state of consciousness. In an altered state, the experience becomes a reality, rather than merely an exercise using the imagination.

Consciousness

The term consciousness derives from the Latin *conscius*, a root that means 'experience with knowledge' (Laughlin et al. 1992: 82). In the Abhidhamma scriptures of

Buddhism, consciousness is said to comprise some eighty-nine distinct elements, such as feeling, perception, will and concentration. For more detail of the eighty-nine distinct types, the reader may refer to Narada Maha Thera (1975) and Guenther (1976). Of these eighty-nine types, there are seven discrete elements present in all. These are variously interpreted as: contact, feeling, perception, volition, attention, one-pointedness and vitality (Thera 1975: 127, fn. 40), or awareness, feeling, perception, will, attention, concentration and psychic energy (Laughlin et al. 1992: 80–1). Emotion, cognition and volition are principal elements of consciousness. Emotion defines the attitude; cognition refers to how segments of information are related to one another; and volition is the process by which attention remains focused on a certain range of stimuli, instead of moving on to others (Csikszentmihalyi and Csikszentmihalyi 1988: 19). Consciousness corresponds to subjectively experienced reality.

Building on the work of Bohm (1965), Gibson (1969) and Piaget and Inhelder (1969), Laughlin et al. (1992: 34) point out that the nervous system constructs the world of everyday experience and that we normally operate upon our *cognized models of reality* (their emphasis). That is to say, we experience our models of reality *as though* they are reality, constructing models in experiential interaction with reality, and then *project* the model into our experience as reality. (This, of course is only one explanation, and might not be endorsed by people in some of the other cultures discussed in this book.) Consciousness corresponds to subjectively experienced reality that is interpreted according to *culturally defined concepts*, an important point to bear in mind when considering experiences in altered states of consciousness; certain experiences that may be pan-human become endowed with culturally specific symbols, language and interpretations.

Alterations in Consciousness

While 'normal' or 'ordinary' consciousness entails the separateness of the perceiver and the perceived, often people in an ASC, such as a trance state, do not experience this distinction: the two become one, and sometimes the notions of time and space are distorted. William James points out that various religious teachers attained their power to influence humans in essentially the same way – by going into trance. Trance has been defined as 'a condition of dissociation, characterised by the lack of voluntary movement, and frequently by automatisms in act and thought, illustrated by hypnotic and mediumistic conditions' (Lewis 1989: 33). Australian occult artist, Rosaleen Norton, experimented with trance states that provided the images she subsequently portrayed in her paintings. Her initial foray into trance is described in detail in chapter 7 (see p. 124), but note here how she felt the need to provide herself with the symbols, fragrances and ambiance that might move her into trance (Drury 1988: 30):

> ... I collected together a variety of things such as aromatic leaves, wine, a lighted fire, a
> mummified hoof, etc. ... all potent stimuli to the part of the unconscious that I wished to
> invoke. I darkened the room, and focusing my eyes upon the hoof I crushed the pungent
> leaves, drank some wine, and tried to clear my mind of all conscious thought. This was a
> beginning (and I made many other experiments which were progressively successful).

Blocking logical, rational thought processes (what yogis call 'stopping the oscil-
lations of the mind') is an important part of moving into a trance state. Gary Doore
uses the word 'entrainment' to refer to the induction of altered states by the fixation
of attention on stimuli, especially a regularly repeating pattern of stimuli, such as
percussion sound (Doore 1988: 217).

Some theorists make ad hoc distinctions between light, medium and deep trance.
In light trance the subject is clearly aware of more than one context of consciousness,
but this awareness declines as trance deepens. The induction of what is known as a
'shamanic state of consciousness' (Harner 1990) can vary from a very light to a
comatose condition. In a light level, shamans alter their consciousness to interact
with the spirit world and can undertake journeys in those realms, but at the same
time they are at least marginally aware of what is occurring around them in the
material world. For example, while on a journey to the 'upper' world, they might
adjust the drumbeat of their assistant when it is not being executed effectively. They
may be able to avoid physical obstacles in their path while dancing and 'travelling'
in the spirit world. They may also continue to interact with a patient or an audience
and even answer their questions. At the opposite end of the trance spectrum they are
completely oblivious to the material world and may appear comatose. Nevertheless,
they consciously determine their entry and exit from this state.

Trance may be accompanied by visions and can be induced by hypnosis, rapid
over-breathing, inhaling substances, ingesting drugs, dance, music or ascetic
contemplation (Lewis 1989: 34). The key to bringing about a change in consciousness appears to be in the continuous and sustained use of any method. Both sensory
deprivation and sensory overstimulation can result in a trance state. The non-
mystical explanation of a trance state is that it is a dissociative mental state having to
do with the central nervous system. Prolonged immobility, fasting, sleep deprivation
and even self-inflicted injury can produce a trance state, as can participating in
'numinous moments', such as sacrifices, initiations, seances or 'shamanic-looking'
consultations. Gary Trompf adds to this list the blowing out of scented breath or
smoke, and gives the example of a Melanesian taro cult whose members chewed
wild strawberry leaves as a vehicle for dance trances (Trompf 1991: 127).

Often trance is accompanied by bodily shaking. For example, in Kenya the
Samburu men poised between boyhood and mature male regularly go into trance,
shaking their whole bodies (Lewis 1989: 35). The Shakers (and the early Quakers)
were often beset by uncontrollable bodily shaking and trance states achieved in
emotionally charged church services. These instances were regarded as mystical

and a manifestation of the Holy Spirit. Haitian Vodoun spirits are said to 'ride' their earthly hosts like a horse, and when this occurs, those possessed go into shaking and trembling and are often unaware of what they are doing. Some American black Baptist churches in places like New Orleans exhibit bodily trembling and epileptic-like states after highly charged emotional singing.

Altered states of consciousness are widely reported, especially during immersion in religious activities. Charles Laughlin explored his own experiences of Tibetan tantric Buddhism during the seven years (1978–1985) he spent as a participating monk. In these years he specifically sought, but also had spontaneously occurring, transformative experiences. One that he relates concerns *dumo* (psychic heat/energy often associated with increased sexual arousal) that can lead to a blissful state. While meditating and concentrating on loving kindness, he felt, at one point, an explosion of a 'rapidly expanding sphere of rose-colored energy'. Laughlin writes (1994: 109):

> Within a split second, my consciousness was in a state of intense absorption upon boundless space filled with pulsing, shimmering rose-colored particles and ecstatic bliss. There then followed the eruption of a soundless scream and another energy explosion from the depths of my being that culminated in the awareness of the visual image of a tunnel or birth canal. When corporeal awareness gradually returned, I spent a couple of hours in complete tranquility...

Reflecting on this and other experiences, he became convinced of the significance of transpersonalism (a term used by Walsh and Vaughan (1980: 16) to identify the experiences of extension of identity beyond both individuality and personality among people practising various consciousness disciplines).[5] Some anthropologists, who are investigating the relationship between consciousness and culture, altered states of mind and the integration of mind, culture and personality, use the term 'transpersonal anthropology'. Laughlin himself seems able to embrace different kinds of explanations for the phenomenon, thus contributing a multifaceted approach to the experiences themselves. He is one of the authors in *Brain, Symbol and Experience: toward a neurophenomenology of human consciousness*, which carefully explains the importance of the autonomic nervous system and its part in the alteration of consciousness, briefly summarized as follows.

The autonomic nervous system plays a large part in consciousness alteration. The autonomic nervous system is divided into two complementary subsystems: the sympathetic (ergotropic) system and the parasympathetic (trophotropic) system. Activation of the sympathetic nervous system results in diffuse cortical excitation, and a bodily response of a waking mode of consciousness and adrenal stimulation. The sympathetic nervous system energizes adaptive 'fight-flight' responses to conditions arising in the cognized environment and is experienced as bodily arousal or stress. Activation of the parasympathetic system leads to decreased cortical excitation, and a bodily response of relaxation, sleep, coma and, ultimately, death. The parasympathetic energizes vegetation, repair, growth and development and is experienced as relative bodily relaxation, calm and tranquillity (Laughlin et al. 1992: 146).

The normal state of balance within the autonomic nervous system breaks down under intense stimulation of the sympathetic system, leading to a collapse into a state of parasympathetic dominance. This pattern of parasympathetic rebound or collapse is a fundamental mechanism used by shamanistic healers to induce an altered state of consciousness. Diverse ASC induction procedures induce a state of parasympathetic dominance in which the frontal cortex is dominated by slow-wave discharge patterns originating in the lower centres of the brain. A wide variety of conditions will evoke the sequence of excitation and collapse. Agents such as hallucinogens, amphetamines, opiates and the like, as well as certain procedures, such as bodily exhaustion (as in long-distance running), drumming and chanting, meditation, sensory deprivation and dream states, and traumatic accidents and injuries, and hereditarily transmitted nervous system sensitivities, can all invoke high-voltage slow-wave electroencephalograms (EEGs) (Winkelman 1997: 397–9). Transcendent states manifest high-voltage slow-wave (EEG) activity.

Simultaneous discharge of both the excitation and relaxation systems may lead to profound alterations in consciousness (Gellhorn and Kiely 1972: 399). The range of driving mechanisms that may result in simultaneous discharge is wide and, as well as the rhythmic stimuli already mentioned, can include various privations, ordeals, harassment, social isolation, sensory deprivation and drugs (Laughlin et al. 1992: 146). The various driving techniques simultaneously excite numerous neural centres. In any given ritual, one specific practice may be sufficient to establish a state of trance. Manifold driving techniques would increase the possibility. So, in any one ritual that employs multiple driving techniques, the possibility of moving into trance would be higher.[6] Hyper-excitation, such as that experienced in the (North American) Sun Dance, the Balinese Kris Dance or a West African spirit ceremony, will lead to experiences phenomenologically different from those induced by hyper-relaxation, such as Zen meditation. The interpretation of experiences in ASCs depends to a great extent on situating the experience within a cultural and/or religious cognitive framework. A similar somatic experience might translate as divine revelation, an encounter with divas or as schizophrenic hallucination. In some cultures experiences are encouraged; in others they are discouraged. In some they fall under the domain of the religious specialist; in others they are common among all people, or negated completely.

As people move into altered states they may experience physical sensations of corporeal shrinkage or expansion, which may be accompanied by a feeling of lightness or rising up, as expressed by St Theresa, a Spanish Roman Catholic nun of the sixteenth century (Streng 1985: 121):

When I tried to resist these raptures, it seemed that I was being lifted up by a force beneath my feet so powerful that I know nothing to which I can compare it, for it came with a much greater vehemence than any other spiritual experience and I felt as if I were being ground to powder. It is a terrible struggle, and to continue it against the Lord's will avails very little, for no power can do anything against His.

Sometimes this lightness turns into the sensation of flying and/or becoming transformed into another creature, especially a bird, at which time visual perceptions indicate a sense of looking down from above. At other times the person may feel as if they are being drawn into a vortex, perhaps a tunnel, and they may experience physical constrictions and breathing difficulties. The physical body may begin to 'vibrate', sounds may be heard and a bright light or lights may be seen. Sri Ramakrishna, a Hindu who performed priestly duties in a temple of Kali, the Divine Mother, in India, in the nineteenth century, wrote (Isherwood 1965: 66):

No sooner had I sat down to meditate ... than I heard clattering sounds in the joints of my body and limbs. They began in my legs. It was as if someone inside me had keys and was locking me up, joint by joint, turning the keys. I had no power to move my body or change my posture, even slightly ... When I sat and meditated, I had at first the vision of particles of light like swarms of fireflies. Sometimes I saw masses of light covering everything on all sides like a mist ... I didn't understand what I saw ... so I prayed anxiously to [the Divine] Mother ...

The term 'ontic shift' refers to those experiences where people feel a 'reality shift', that is, a sense that they are no longer dealing with the world as it is known ordinarily, and that this new state is highly significant (Howell 1989: 86). Being conscious of the 'shift' itself enables one to experience the change as having its origins in an 'other reality'. This ontic shift complements the Western physiological theoretical approach, which needs to make a distinction between 'real' and 'not real'; other cultures, however, which hold different views about what constitutes 'reality', might not make such a sharp distinction. Our beliefs are based on perceptual, behavioural and affective activities that lead to an existential world view from which we derive our sense of the 'real'. This world view does not necessarily have a cognitive component, that is, our emotions and beliefs are not necessarily informed by our reasoned thinking, which might explain why, for example, a scientist could believe in a particular religion or the existence of a spirit world (existential world view), while maintaining the rigours of an academic discipline (cognitive component).

The main components of trance induction that lead to extraordinary experiences are a combination of triggers: repetitive sounds, such as drumming, chanting, clapping, and so on (sonic driving); rhythmic movement, such as dancing or swaying; heightened emotions; focused attention; total participation in the activity; and cultural immersion or cultural knowledge. This sensorial 'formula' for trance induction appears to be universal, from Western Pentecostal services to Islamic-based Sufi ecstatic circles, to the Kalahari San in South Africa. Additional components that enhance such a combination of triggers might be donning a mask, painting the body, inflicting pain and the use of aromas, such as incense, and drugs. Not all the components have to be employed at the same time. Sensitive individuals may move through a portal using only one of these triggers, and some may even have a spontaneous experience without any of the triggers.

Emotion

While other studies have demonstrated the importance of particular techno-logies, little has been said about the important part played by the emotions. A recent exception is the edited collection by Kay Milton and Maruska Svasek, entitled *Mixed Emotions: anthropological studies of feeling* (2005), with its work on an anthropology of the emotions, which advocates discussions of the 'multiplex sensations experienced by fieldworkers' in trying to understand the incoming sensory data experienced in 'being there' (p. 55). Elizabeth Tonkin's article in this collection calls for anthropologists to raise their awareness, as well as to document and analyse their own social, interactive and emotional fieldwork encounters that largely involve both cognitive and bodily intuitions (p. 65). Anthropologists have recently become less loath to discuss the importance of emotion in fieldwork. Indeed, the edited collection by Hume and Mulcock (2004) reveals the awkwardness of positioning oneself in the field, and the gamut of emotions that are encountered once one is engaged in fieldwork – fear in high-risk situations, despair over the suicide of a close informant, the mixed emotions of being an insider/researcher and the discomfort of being an outsider. Clearly, anthropologists now realize that the distanced rational observer is a myth that needs to be dispelled. Indeed, Leavitt (1996: 530) writes that emotions 'bridge the domain of cultural meanings and bodily feelings'. Fieldwork and emotional intersubjectivity, in fact, are probably essential to good ethnography. Wikan (1992: 471) insists that the importance of 'resonance' cannot be underestimated, and one should willingly 'engage with another world, life, or idea', and use one's experience to try to grasp the meanings and values of members of other cultures. This deep engagement with alternative religious groups has produced some very exciting work in the field of the anthropology of religion (see for example, Rountree (2004); Blain (2002); Greenwood (2000); and the classic, Young and Goulet (1994), *Being Changed by Cross-cultural Encounters*), where fieldworkers have plunged into the beliefs and ritual practices and experienced at first hand the events described by informants.

Christian theology and many academic approaches to religion have under-emphasized, and at times studiously denied the emotions because they detract from a scientific investigative approach; indeed some seem to find emotional displays rather embarrassing. Yet most spiritual experiences are intensely emotional, and seem to form an intrinsic part of the experience, as the following quote of a Caribou Arctic shaman demonstrates (Rasmussen 1927, cited in Larsen 1976: 77):

> I tried in vain to become a conjurer up of spirits with the help of others. I never succeeded. I visited many famous shamans and gave them large presents, which they immediately passed on to other people [...] Then I went out into the solitude and soon became very melancholy. In a mystical fashion I used to break into complaints and become unhappy, without knowing the reason. Then sometimes everything would suddenly become quite different and I felt a great and inexplicable joy, a joy so strange that I could not control it. I had to break into song, into a mighty song that had no room for anything but this word: Joy! Joy! Joy! And in the midst of this mysterious bliss I became a shaman, without knowing how. But I was a shaman. I could see and hear in an entirely new way.

Every shaman, he says, has to feel illumination in his body that gives him the power to see with closed eyes into the darkness, the future, or into another person's secrets. After the experience described above he felt that he was indeed in possession of this incredible ability.

In Christian religious experiences when one talks about being 'born anew' or 'born again', there is a very strong emotional component. Deep emotions give rise to hymns of praise, glossolalia, trembling, loud shouting, spontaneous and joyful singing, and even devotional poetry. The emphasis is on the personal, direct experience of spiritual power (Streng 1985: 35). Worship that focuses on love felt toward the Holy Spirit, or the Holy One (however it is perceived), creates surges of emotion so strong that the individual feels personally transformed. The sensation of a personal, experiential consciousness of the real presence of God might 'flood[s] the soul with joy' and bathe the whole inward spirit with 'refreshing streams of life' (Streng 1985: 136). It has sometimes been described as an 'awesome-loving experience' (p. 37). Similarly, ecstatic fervour dominates devotional movements in many African Christian services, in Hare Krishna practices and in some new religious movements.

The emotional element also seems highly significant to the success of many rituals, especially those that involve calling on spirits for healing purposes. Cultures as vastly different as the Ndembu (Africa), the Kalahari !Kung (Africa) and Western Pentecostalists all employ heightened emotion in their healing services. Likewise, the Sufi notion of 'heart' demonstrates the importance of emotions. While fear and anticipation of heightened emotions are expressed among the !Kung (this is further explored in chapter 4, Dance and Movement), the following example from the Sufis emphasizes a different kind of emotion, that of 'heart', in bringing something into manifestation.

The Sufis: *Qalb* and *Himma*

The thirteenth-century Sufi mystic, Ibn 'Arabi, (1165–1240), recounted how, when he was still a 'beardless youth', the philosopher Averroës appeared to him in an ecstasy (Corbin 1969: 42):

> [...] in such a form that between his person and myself there was a light veil. I saw him through this veil, but he did not see me or know that I was present. He was indeed too absorbed in his meditation to take notice of me. I said to myself: His thought does not guide him to the place where I myself am.

It is important to note that in Sufism, the material world of the apparent, the external and the exoteric (*zahir*) has its corresponding hidden, spiritual, internal, esoteric side (*batin*). This is the central postulate of esotericism and of esoteric hermeneutics (*ta'wil*) (Corbin 1969: 78). The *ta'wil*, writes Corbin, is 'essential symbolic under-standing, the transmutation of everything visible into symbols, the intuition of an essence or person in an Image which partakes neither of universal logic nor of sense perception' (p. 13). The *batin* is a world of Idea-Images, of subtle substances and 'immaterial matter'; it is the scene on which visionary events and symbolic histories appear in their 'true reality'. It is an intermediate universe 'where the spiritual takes body and the body becomes spiritual', and the organ of this universe is the 'active Imagination' (p. 4).

One of Ibn 'Arabi's first visions occurred when he fell gravely ill, to the point where it was thought he was dying. Indeed, those around him, including his father, thought him dead, and his father began reciting the thirty-sixth sura of the Koran, which is intoned specifically for the dying. Ibn 'Arabi later said that during this time he was 'besieged by a troop of menacing, diabolical figures', but then something else occurred. There arose, he said, 'a marvellously beautiful being, exhaling a sweet perfume who, with invincible force repulsed the demonic figures'. When Ibn 'Arabi asked him who he was, he replied, 'I am the Sura Yasin'. This response meant that the figure was the form of a person that corresponded to the energy released by the spoken Word. Ibn 'Arabi had communicated with the *'alam al-mithal*, the subtle, supersensory intermediate world between the corporeal and the spiritual. He was to have this experience again at other times (Corbin 1969: 39).

In his autobiography (*Risalat al-Quds*), Ibn 'Arabi tells how he was able to evoke the spirit of his *shaikh*, Yusuf al-Kumi, whenever he needed his help. A disciple of Ibn 'Arabi wrote that Ibn 'Arabi 'had the power to meet the spirit of any Prophet or Saint departed from this world, either by making him descend to the level of this world and contemplating him in an apparitional body (*surat mithaliya*) similar to the sensible form of his person, or by making him appear in his dreams, or by unbinding himself from his material body to rise to meet the spirit' (Corbin 1969: 224). However, although this is said to be possible, the greatest mystics were contemptuous of the use of such power and refrained from its use, partly because it could lead to thoughts of self-power rather than acts of devotion.

Ibn 'Arabi said that God would remain 'veiled' to those who merely prayed for God to have compassion with them, but the intuitive mystic, or gnostic, who asks that divine compassion should come into being through them, is able to lift the veil. Rather than imploring God to be compassionate, the gnostic 'actualizes' the divine Being, as he aspires to be *through* and *for* him who is praying and who 'in his very prayer' is the organ of His passion (Corbin 1969: 117).

The heart (*qalb*), is said to be one of the centres of 'mystic physiology', and although it is connected to the physical organ of the heart, it is, like the chakras, distinguished from the bodily organ (Corbin 1969: 221). The power of the heart signifies ardently desiring a particular goal while in the act of meditating, imagining and projecting that goal. While love is related to the heart, the specific centre of love in Sufism is said to be *ruh*, *pneuma* or spirit. *Qalb* produces true knowledge, the gnosis of God and the divine mysteries and comprehensive intuition. The power of the heart is said to be a secret force or energy (*quwwat khafiya*), which perceives divine realities by a pure hierophantic knowledge (*idrak wadih jali*). The heart is believed to be 'the mirror in which the Divine Being manifests His form'. In its *un*veiled state, the heart is 'like a mirror in which the microcosmic form of the Divine Being is reflected' (p. 77).

Himma has been translated as intention, desire and force of will. When a Sufi meditates with ardent desire and strong will, the force of the intention is said to be so powerful that it can project and realize (essentiate) a being external to the person. Thus, 'If the heart is the mirror in which the Divine Being manifests His form [...] the Image which the heart projects is in turn the outward form, the "objectivization" of this Image' (Corbin 1969: 224). The function of *himma*, the concentration of the heart, is the organ which makes it possible to achieve knowledge that is inaccessible to the intellect, and this is regarded by the mystics as 'true' knowledge.

What the Sufis called 'science of the heart' involves creative imagination: entrance into the *'alam al-mithal* (the intermediate world) is possible through the active imagination. As a general rule, everyone is able to imagine something in their 'mind's eye', but in addition to this, the gnostic uses his *himma* to create something which exists outside the mind's eye. In both cases the imaginative faculty is used, though with different results. The word 'create' is specifically used in the Sufi writings, according to Corbin (1969: 223). By concentrating the active imagination one is capable of *creating* objects and producing changes in the outside world. The object on which a person concentrates his imaginative meditation becomes the apparition of an outward, extra-psychic reality. This is what Ibn 'Arabi designates as the detached imagination, as it is separable from the imagining subject. Thus it is possible to 'produce something which breaks away from it (*khayal munfasil*)'. This creation can exist as long as the *himma* maintains it, and this forms a part of mystic perception (*dhawq*). There is, then, the possibility of being able to transmute all the objections of sensory perceptions (p. 237).

The power of the heart is a secret force or energy (*quwwat khafiya*) which perceives divine realities by a pure hierophantic knowledge (*idrak wadih jali*) (Corbin 1969: 226):

> When Ibn 'Arabi says that a gnostic *creates* something through his *himma*, through the creativity of his heart, he means [...] that the gnostic causes to appear, in the *Hadra* of the sensible world ... something which already exists *in actu* in a higher *Hadra*. In other words, the heart creates by 'causing to appear', by 'preserving' something which already exists in one of the *Hadarat*. By concentrating the spiritual energy of *himma* on the form of a thing existing in one or more of the 'Presences' or *Hadarat*, the mystic obtains perfect control over that thing, and this control preserves the thing in one or another of the 'Presences' as long as the concentration of *himma* lasts.

The projection brought about by the mystic's heart with the help of his active imagination (called theophanic imagination) and concentration appears as endowed with an outward reality, even if it is visible only to other mystics.

So, in the Sufism of Ibn 'Arabi, we find strong emphasis on other-worldly realms, emotion as will and desire, on creative and active visualization, intention, projection of a thought form and spiritual energy. These ideas are also contained within a different, yet related, set of ideas from Western occultism. I refer to W.E. Butler as a modern representative of this system.

Western Occultism and Esoteric Spirituality

The term occult generally means that which is mysterious and beyond the range of ordinary knowledge; and esoteric refers to knowledge that is gained by initiation into the mysteries. Illuminated knowledge is often called gnosis, and knowledge in this sense is knowledge of spiritual mysteries. The gnostic is one who searches for answers to the mystery of existence, and the desire to know the divine and the true nature of oneself.

While esoteric spirituality takes in a range of spiritual forms, it is possible to talk about a form confined to the West. By this general term, I refer to what Faivre (1995: xiii) calls the 'Latin West', which is the Greco-Roman whole encapsulating Judaism, Christianity and Islam, along with philosophers and thinkers who moved beyond the doctrines and dogma of these mainstream religions. Western esoteric spirituality conflated many diverse yet linked ideas from the time of the Renaissance, especially around the end of the fifteenth century (p. xiii). Some of the common threads of esoteric spirituality include Stoicism, Gnosticism, Hermeticism, neo-Pythagoreanism, Neoplatonism, the Jewish and Christian Kabbalah and alchemy.

Indeed, the Kabbalah constitutes an integral part of Western esotericism. It is not so much the history of the ideas that form esoteric spirituality that is of interest here, but the common strands that tie such a large array of ideas together.

Contemporary esoteric spiritualities, unlike the mainstream Western monotheistic religions, place little emphasis on belief, focusing more on the faculties of intuitive knowing, imagination, observation and personal experience. Antoine Faivre identifies four fundamental intrinsic characteristics of modern Western esoteric spirituality: correspondences, living nature, imagination and mediation, and the experience of transmutation or metamorphosis (Faivre 1995: xv).

Accompanying the notion of the microcosm as a reflection, in miniature, of the macrocosm – 'that which is above is like that which is below, and that which is below is like that which is above', a saying attributed to Hermes Trismegistus – is the idea of correspondences. Correspondences are symbolic and/or real links (metals, planets, parts of the body, colours, plants, gems, and so on) that help to bridge the gap between the visible and invisible worlds. The notion of correspondences was common to thinkers like Cornelius Agrippa and Swedenborg, as well as the Neoplatonists.

Living nature is the idea that God, Humanity and Nature are interconnected. All are essentially alive in all their parts, a philosophy of metaphysics that tends to be monistic rather than dualistic. Imagination and mediation are two linked and complementary ideas. While mystics aspire to a more or less complete suppression of images and intermediaries (because they are hindrances to the experience of union with God), esotericists are more interested in images that are revealed by looking within themselves through their creative imagination. Indeed, one becomes conscious of a transcendent reality through focusing on the interior world of the self. It is recognized that divinity is within the self and is a reflection of the divine outside the self. With the aid of symbols and images, the individual seeking gnosis endeavours to discover and to know the interior self by the inner gaze and communication with the mediating entities between the divine world and the natural world. This is aided by the tool of creative imagination, what Henry Corbin calls the *mundus imaginalis* of the Sufis.

While the mystic aspires to union with the divine, esotericists prefer to discover, see and know the mediating entities between the divine world and Nature. However, the distinction is not always as clear-cut as this and there is sometimes a great deal of esotericism in the mystics (for example, St Hildegard of Bingen), and a mystical tendency can be seen in many esotericists (Louis Claude de Saint-Martin, for example) (Faivre 1995: xvii).

The terms transmutation (a term from alchemy) and metamorphosis mean change that accompanies self-knowledge. 'If one wishes lead to become silver or silver gold, one must not separate knowledge (gnosis) from interior experience, or intellectual activity from active imagination' (Faivre 1995: xviii). It is through the imagination that a person can establish rapport with the metaphysical world.

To W.E. Butler, a twentieth-century practitioner of Western esoteric spirituality, the aim of all magic (which he defines as the art of producing changes in consciousness at will) is to obtain mystic union with the indwelling Self, the God within (Butler 1970: 159). If one accomplishes this, one may 'surrender in loving service', the lesser personality to the 'indwelling spiritual Self', so that the 'will of the eternal may be carried out among the living' (p. 156). Although some magicians may not aspire to such altruism, Butler insists that this is the true goal of the inspired magician.

One of the 'keys' in magical work is recognizing that the conscious mind can act upon the subconscious mind, and that by changing consciousness it is possible to act directly upon the inner worlds and thus, ultimately, upon the objective world. This idea reflects the philosophy of Hermes Trismegistus discussed earlier. 'True magic', writes Butler, 'brings one into conscious union with the indwelling Self, the God within, and though the practice of the magical arts may stop at some point perhaps remote from this, yet in the end the aspirant will find an inner compulsion to complete the journey and find his true peace' (Butler 1970: 158). The rites and ceremonies of magical works are specifically designed to make contact with the 'inner temple of the heart' (p. 91). The tools and devices used to train the novice magician are all designed to bring about a willed dissociation of consciousness.[7] This in turn eventually leads to the willed integration of the individual with the divine, according to Butler.

A person's emotional state can generate different energy patterns, and sustained and continued emotional 'brooding-over' some problem can generate strong thoughts that have their own forms (Butler 1970: 109). As highly emotional thoughts can generate energy, emotion is an important part of rituals. When accompanied by particular sigils, emotion can be used in magical work to attain certain goals. If one mentally visualizes the sign of the cross, for example, while evoking strong emotions and engaging in sustained prayer, it is possible to build up a thought image that can take on a form and shape of its own, independent of the person's imagination. If the same image is reinforced by making the sign with one's hand in the air, then the effect of the gesture is to cause the energy of the thought-form to become more clearly defined and stronger. All this depends to an enormous extent on concentrating the mind on the pictorial image. 'The mind', writes Butler, 'supplies the forms and channels through which the forces [energies] work, and the more definite the channel, the more control can be exercised over the forces flowing therein' (p. 39).

Thus, focused thought, strong will, emotion, visualization and signs and gestures can all combine to create the magical action intended by the magician. Central to all this is the belief in energy (which is integral to Western occultism) and the idea that thoughts have energy and form and can exist outside the mind as mental projections that can take on a form independent of their creator.

To summarize some of Butler's ideas that parallel those of the Sufi, Ibn 'Arabi: there is a spark of the divine in the human; there is a metaphysical world which is separate yet linked to this world; it is possible for communication to occur between the two; it is possible to evoke into visible appearance, that which is normally invisible. In order to open the veil, one can perform certain actions, meditate upon the inner meaning of signs and words, incorporate strong emotional content into the meditations, have a clear goal of the desired outcome and employ strong visual components to the image. All these ideas are far removed from religions that urge their followers to refer to doctrine, follow dogma and believe by faith alone. The early gnostics argued that one's own experience is the ultimate criterion of truth and takes precedence over all tradition and second-hand testimony. Unlike orthodox Christianity, a major premise of the gnostics was that the psyche bears within itself the potential for liberation or destruction, and this was more important than doctrine and clerical power (Pagels 1979: 53, 132, 135). According to the Gospel of Thomas (32:19–33:5 in the Nag Hammadi Library 118) (one of the gospels that was omitted from the New Testament), Jesus proclaimed the Kingdom [of God] as being inside and outside (Pagels 1979: 136):

> ...the Kingdom is inside of you, and it is outside of you. When you come to know yourselves, then you will be known, and you will realize that you are the sons of the living Father. But if you will not know yourselves, then you dwell in poverty ...

The gnostics insisted that it was only on the basis of immediate experience that one could create the poems, vision accounts, myths and hymns that they prized as proof of the attainment of gnosis. Luke 17:21 reveals, 'The Kingdom of God is within you', and Pagels suggests that the term 'Kingdom' symbolizes a state of transformed consciousness (Pagels 1979: 137).

With both the Sufis and Western Esotericists, the principal quest is to gain knowledge that is inaccessible to the conscious intellect. Such knowledge is often referred to as 'true knowledge', or 'seeing things clearly' by lifting a veil that normally obscures pure consciousness. Healing the body and the mind, making one 'feel good' and personal growth are all by-products of passing through the veil.

It is to the experience of opening the doors of perception and knowledge that I turn to in the following chapters. The book is arranged in the following way. Chapter 2 looks at visual perceptions, the use of objects such as mandalas and esoteric symbols, and how visualization techniques aid in the training of novices to 'see' more clearly. Chapter 3 concentrates on the sense of hearing and the effect of sound, sound vibrations, emotional songs that 'uplift the soul' and ethnomusicological comments on 'beats' and 'tones'. Chapter 4 moves to dance and other movement. Chapter 5 focuses on touch and pain and how the physical effects of pain can move an individual into transcendent states. Pain has been used for this purpose by medieval mystics and modern primitives alike, with the use of self-flagellation and other acts of penitential self-torture. Chapter 6 discusses the lesser documented olfactory senses, with a section on breathing. Chapter 7 covers the controversial area of drugs and other substances that are designed to open up gateways, investigating the use of entheogenic or psychedelic substances employed with the express purpose of transcendence. Chapter 8 will address questions that have been raised throughout the book, as well as posing questions about the nature of reality, and will suggest areas for future multidisciplinary research that requires a willingness to be open to all sorts of exciting possibilities.

–2–

Mandalas and Visual Symbols

When mental images are formed, these mechanisms would respond in much the same way as they do when objects and events are observed, resulting in the sensation that an image can be 'seen' as if it were an actual object or event. Further, the more vivid the image, the more strongly these mechanisms would respond, and the more similar to actual objects or events the mental image would appear.

> R.A. Finke, 'Levels of equivalence in imagery and perception',
> *Psychological Review*

The hallmark of the shaman is his ability to control his visions – to begin, manipulate, and end them at will.

> L.G. Peters, 'Trance, initiation, and psychotherapy in Tamang shamanism',
> *American Ethnologist*

In the previous chapter I discussed briefly the importance of visualization in both Sufism and Western esoteric spirituality. In this chapter visualization and mental imagery cultivation will be elaborated on in more detail, using examples from various religious practices and cultures. It will be seen that the practice of visualization and of cultivating mental imagery in order to visualize is widespread, and is used to gain knowledge from extra-mundane sources for a number of reasons, principally in order to assist in affairs of this world and to bring about healing. Although the acquisition of such knowledge is not limited to the techniques of visualization, I focus on the visual in order to highlight its importance in the scheme of the senses.

R.A. Finke's comment above (1980: 113) is a result of his review of experimental work on mental imagery. Finke suggests that mental images can stimulate visual processing mechanisms directly, triggering many of the same information-processing mechanisms that are activated during ordinary visual perception. The more vivid the image visualized, the more strongly such mechanisms respond, and the more similar to actual objects or events the mental image appears. The imagined object viewed via mental imagery is just as real to the individual perceiving it as the 'real' object is in the material world, so a 'vision' of a tree (for example) is as real a perception as a 'real' tree, and when a shaman (or anyone else for that matter) 'sees' or experiences 'spirit', it is as real as anything that he or she might experience in the mundane world. Both experiences are valid and real to the perceiver. This led Finke to propose his theory of 'levels of equivalence', which has profound consequences for a Western understanding of shamanism. It may be, as Richard Noll (1985: 446) suggests, the 'Ariadne thread' that links the numerous reports of visionary journeys to different 'worlds'/planes of existence, or related phenomena (vision quests, shamanic flight, mystic visions, encounters with spirits), with a psychologistic paradigm that is acceptable to a Western audience. Other cultures or religions that have their own interpretive framework do not need to be persuaded.

The Shaman's Inner Eye

The symbolism of divine or magical perception through an eye that sees all, or sees into the inner thoughts and feelings of people, is consistent and pervasive: the Egyptian eye of Horus, the eye of the Freemasons, the Rosicrucians, and the mystical alchemical eye of Jakob Boehme, the disembodied eyes appearing on many Buddhist stupas, the omniscient eye of God, the 'evil eye' that can harm and the mystical third eye of Hinduism. Developing the 'inner eye' forms part of much shamanic training, and accounts are very similar in places as geographically distant as Australia and Africa. The Aboriginal 'clever man', for example, acquired special sight during arduous training, when quartz crystals were 'sung' into his forehead in order to activate the ability to 'see with the inner eye', detecting illnesses that were not visible, and to have 'x-ray vision' so that he could see through objects. He could also perceive a psychic light about a dead person's grave for a short time after death (Hume 2002: 138–40). Berndt and Berndt write of the father of a young sorcery victim who called on the services of a clever man to help ease his son's pain. After waving emu feathers over the afflicted part of the patient's body, the clever man 'stared at the wound ... his eyes were glazed and his X-ray vision was centred at the middle of his forehead ...', and after various procedures, the clever man drew an object out of the boy's body (Berndt and Berndt 1993: 261).

The ability to see the internal organs of a person's body and detect illness is also understood to be a quality of the !Kung Bushman (Africa) healers. The following quote is by an experienced !Kung Bushman, commenting on the qualities of a younger, less experienced healer (Katz 1976: 106):

> You see him staggering and running around. His eyes are rolling all over the place. If your eyes are rolling, you can't stare at sickness. You have to be absolutely steady to see sickness, steady-eyes no shivering and shaking, absolutely steady ... with a steady-gaze ... you need direct looking.

'Seeing properly' allows the !Kung healer to see things that are normally invisible to human sight. Such a person is said to be able to locate, diagnose and heal sickness. During their healing dances this special kind of seeing makes it possible to see energy, to see inside people and to 'see the insides of the one the spirits are trying to kill·[…] you see the spirits and drive them away' (Katz 1989: 211). Once the illness is discerned, it can be 'pulled out' of the sick person's body, by the healer directly placing his/her vibrating hands close to or on the patient's body and pulling it into their own bodies, then expelling it by throwing it away.

Shamanic training in vision cultivation often consists of a two-phase process; the two phases are not necessarily discrete and may be sought concurrently. First, the neophyte shaman is trained to increase the *vividness* of his visual mental imagery through various psychological and physiological techniques, and then to increase the *controllability* of the image. The purpose is to block out the 'noise' produced by the external stimuli of perception and to attend to internal imagery processes, thus bringing them into focus more clearly (Noll 1985: 445–7). Fechner described this process in 1860 when he said that 'in imaging, the attention feels as if drawn backwards towards the brain'.[1]

The first phase of shamanic vision cultivation is to induce a cognitive figure-ground reversal by increasing the vividness of mental imagery until it is attended to as primary experience (figure), and diminishing the vividness of percepts until they are attended to as secondary experience (ground). Once a novice shaman reports highly vivid images, a second phase of mental imagery training is aimed at, that of increasing the controllability of the visual imagery contents, which entails actively engaging and manipulating the visionary phenomena. The goal is to be able to hold the image for some time, and eventually to evoke and change the image at will. Exercises that enhance images also produce more sharply focused images, turning something nebulous or hazy into something that is very clear and very real. Sometimes this is referred to as developing the 'inner eye', 'spiritual eye', 'third eye', or some similar metaphor. The hallmark of the shaman is not only the ability to control visions, to manipulate them, but also to end them at will. (Herein lies a major difference between a shaman and a person with a mental disorder.) The ability to recall dreams easily, and to successfully mentally rehearse an event are correlated with the ability to control imagery. The enhancement of mental imagery also aids memory. Visual representation is a powerful mnemonic strategy and it is easy to see why visual enhancement, particularly in non-literate societies, would contribute to recalling vital components of a long myth sequence, or to remembering tracts of land across a wide geographical area. The Pitjantjatjara women of central Australia, for example, use visualization and songs as a cognitive map for remembering large tracts of country traversed by the Ancestral Beings as they wandered across the country during their journeys long ago (Payne 1993).

Mental imagery cultivation, defined by Noll as 'the deliberate, repeated induction of enhanced mental imagery' (1985: 444), exists in a wide variety of societies throughout the world. While it is usually the domain of select individuals such as shamans, it is possible to be cultivated by everyone. Mental images that are enhanced by concentration and will, using techniques such as creative visualization, can project an image from the 'mind's eye' to an image that is projected outside the individual. This practice, whether explicit or implicit, is the experiential core of many mystical and magico-religious traditions.

I now turn to three very different religious traditions in which visualization and mental imagery cultivation are an important part of their practices: Buddhism, Western esotericism and Sufism.

Buddhism

In the various branches of Buddhism, the central focus is on: the Buddha (an enlightened being who has seen the truth, the dharma (the teachings of Buddha) and the sangha (the order of monks and nuns who carry on the teachings); and the principle way of following these three central tenets is through leading a life that is appropriate to the teachings, especially through meditation and devotion, with the goal of reaching enlightenment. In all these teachings, meditation practices include techniques of visualization that are designed to assist the meditator's concentration.

Visualization, or 'thinking in pictures', is highly encouraged and is used to optimum advantage in Vajrayana, or Tantric Buddhism, as a rapid means of reaching enlightenment (Noll 1985: 451). The practice of the Vajrayana path involves complete identification of body and mind, with an enlightened being, and seeing one's environment as a 'pure realm'. Focusing attention on a mental image of an enlightened being (such as Tara or Avalokiteshvara) is recommended as a means of developing single-pointed concentration. One focuses on the qualities of the enlightened being, such as compassion, wisdom, love and strength, in order to open the heart to these qualities and contemplate one's 'own true nature' as reflecting those qualities. The aim is to produce a positive, joyful meditative experience, and to remind the meditator of the experience of enlightenment until it becomes a living reality (McDonald 1990: 111–12).

The Vajrayana tradition of Buddhism involves intensive visualization training based on a series of elaborate icons that must be successfully reproduced in full detail in the 'mind's eye' during meditation practice. The more highly detailed the images (colours, implements, hand gestures, posture, which all symbolize different aspects of the path to spiritual fulfilment) that one can hold in one's mind, the more successful the visualization. If one selects Tara (a buddha representing skilful activities) for the exercise, one could image her body as emerald-green light, translucent and radiant, dressed in clothing of 'celestial silk' and adorned with precious gems. She could be seated in a spiritually meaningful posture, holding a blue flower and smiling lovingly at the meditator. The visualization could include thoughts of Tara's inexhaustible loving kindness and of opening one's heart to this energy (McDonald 1990: 120).

While Richard Noll speaks of enhancing the vividness and controllability of an image, Buddhist meditators using Vajrayana meditation techniques talk about analytical and stabilizing techniques. To construct an image, analytical thinking is needed, but to develop clarity of image, one needs to stabilize the image, that is, hold it with 'single-pointed attention'. In this manner, visualization increases familiarity with positive images and strengthens the ability to control and concentrate the mind (McDonald 1990: 112).

Training involved in the enhancement of image-building in this tradition involves visualizing familiar objects, such as the face of a friend, or the view from the window of a house. Gazing at a picture or statue of an enlightened being, and then closing the eyes to recall details of the picture or statue, is also recommended as a means of developing visualization and creating the feeling of being in the presence of an enlightened being.

Western Esotericism

It is not surprising that these skills are also taught in many of the Western occult schools, in order to promote imaginal ability. People who fantasize often, who see, hear, smell and touch and fully experience what they fantasize (what Wilson and Barber (1982: 340) call the 'fantasy-prone personality'), are more easily trained than others. Wilson and Barber list the following characteristics of fantasy-prone personalities: the ability to hallucinate voluntarily, the ability to recall vividly memories of life experiences, and psychic ability or sensitivity (p. 340), which are also attributes of shamans.

Practitioners of the Western esoteric spiritual path[2] believe that knowledge which is normally hidden from humans is accessible if one learns to 'open the doors in the right way' (Butler 1970: 90). Symbols within a particular system of esoteric knowledge act as 'doors' to this knowledge, and to powers that are associated normally with the metaphysical. One of the 'paths' used by some contemporary occultists is their own adaptation of the Kabbalah (which may not have the rich history and philosophical underpinnings as the Jewish Kabbalah) as a meditation system. The Kabbalah, as they see it, is based on a philosophical system whose main principles are monism (the unity and oneness of all) and the notion that the microcosm (this world) is but a reflection of the greater universe, the macrocosm. Employing a system of correspondences, it is possible to evoke that which is within (immanence) as a separate manifestation of that which is 'without' (transcendence). The glyph of the Tree of life illustrates these principles in diagrammatic form, with a series of Sephiroth and pathways that lead from one sephirah to another. The sephiroth on the Tree of Life represent the points by which the individual subjective consciousness makes contact with the greater spiritual universe. By training the 'mind's eye', the novice learns to link, deliberately and consciously, a symbol with its appropriate 'force' or 'energy' (Butler 1970: 42).

The key to metaphysical knowledge opens the door to the forces and powers that are both outside the individual, yet contained within the individual. One aim of the occultist is deliberately to *will* the opening of the veils between the physical and the metaphysical. Although in some of the literature one may construe metaphysical realms as a 'place' or 'places', some occultists regard this notion as obscuring the most important point, that the next phase of existence is actually a state of consciousness (Butler 1970: 48).

To facilitate the imaginal process and become proficient at visualization, certain exercises are recommended. An image held in the 'mind's eye' is cultivated so that the image itself can be projected from the mind and 'seen' outside the imagination. In Noll's terms, the mind is trained to create an image, to hold the image, and to improve the vividness and controllability of the mental visualization. With practice, a reflexive process occurs: the mere thought of the emotion associated with the form will evoke in the waking consciousness the symbol-form concerned, and, conversely, the symbol will evoke the emotion. When proficiency at mental imaging is attained, the practitioner can perceive things directly on the 'astral levels' or 'astral planes', without the need for symbols.

Several techniques are suggested to enhance the practice of visualization. One exercise is to close the eyes and imagine the face of a familiar person, to picture the shape, colour and texture of the face, and to hold the image for as long as possible. When one has attained the ability to sustain the mental image for more than a fraction of a second, the aim is then to attempt to project the image on to a blank wall. When this is achieved, the next step is to be able to 'see' this image on the wall with the eyes open, as if it were an entity in itself, and to maintain this image without allowing other thoughts to enter (Hume 1995). The intensity of the mental image can vary from a less cultivated image to seeing for a brief flash, to the vivid and sustained image.

The ability to visualize is important in moving the practitioner beyond the physical realm to the metaphysical realm. In *The Magician*, Butler (1970: 61) writes:

> For successful magical work it is absolutely essential that the operator should be able to build up mental images, since [...] the forces of the Astral Light are directed and controlled by such mental images. It is therefore evident that the would-be magician must gain proficiency in this image-building if he is to do any effective work.

By training the 'mind's eye' one is able to evoke images of god-forms, for example, so that the 'force' or 'energy' of the god-form can be used for magical purposes. One technique for evoking is to imagine a particular god-form (such as Isis) surrounding and coinciding with one's own physical body. While breathing rhythmically, the name of the god is then frequently vibrated. (This might take only a few minutes or up to an hour.) As concentration becomes more intense and profound, the form is said to become vitalized by streams of dynamic energy and power, and the mind is invaded by light, intense feelings and inspiration (Regardie 1979: 36).

W.E. Butler discusses two different forms of image-building (1970: 62): the first is the 'creation of images', where the mind is trained to intentionally construct some image; the second is the 'evocation of images', where the mind is held by the will in a quiet and passive condition, and images are allowed to rise in consciousness. Regular practice of both types of visualization will 'establish a channel' by which many mental conflicts held in the unconscious may come to the attention of the conscious mind. These exercises are believed to assist the individual on the path of self-knowledge, and at times they engender highly emotional experiences that are thought of as a necessary purging process on that path. In addition to the sense of mental and physical well-being that these exercises produce, their more important goal is spiritual, as they create openings to the metaphysical realm. Concentration on the task at hand is said to be crucial in any occult work as 'the mind supplies the forms and channels through which the forces work, and the more definite the channel, the more control can be exercised over the forces flowing therein' (p. 139).

Other sensory modalities – hearing, smell, taste and touch – can be enhanced with training techniques that are similar to those employed for image enhancement. Training for heightened audible sensitivity is done through the use of a gradually diminishing sound, and the projection of audible forms is assisted by using aids such as large seashells. The advanced adept becomes familiar with these practices until there is a shift in consciousness and this state can be attained at will. The combination of enhanced sensory faculties is said to exalt the person's consciousness, 'lifting the mind to another interior plane where there is a perception of the meaning and transcendental nature and being of the god' (Regardie 1979: 39).

Occultists such as W.E. Butler, Israel Regardie and Franz Bardon insist that the most important thing in the art of invocation is imagination, as it develops 'inner sight' and raises awareness of other realms of existence. Prolonged meditation can result in physical body numbness, with the eventual disappearance of any somatic feeling. Awareness of the body is then replaced by another kind of awareness.

Islam and the Sufis

In Sufism, it is important to attain a balance between one's inner and outer dimensions, so all external activities are intended to enhance the inward attention of the Sufi to empty the mind of worldly preoccupations in order to be plunged deeply in ardent love of God, filling one's thoughts only with God. In order to 'remember' that which we know (but have forgotten), we need to invoke 'recollection' (*zikr*) of that which is in our deepest core. When the mind is emptied of all other thoughts, with God as the absolute focus, one is more likely to attain the goal of 'remembering' (Netton 2000: 35–9). This can be achieved by listening profoundly with the 'ear of the heart' to music or poetry, engaging in recitation or other activities that lead to the same goal. One such recitation is: 'God is with me; God watches me; God witnesses me'; and this is repeated over and over again each night until a 'sweetness' manifests in the heart (p. 48). The Sufi is also advised to stay responsive to divine communication and to keep the heart in a constant state of alertness (p. 77). Visualization is very important to this endeavour and there are specific exercises one can practise in order to gain proficiency. Another exercise is to recite the name 'Allah', or the Arabic names of God (mentioned in the Koran), while employing breath control techniques (see Ernst and Lawrence 2002: 29–30), for example, concentrating on moving the divine names from the lower to the upper body and visualizing letters, words or complex visions while doing so (p. 29):

> While holding the breath seven times one gradually raises the visualization of the name Allah from beneath the navel up to the throat where it becomes *hu*. When the seventh repetition is completed gradually release the breath and repeat.

The effect, it is said, is immediate and 'obvious'. Note again, that there is more involved here than visualization; breathing (which will be covered in more detail in chapter 6) is also quite crucial and is a technique that accompanies visualization, along with focused attention on the total physical body.

In the Sufism of Ibn 'Arabi, the term *'ilm al-khayal* means 'science of the Imagination', which is used in the attainment of spiritual experiences (Corbin 1969: 216). Imagination and visualization are so important that Ibn 'Arabi declared: 'He in whom the Active Imagination is not at work will never penetrate to the heart of the question' (p. 38). On the power of the imagination, he said of his own visionary experiences (Futuhat II, 325, cited in Corbin 1969: 382):

> This power of Active Imagination [...] has visually represented to me my mystic Beloved in a corporeal, objective, and extra-mental form, just as the Angel Gabriel appeared to the eyes of the Prophet. And at first I did not feel capable of looking toward that Form. It spoke to me. I listened and understood. These apparitions left me in such a state that for whole days I could take no food. Every time I started toward the table, the apparition was standing at one end, looking at me and saying to me in a language that I heard with my ears 'Will you eat while you are engaged in contemplating me?' And it was impossible for me to eat, but I felt no hunger; and I was so full of my vision that I sated myself and became drunk with contemplating it, so much so that this contemplation took the place of all food for me. My friends and relatives were astonished to see how well I looked, knowing my total abstinence, for the fact is that I remained for whole days without touching any food or feeling hunger or thirst. But that Form never ceased to be the object of my gaze, regardless of whether I was standing or seated, in movement or at rest.

Visions, to Ibn 'Arabi and his followers, whether they are experienced in a waking or dream state, are themselves *penetrations* into the world of another dimension.

In Sufi cosmology, there are five hierarchical planes of being, called 'Presences' (*Hadarat*), and the relations between them are determined by their structure. On each plane there is a bi-unity whose two terms stand in a relation of action and passion to one another. Each lower Presence is the image and correspondence (*mithal*), the reflection and mirror of the next higher image. Thus everything that exists in the mundane world of the senses is a reflection of what exists in the world of Spirits, writes Corbin (1969: 226):

> Because of their correspondences one and the same being can exist simultaneously on entirely different planes, in forms which are in correspondence by virtue of the homology between the world of Spirits and the sensible world.

According to Ibn 'Arabi, prayer is an intimate dialogue with God, and to be successful, it must open out into contemplative vision. For this to occur, the faithful need to 'imagine' (*takhayyul*) God as present and must 'attain intuitive vision' (*schuhud*) or visualization (*ru'ya*). They should contemplate God in the subtle centre, which is the *heart*, while simultaneously hearing the divine voice vibrating in all manifest things to the extent that nothing else is heard. The Sufi says, 'When He shows Himself to me, my whole being is vision: when he speaks to me in secret, my whole being is hearing' (Corbin 1969: 251).

Progression from being a simple believer to experiencing a mystic state is accomplished through an increasing capacity for making oneself 'present to the vision by the Imagination'. One can move from mental vision by way of dream vision to verification in the station of *walaya*, imaginative witnessing vision. The mode of presence conferred by the imaginative power (*hudur khayali*) is not considered to be an illusion, but a 'truthful witness' as it 'sees directly'. To the mystic, the image will be a vision of the 'Form of God' corresponding to his own innermost being, as he is the microcosm of the Divine Being (Corbin 1969: 232–4).

Active imagination is said to guide, anticipate and mould sense perception, and to transmute sensory data into symbols. A distinction is made between imagination and fantasy. The former, *Imaginatio*, is the *magical* production of an *image*, which produces the Spirit in forms and colours, and is 'the fulfilment of being in an Image and a transposition of the Image into being' (Corbin 1969: 282). While fantasy is considered to be the 'madman's cornerstone' (p. 179), imagination is linked to *'alam al-mithal*, 'the world of Idea-Images, the world of apparitional forms and of bodies in the subtile state' (p. 217). Imagination is the intermediary between the world of pure spiritual realities, the world of mystery and the visible, sensible world. The imagination has metaphysical status.

Ibn 'Arabi distinguishes between imagination that is *conjoined* to the imagining subject (it is inseparable from the person), and a self-subsisting imagination *dissociable* from the subject. Imaginations that are conjoined to the imagining subject are provoked by a conscious process of the mind, while those that are dissociable from the subject present themselves to the mind spontaneously like dreams (or daydreams). The specific character of the conjoined imagination is its inseparability from the imagining subject, with whom it lives and dies.

The imagination separable from the subject, on the other hand, has an autonomous and subsisting reality *sui generis* on the plane of the intermediary world, the world of idea-images.[3] Exterior to the imagining subject, it can be seen by others, such as mystics or psychics. The separable images subsist in a world specific to them, so that the imagination in which they occur 'has the status of an "essence" (*hadrat dhatiya*) perpetually capable of receiving ideas and Spirits and of giving them the "apparitional body" that makes possible their epiphany ...' (Corbin 1969: 219). All this demonstrates the extraordinary role of the image in the spirituality of Ibn 'Arabi, and the importance of developing the imagination.

If one imagines, say, a pool of water, then the pool of water is a 'new creation', and precisely because it is 'imagined', the image, once recognized as such, becomes real and meaningful rather than illusory. Finke's theory of 'levels of equivalence', mentioned at the beginning of this chapter, can be partially employed here, in that what the Sufi sees through *himma* is perceived to be just as real as an object that is perceived through everyday sight. However, the Sufis are taking this a step further, as the distinction is made between imagination that is conjoined and imagination that is dissociable. In the latter case, the image has a life apart from the subject, existing separately.

The purpose of enhancing the function of *himma*, or the imaginative faculty, is to perceive the 'intermediate world' in order to raise sensory data to a higher level, so as to permit Sufis to 'fulfil their theophanic function' and thereby gain greater understanding of knowledge of the Divine (Corbin 1969: 239).

> ...O resolute seeker! Enter with me into the Ka'aba of the Hijr, for that is the Temple that rises above all veils and coverings. It is the entrance of the Gnostics; there is the repose of the pilgrims engaged in the processional.[4]

In each of these three quite different religious traditions it is clear that visualization and the imagination play important roles, and each one incorporates similar training exercises in order to attain comparable goals: to be in the presence of the Divine, however interpreted, for the purpose of gaining knowledge, inner awareness or closer attainment of a spiritual goal, or to put such knowledge to use in this life. It should be reiterated that while this chapter highlights visualization as well as using the imagination to enhance visualization, multiple senses are employed, and particular combinations depend on the culture under study.

Religious and Cultural Context

While each religious tradition might employ similar techniques, the theologies associated with each one are quite different. Herein lies the major setback for the argument that 'all religions are the same really'. While technologies and even neurophysiological aspects are most likely constant, the interpretive frameworks for the knowledge gained are very diverse. This explains why seeing a 'light' might be interpreted as a specific deity, iconic religious figure, an enlightened being, and so on, or 'proof' of the veracity of a believer's religious doctrines.

The 'rational' interpretation of an experience, in the cold light of day, calls on the logical mind to explain the experience. The gap between the experience and the telling of the experience seems to be wide. Not only are there bits missing, but the experience is interpreted in the light of what one knows consciously: by recalling culturally appropriate myths, textual narratives, iconic paintings, and so on; thus the actual experience can be quite drastically altered in conveying it to others. It is somewhat like being in a dream, then trying to remember the details of the dream when one wakes up. How we process an image depends to a large extent on what we can recall from our own past image experiences. Most paintings of Christ depict him as a slender male with shoulder-length hair and a beard, and with the marks of the crucifix nails going through the palms of the hands. This is also how most 'visions' of Christ are reported. Research, however, points to the fact that the weight of a mature male body would not support a person nailed to the cross through the palms of the hands, but might support such a weight if the nails were put through the wrists. But few people know this. Rudolf Arnheim writes that a person's direct observation is 'an exploration of the form-seeking, form-imposing mind, which needs to understand but cannot until it casts what it sees into manageable models' (cited in Eck 1985: 15).

To See and Be Seen

The eye is deemed to be the mirror of the soul, and has long been associated with secret mysteries. The words 'mystery', 'mystic' and 'mist', come from the Greek root, *muein*, which means to close the eyes. Initiations into mystery religions involved closing the eyes in contemplative practices in order to discover the mysteries of life. In the Hindu religion, *Dars'an* means 'seeing', especially religious seeing, or 'the visual perception of the sacred'; it is sometimes translated as the 'auspicious sight of the divine'. Eck tells us that from the point of view of the lay person, the central act of Hindu worship is to attend a temple in order to 'stand in the presence of the deity and to behold the image with one's own eyes, to see and be seen by the deity'. It is through the eyes that one gains the blessings of the Divine. Sacred perception, which is the ability to see the divine image, seems to be a reciprocal process: a deity presents itself to be seen in its image, and the worshipper 'truly' sees the deity through the image. Contact between devotee and deity is exchanged through the eyes (Eck 1985: 3, 6–7).

It is not surprising that the eye appears often as a religious symbol; we see and understand things with our outer eyes. When our eyes are closed, the eyelids act as veils that cover our perception of the material world. But even with eyes closed, as in dreams, we perceive things and can sometimes gain knowledge through the symbols contained in those dreams. We can also 'see' with our 'mind's eye', anticipating an event, visualizing a particular scenario, or imaging an object. Upon intense meditation on a particular object, the object might undergo a physical ontic shift, and sometimes appear as something other than it is. Focusing on a fixed point in the centre of the visual field, and at the same time being aware of the peripheral field, it is possible to 'see' things that, on closer inspection, are not physically there.

Generic Symbols

The following are generic symbols that 'pull' the viewer into the centre and act as portals:

Spiral:

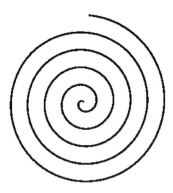

Concentric circle:

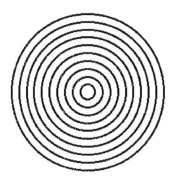

Concentric square:

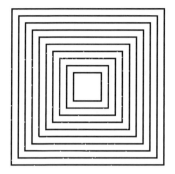

These symbols direct the eye inward and outward, providing a cognitive or optical figure-ground reversal, and then the image can be seen in third-dimensional form, with the 'spaces between' being more prominent if focused on. The eye/mind is drawn into the centre and out again, as if through a vortex. With the eye thus focused, images begin to arise in the conscious mind and one can go into a light trance.

Intense concentration on a particular symbol can centre the mind, stimulate non-analytical modes of knowing and operate as a door or passageway. Iconic symbols appear to be highly effective in contacting a particular spirit or iconic figure. For example, intense devotion to an icon of the Virgin Mary may produce a vivid and highly significant experience for a Roman Catholic; likewise a vévé (ground drawing, usually made in cornmeal, associated with a particular spirit) for a practitioner of Vodou; or a tarot card image for a Western occultist.

Entoptic Phenomena

Various geometric designs, such as lattices or grids, parallel lines, dots and flecks, zigzag lines, wavy or undulating lines, bright dots or flecks, circles, as well as meandering lines and other similar phenomena (such as those found in the caves mentioned in chapter 1), form part of entoptic (visual) phenomena. They are generated in the eye and within the optic system beyond the retina. The images are believed to derive from the structure of the nervous system (Blundell 1998: 4–5).

Lewis-Williams and Dowson call such images 'form constants', 'phosphenes' and 'entoptic phenomena' (1988: 201–45). Entoptic phenomena produced by inducing altered states of consciousness are very similar in geometric form among people as geographically distant as the San of South Africa (Blundell 1998: 3–12), the northern Paiute of California (Patterson 1998) and Western student subjects in a laboratory setting (Patterson 1998: 44–5).[5] They are known to appear during the first stages of a trance state. The images can be experienced as luminous and animated, and can fragment and reduplicate themselves, as well as rotate in the field of vision.

They can also integrate, superimpose and juxtapose with one another. Although these various shapes may be experienced the same way universally, they might be interpreted according to cultural expectations. However, in spite of different cultural backgrounds, everyone has the potential to see them.

Building on the work of Ronald Siegel, Lewis-Williams and Dowson suggest a three-stage model, based principally on entoptic phenomena, for understanding the progression of altered states. Although three stages are mentioned, a person might go directly to the second and third stages without experiencing the first stage. The first stage is a description of the various geometric visual percepts that people experience when initially entering an altered state. In the second stage, the 'construal stage', people try to make sense of the phenomena. It is at this stage that an experience is interpreted according to cultural, subcultural or belief-specific ways, as well as in accordance with their individual emotional states. They may then move to the third stage, the 'iconic', where they become drawn into the images. This may be accompanied by a variety of sensorial experiences: olfactory, tactile, aural and somatic.

At the transition between the second and third stages, many people feel they are passing through or being drawn into a vortex, on the sides of which there may be a lattice or grid. Some describe the vortex as a whirlpool or whirlwind. They may experience difficulty in breathing, constriction or a sensation of being swallowed up. The vortex may turn into a tunnel that leads underground to another realm.

In the third stage, a deep trance occurs. Here, entoptic phenomena are combined with iconic images of people, animals and monsters. In this stage also, people feel themselves blend with the images or transform (partially or fully) into animals. There may be an experience of rising up and flying and/or of being transformed into a bird, with accompanying changes of a view from above. They may also believe they can travel beyond their human bodies. Taking these different experiences into consideration, it is not surprising that shamanic societies hold a three-tiered system of the cosmos: one that is above, one that is below and the mundane level between.

Certain motifs in rock art show significant similarities to the imagery experienced in altered states of consciousness. Blundell raises the point that particular entoptics dominate in certain areas, and ponders that it may be because of different methods used for inducing altered states of consciousness. Jeremy Dronfield, who has worked on Neolithic passage-tomb art, argues that the concentric imagery of the tombs is located on the walls so as to be visually related to the passages. Further, that 'concentrics and passages were intended to be, respectively, representations and reconstructions of subjective tunnel experiences' (Dronfield 1996: 37). Dronfield also considers the position of lattice and lozenge motifs near human skeletal remains in Neolithic times, suggesting that these images might have been mnemonic devices and symbols used in the process of negotiating access for the recently deceased. By linking entoptic imagery to the symbolic construction of space at Irish Neolithic passage-tombs, Dronfield attempts to move beyond identifying and classifying entoptic imagery as an end itself. Indeed, the entoptic designs may be only part of the picture, perhaps precursors to deep trance, alerting the person that the way is opening up for the deeper trance experience.

Discussion

In this chapter, although I have taken examples from a broad range of religions, cultures and historical epochs, certain themes cross-cut all of them with regard to the role of visual portals. Enhanced visualization and focused attention is a technique and a training procedure that is emphasized by shamans, Western esotericists, Buddhists and Australian Aborigines, in order to develop the 'inner eye' – however this is expressed. Another theme is that metaphysical knowledge opens the door to forces and powers that are both external to, and residing in, the individual. Visualization and meditation, when accompanied by strong emotions, are key concepts to attaining some sort of attunement with another presence or power that is greater than the individual. The interpretation of this invariably ineffable experience is often expressed poetically or in metaphors, and has to rely on the inadequate use of words to convey their true impact. Also, the astounding nature of what is seen/felt/heard is communicated through cultural filters. As the discussion in this chapter focused on the visual, and the eye is the mechanism for seeing, I now turn to August Reader (1995), a clinical professor of ophthalmology, to articulate the West's difficulty in accepting any metaphysical experience without resorting to a Western science paradigm.

The physiology of the visual system and its role in occurrences of a mystical nature was investigated by August Reader after he had an intriguing episode that involved what has been described in the literature as a typical near-death experience. At 1.30 a.m. he suffered severe chest pain which radiated with heat down his left arm and up into the left part of his neck. As the pain increased and his breathing started to lessen, his heart suddenly stopped beating. As a physician, he immediately recognized the signs of cardiac ischemia and was convinced that he was dying. He broke out in a sweat and seemed to become paralysed. Many anxious and troubling thoughts arose in his mind as he lay there thinking of all the things that needed to be done, of his family, his practice and his life. Then, in the midst of these thoughts, he remembered being told as a child that when facing death one should let go of everything and turn to God. When he decided to let himself go and release himself 'to the arms of God' he felt a sense of bliss and understanding, and he experienced (Reader 1995: 55):

> holographic flashes of everything that occurred in my life, from the most trivial detail to the most important events, all displayed equally and with no favor, connected by golden threads, showing me that everything that had occurred to me in my life was important, was part of who I was, and was essential to who I had been. And in that knowledge

was the understanding that my life had been worthwhile and I had nothing to regret in dying.

That vision lasted, he said, only half a second, and then he was projected down a long rocky tunnel of greyish-brown, with a bright light at the end; this bright light then turned golden-white and began to surround and suffuse through him, and at the same time he saw the faces of everyone he had known, both alive and dead, including his own father who had been dead for seven years. He was asked if he would like to 'join the dance', but he said no, and then he 'awoke' to the sound of his alarm clock.

A Western rationalist approach tends to explain away this incident as being attributable to a vivid dream (itself an intriguing concept), and instead of exploring metaphysical literature on the topic, or delving into religious or cross-cultural sources for similar phenomena, Reader chose instead to investigate the neurological foundations of the visual system that might have created the experience, and to limit his explanation to one that might be palatable to an academic readership. Briefly, these are his findings (Reader 1995: 55–9).

Reader's scientific physicalist explanation is that the stimulation of the sympathetic nervous system can lead to an increase in visual imagery, which produces images such as angels, elves, ghosts, the Virgin Mary, and so on, and this is due to a release of the memories in the right temporal lobe, mediated through the amygdala and limbic system as part of the fight-or-flight mechanism. When there is excessive stimulation of the sympathetic nervous system, the visual imagery can be vivid and can generate the experience of a white light. When this light occurs, there is a profound and sudden decrease in peripheral vascular resistance due to the excessive parasympathetic stimulus; the sudden release causes a rapid increase in blood flow through the entire body, which gives a sensation of energy or light being transmitted. As the white light develops, blood is 'shunted away from the occipital lobe', which enhances the white light experience and, at the same time, causes the tactile sensation of an energy flow through the body.

In short, there is marked peripheral vasodilation that leads to cortical ischemia, and this, suggests August Reader, is what occurs in profound mystical states such as those experienced in Zen Buddhism and Hinduism. There is also a psychological component as the events are enhanced when there is extreme fear or panic (high emotional states), which comes into play whenever the sympathetic nervous system is stimulated in a fight-or-flight response. The occipital lobe (say proponents of this explanation) is of major importance to the white light experience and the temporal lobe for visual imagery.

The autonomic nervous system, comprising both the sympathetic and para-sympathetic nervous systems, acts as the automatic regulatory mechanism within the body and in balancing the stresses that assail the physical body, both internally and externally. There is at play (Reader 1995: 62):

a complex system of reflexes that mediate ischemia to the cerebral cortex, stimulating 'release' of the occipital poles and the rostral midbrain to discharge these images in any profound state of cellular agony. These vascular events are mediated by way of the autonomic nervous system.

This scientific explanation provides convincing evidence about what the body is undergoing while something of this kind is being experienced, yet such an explanation is limited as it does not really account for the entire phenomenon. While many readers might seem convinced of the above argument, which dismisses the encounter by offering the systemic mechanics of any unexpected encounter as a total explanation, Reader himself, in spite of turning to this scientific approach, remained somewhat perplexed, and concluded by posing the question: why is the experience (his own and that of others) accompanied by such a 'profound feeling of Spirit', and 'a love that is so profound, deep, and unifying that it seems it can only come from a Universal Presence, and from nowhere else' (p. 61).

There are two aspects of the near-death experience that cannot be fully explained physiologically, writes Reader (1995: 60), who continues to be baffled by the experience. One is the initiation of the near-death reflex; the other is the subjugation of will to a higher power, which subsequently changes the way one lives in the world after the experience. Not everyone who has a cardiac arrest has a near-death experience with the classic features of entering a tunnel, seeing a white light and encountering spiritual beings. It seems that the emotional factor of fear that is generated by the realization that death is near – as well as the hope of rescue in a high power, and the subjugation of will to that higher power – is Reader's tentative explanation. Nevertheless, he concludes his article thus (p. 62):

> ...the internal mysteries of the brain will always hide the Inner Mysteries, although the heart will always have a way of finding the right answers.

This final statement indicates his own ambivalence about reducing such phenomena to only one component – the physiological – in spite of concerted efforts to do so.

While most recorded near-death experiences report a positive and overwhelming feeling of assurance that death is not to be feared, and many transform their lives as a result of their encounter, not all near-death adventures are positive. Some individuals have had terrifying experiences (see Bush 2002), which have led them to harbour forebodings of death and to fear it. But that is another story which I will leave the reader to pursue.

It is clear that there are many ways of approaching such phenomena and we should not restrict our understanding to purely physiological explanations. Such confined reasoning is limiting and deprives us of exploring exciting alternatives that might greatly add to, and complement, a Western scientific approach. It also undermines thousands of years of deep insight gained by people in other cultures on the vast and seemingly limitless possibilities of mind, body and spirit.

Portal symbols, write Laughlin et al. (1992: 237), are 'like doors between rooms, or perhaps keys to the doors between rooms', and myth forms a narrative bridge that gives context and meaning to symbols. Myths equip the listener with a set of symbolic images that often can be used as access points, or portals. Many of the visuals discussed in this chapter aid the practitioner in opening those doors; sometimes symbols are imaginally inscribed on doorways or other portals in order to facilitate entrance to and exit from invisible realms. Visual technologies are a strong method of moving through portals and can be used alone or as an accompaniment to other technologies, such as sound or physical movement. In the next chapter, sound technologies will be the focus of the discussion.

–3–

Portals of Sound

You look, but you do not see. You touch, but you do not feel. You listen, but you do not hear. Without sight or touch … one can learn a great deal. But you *must* learn how to hear, or you will learn little about our ways.

Songhay sorcerer[1]

Marsilio Ficino (1433–99), humanist of Renaissance Florence, attributed magical power to music. Like others before him, Ficino thought that 'all realities emit vibrating rays which together compose the harmonious chorus of the universe', and that 'each sonic emission is attuned to other resonances which reverberate in accord with the first sound because they resemble it in some measure' (Sullivan 1997: 2). When, for example, one string of an instrument is plucked, another string 'trembles' in accord with the first one because they are 'tuned in the same consonance', and, in turn, 'carry-on echoes' evoke 'continuing syntonies which reverberate in shifting patterns throughout the entire cosmos' (p. 2). A medical physician who was knowledgeable about the scientific advances of his day, Ficino nevertheless was convinced that music was more effective than medicine in healing certain physical complaints because music was attuned to celestial benefits. He spent much of his life working on translations of pagan and magical texts attributed to Hermes Trismegistus, which he believed contained secret wisdom. Ficino expounded his 'music-spirit theory' in his *Three Books On Life*, devoted to the potential role of music in curing disease, and suggested that music also played an instrumental role in theurgy, or the invocation of the gods. He even offered practical techniques for creating songs to employ planetary emanations that would counteract melancholia. His musico-magical doctrines suggested that certain kinds of songs had the potential to summon demons, an idea that, although anathema to orthodox Christianity, achieved prominence in the late sixteenth and early seventeenth centuries (Gouk 2000: 9–10).

Many of the religious communities discussed in the collection of articles in Sullivan's edited book, *Enchanting Powers* (1997), demonstrate similar notions about the enchanting power of religious music, and its ability not only to attune itself to other realities, but to provoke other realities into resonating in tune with it. In medieval Java, for example, where tantric practices were maintained after long years of study with a spiritual guide, focused yet relaxed listening to certain kinds of music was believed to be a vehicle of transportation to the mystic union with deity, or for the descent of a personal deity (Beckert 1997: 16, 49).

43

Having one's ears 'opened' to the significance of sound is highly significant to an apprentice Songhay (Nigeria, Africa) sorcerer, as indicated by the quotation at the beginning of this chapter. Paul Stoller, who spent several years among the Songhay as an apprentice sorcerer, relates that once he accompanied his sorcerer instructor to the top of a dune (where Songhay women traditionally sift millet seed from husk) in search of a sick man's 'double', or spirit. After sifting through the millet seed for some time, the sorcerer suddenly jumped up, exclaiming that he had sensed a sick man's 'double'. He then asked Stoller whether he had heard, felt or seen the same thing, but the bewildered Stoller had to confess that he had not. So began Stoller's apprenticeship in Songhay hearing, which changed his own epistemological presuppositions. The Songhay believe that sound is a phenomenon in and of itself, and is the carrier of powerful forces. Words not only convey knowledge or information, but they are also power and energy themselves. Indeed, Stoller's fieldwork experiences led him to suggest, like Favret-Saada (1980), that there is efficacy in magical utterances, words have power and sound is very powerful indeed.

In the Bocage area of rural France, where Favret-Saada carried out her fieldwork, 'the act in witchcraft', she says, 'is the word' (1980: 9). When she started questioning the local people about witchcraft, she was asked, 'are you strong enough?' (p. 11), implying that only a strong person would be able to sustain the physical and mental dangers of the enquiry. The more she delved into witchcraft, the more she became personally involved in the intricacies of local beliefs and 'caught' in them herself. Belief in witchcraft is still very much alive, and although no one admits to being a witch or uttering harmful spells, people say that they have been bewitched, and others are known to be 'unwitchers' (spell-breakers).

The people of the Bocage say that the witch has a certain amount of magical 'force' and can deplete a person's vital energy so that they become ill. Also, the witch can cause accidents by means of rituals and incantations. Many of the people who confess to having been 'caught' by witches, say they must not talk about it; for the less one talks, the less one is likely to be 'caught' again.

A bewitched person tries to avoid death or loss of their vital life force by calling on a known 'unwitcher' (itself a precarious occupation, as an unwitcher may afterwards be accused of being a witch) who is capable of combating the power of the witch. What actually circulates, say the people of the Bocage, is vital force, but what causes it to circulate is magic force. Naming or talking about a person who is accused of being a witch can be dangerous, and love can quickly turn to hate if even a close friend is suspected of being a witch. As Favret-Saada confesses, she experienced terror and confusion (1980: 127) as she watched a chain of thoughts play out: a man died in a car accident, she herself was involved in a series of car accidents, people in the community subsequently remembering spells that were uttered or believed to be uttered, and the general feeling that all these events were due to witchcraft. Thus, following an unfortunate event, innuendos and gossip fly about with very little to restrain them. All this was happening in late twentieth-century France, and Favret-Saada must have felt that she had stepped back into the height of the witchcraft craze in the Middle Ages.

It seems that very little has changed in some areas of rural France with regard to beliefs about witchcraft. Consider Favret-Saada's comment (1980: 133):

> When I heard about the inescapable death of Pierre Coquin, I was thus '*caught*' in the discourse of the bewitched. So convinced was I of its reality that I did not even wonder whether there was any other way of 'reading' this drama. It had been enough that my subjective landmarks should have dissolved on one occasion in which the possibility of my own death had become a fact. It was as if, for a few hours, I had accepted as the only possible truth the affirmations of the bewitched, according to which, in spells, one can never expect any sort of statement from witches, since they never admit being one, they pretend they do not believe in it all, and they treat those who accuse them as backward people who would be better off applying the rules of the experimental method more rigorously.

Thus, the power of words, or the innuendos that lead to the belief in the power of words, can be very powerful indeed. When communities of people believe so implicitly in witchcraft, as Favret-Saada found, it is extremely difficult not to get caught up in the discourse of witchcraft and the beliefs if one stays in that community. Favret-Saada's experience mirrors that of Tanya Luhrmann (who studied contemporary witchcraft in England), which she later termed 'interpretive drift' (1989: 312), to describe the slow, often unacknowledged, but significant shift in the way events are interpreted as one becomes more ensconced in a particular activity. The researcher becomes progressively more skilled at seeing a different pattern to events, one that accords with the group under study. One could say that researchers enter and engage with another kind of reality, one that is every bit as real to those engaged in it, as any other set of realities in any other community. Thus it is not difficult to see that with the addition of other technologies (sound from objects such as drumming, mandalas, and so on) one can move into another frame of mind and drift even further.

In some cultures, the focus on listening takes precedence over oration and rhetorical skills. For example, Veit Erlmann writes that for Muslim theologians and philosophers, the beauty and perfection of the divine message of the Koran is transmitted to followers through listening; one needs to open not only one's heart, but one's ears to God (Erlmann 2004: 12). So, as anthropologists, we should develop more sensitivity to listening even more intently in our quest for cultural understanding.

In this chapter I consider sound in various forms, particularly how sound can take one through a portal to the 'other side'. Drumming, chanting, magical words, sound vibrations and emotional songs that 'uplift the soul' will all be considered as means to transport one from the mundane to the transcendent. Sound does not necessarily take one into a trance state, though it can do this, but sounds can have a strong emotional component that put the listener/singer into a different frame of mind, one that is receptive to the transcendent experience. Sounds from instruments, and from the human voice, both have the ability to transcend the ordinary in some traditions. In the next section I start with the emotionally evocative songs and other sonant components that enable contemporary Pentecostals to encounter the healing power of Jesus, and then I move on to sound vibrations, rhythms that 'follow the heartbeat', and the efficacy of drumming.

The Pentecostals

People who undergo a profound Christian religious conversion say that no words can do justice to such an experience. Sometimes the encounter is overpowering and can produce, in some denominations such as Pentecostalism, activities such as speaking in tongues (glossolalia), trembling, loud shouting, repetitive singing or swooning into apparent unconsciousness. Deep emotions also result in spontaneous and joyful singing, hymns of praise or devotional poetry (Streng 1985: 35).

A 'successful' Pentecostal service, where members feel they have encountered the presence of Jesus, would not be possible without the highly charged emotions that are instigated by the music. Indeed, the stage of musicians and musical instruments is the focal point of most services, and the sounds 'symbolize an entrance into the felt presence of God'. The worshipper is elevated to a heightened or ecstatic state in which the presence of the Divine is 'keenly felt' (Stowe 2004: 3). Music functions as an 'auditory icon', embracing and surrounding each of the worshippers; verbal utterances and shouts (such as 'Halleluja!' and 'Jesus!') are 'oral sacred expletives', that help the congregation usher in and sense the Holy Spirit (Albrecht 1999: 143). As well as providing an atmosphere of high excitement, and the expectation that something momentous is about to happen, music is the precursor for other physical expressions of devotion, such as raising the arms and touching others. The encouragement of social interaction helps to prepare and sustain congregants for an emotionally intense session of worship.

A fundamental characteristic of the Pentecostal movement in general is the belief that its followers can tap into God's power through the intensity of their faith. One of Csordas' (1997: 202) informants expressed this idea as follows:

> It's a sort of immediacy of God speaking to the person. It's not like an actor on the stage where an actor speaks in God's name. There's usually a spiritual sense about it. When you hear a prophecy you're really hearing something of God addressing you. It's not just this person.

A 'prophecy' is understood as the direct utterance of God through an inspired speaker (p. 164), after which many in the congregation respond by saying, 'Thank you, Jesus', or 'Alleluia, Jesus'. Glossolalia, or speaking in tongues, is considered a gift of deity, and indicates that the utterer is not his/her normal self. Speaking in tongues is 'a ritual statement that the speakers inhabit a sacred world', since the gift of prophecy and glossolalia are considered a gift from the deity (p. 238). Imagery may also accompany a prophecy: one man had a revelatory image of a multitude of people clothed in white while he was engaged in prophesying, and another pictured a hedge with runners emerging from it (pp. 230, 232). Charismatic imagery might occur at any time and is closely associated with prophetic utterance, but it occurs regularly during prayer; one prophet perceived the prophecy first as an image, and then the words came (Csordas 1994: 75), which is not uncommon. Members of the congregation might open their hands, palms upwards, during the service, in order to receive God's power; and touch is extremely important in charismatic healing, when the power of the Lord moves through the healer (the conduit of power) into the sick person to make them well again. Thus, while words, songs and prayers are highlighted in Pentecostal services, they are not without other accompanying sensory modes.

The spiritual 'gifts' from God, such as prophecy, healing and glossolalia, prove to the Pentecostals the strength of God's power over the limitations of orthodox medicine and the faithless non-believers. Evidence of divine power is demonstrated weekly, if not daily, in the lives of the Pentecostalists through 'signs and wonders' (such as glossolalia, divine healing and prophecy). A part of the Pentecostal discourse emphasizes the power of imagination, visualization and the employment of the right words. The faith of the believers becomes a spiritual energy or power which makes the laws of the spirit world function in that the positive power (God) is activated and the negative power (Satan) is negated (Hunt 1998: 275). Pentecostals speak of 'binding' as the restriction of the powers of evil (demonic spirits of illness, for example), and 'loosing' (allowing the power of God to become active in a particular situation, such as to promote healing or prosperity).

Certain steps are taken during binding and loosing. The person audibly thanks the Lord for having made him/her his representative and for giving him/her authority over devils. S/he then submits to God, 'speaks to the devil' by using scriptures against him and then prays for healing. S/he then thanks God for having done all that has been 'commanded'. In this binding and loosing process, the spoken word appears to be crucial (Hunt 1998: 275–6), and importance is placed on positive thinking and speaking with authority. By 'speaking the Word of God', the speaker can demand authority over Satan and employ the power of the name of 'Jesus' to instigate the healing process ('that cancer has to obey your word') (p. 277). Merely uttering the word, however, is not sufficient in itself; one must have faith in God that his power is transferred to the words for them to have effect.

Hunt compares the practices of Pentecostalist 'Faith' ministries in the USA with the magical practices of shamanism. Both, he writes, invoke metaphysical techniques to bring about change. The neo-Pentecostal Faith ministries of which he speaks teach that health and wealth can be acquired through the atonement of Christ, and the manifestation of God's power to believers. Pentecostalists stress the power of imagination, visualization and 'confessing' the right words in the form of incantations, and this, suggests Hunt, can be likened to magical practice. Although Pentecostalists themselves would no doubt find the idea abhorrent, belief in and practice of miraculous works mirror closely those who use magic to bring about a desired goal. For the Faith ministries about which Hunt writes, 'faith' is a spiritual force, energy or power that makes the laws of the spirit world function. The sacred words become more than symbolic; they become imbued with a spiritual power that can be manipulated by the speakers. Words, writes Hunt (1998: 277), 'are agents in themselves which establish connections between human beings, and between human beings and the world'. They can alter reality.

Although there is no evidence to demonstrate that all Pentecostalists go into trance in their ritual performances, they certainly aim to encourage either a mystical experience, and/or direct communication with their God. In this sense, they are entering a doorway to the divine encounter, and every effort is made to 'develop and maintain pathways' into God's presence (Albrecht 1999: 142). As Albrecht writes, Pentecostal services are a communal affair, with the fundamental aim of constructing an atmosphere in which they may consciously and intuitively encounter God, which is often expressed as a 'felt presence of the divine' (p. 149). During what Albrecht terms 'transcendental ecstasy', people may have a sense of being 'inspired' to speak or act, or, more dramatically, of being acted upon or seized by the (transcendental) Divine, and being infused with the Holy Spirit (p. 186). During these times a person's gestures and facial appearance can suggest to observers that some kind of ecstatic experience is occurring and, ipso facto, that they are in the presence of Spirit. Openness to this orientation underlies Pentecostal spirituality.

Although Pentecostal services may differ somewhat from one culture to another, they all seem to follow a basic structure with regard to the intentional build-up of emotion through music, the invoking of the presence of the Holy Spirit and the belief that God can work miracles through the faithful. The interweaving of music and emotion in Pentecostal groups is particularly fine-tuned; it is carried out so effectively, in fact, that every service is demonstrably successful in bringing about heightened emotions in most of the people present and seemingly desired outcomes of healing, prophecy and glossolalia, all of which are regarded as a sign of the presence of Jesus.

The Halveti-Jerrahi Order of Dervishes

Ritual prayer (*salat*), performed five times a day, is one of the fundamental obligations of all Muslims. Regular recitation of verses of the Koran also forms an important part of Islamic religion, and can sometimes be extremely emotional when performed with others in a mosque. Although the Islamic holy book, the Koran, does not mention how God is to be remembered, the mystical branch of Islam, the Sufis, consider that it is by being close to God, and having the direct experience of God's presence, that one can best 'remember' God.

Among the Sufis, one branch of which is the Halveti-Jerrahi Order of Dervishes, repetitive prayer is known as a form of *dhikr*, which means, in a general sense, 'remembrance of God'. In a more limited sense, *dhikr* refers to repetitive prayer performed to express love of God and a longing for his presence. *Dhikr* can be expressed as: *dhikr* of the tongue (*jali*), *dhikr* of the heart (*qalb*) and *dhikr* of the inmost being (*sirr*), which all involve repeating the name of God 'with concentration and full intention of the heart, and of one's inmost being', and with certain body movements. This practice can lead to an alteration of ordinary perception and cognition, and a loss of the consciousness of self. When *dhikr* is performed in this manner, the mystic experiences *tauhid*, unification, at which time there is a total annihilation of the self (*nafs*) and a dissolution of ego in order to allow the presence of God. Thus, through focused attention, movement, repetitive prayer or chanting, and the belief that it is possible to be in the presence of God, the Sufis attain true *dhikr* (Geels 1996: 229–51).

While songs or chants (accompanied by music or not) can be employed to evoke intense emotional experiences in singers and listeners alike, and are used to great effect in charismatic Christian churches, and repetitive prayer and movement can break through barriers so that the Sufis feel they are in the presence of God, certain instruments such as drums (universally identified as a potent element of emotionally charged rituals), and the more culturally specific didjeridu (which I discuss in this chapter), can trigger the same sort of transformations and lead to intense emotional and physiological changes.

Drumming

The Siberian shaman's personal drum enabled him to move between the three zones of the universe. In the ceremonial performance known as *kamlanie*, the drum symbolically fulfilled the role of a superior animal, on which the shaman journeyed. During *kamlanie*, shamans often placed the drum between their legs and beat it with their drumstick as though whipping a horse or reindeer. If, in the course of the journey, a river blocked the shaman's path, the drum transformed itself into a boat in order for the shaman to proceed on his journey. The drum also gathered together the shaman's spirit-helpers and (among other things) was used to convey the souls of sick people back to their ailing bodies. Drums and rattles promoted 'spectral shifts between inner and outer auditory perception', sounds moved 'in aural streams between foreground and background, between inner and outer soundscapes, between memory and the present, between music, language and noise'. The sounds and vibrations of both voices and drums reverberated in bodies and in acoustical spaces occupied by performers and listeners, linking ordinary humans with extraordinary spirits (Miller 1999: 71–2).

The Kaluli people of Papua New Guinea also recognize the important link between drumming, emotions and somatic experience. The Kaluli believe that everything, including sounds (such as birdsong) and objects (such as drums), has a visible realm (an 'outside') and a reflection realm (an 'inside'); one is the deeper reality of the other. They say that two coextensive realities make up the world: one visible, the other a reflection.

A deceased person becomes a spirit reflection, appearing in the visible world in the form of some animal, or more often in the form of a bird (Feld 1982: 32). Spirits communicate with the living through bird calls; hence, as well as being 'indicators of the avifauna', bird sounds are also the 'talk' of the dead (p. 30). As one Kaluli man told Feld: 'to you they are birds, to me they are voices in the forest' (p. 45). Bird sounds are understood as having 'inside' words (p. 17), and because of their association with the dead, the songs and performances that mimic birds evoke strong emotions of nostalgia and sadness. Weeping, sadness and death are associated with birds, myths, dance and the natural environment. Weeping indicates emotional expression among the Kaluli and is equated with expressions of grief and bird sounds. Performances that portray nostalgia and sadness are deliberately invoked to produce these sentiments in an audience.

When seances are conducted in dark longhouses, they provide an opportunity for the living to hear the voices of the spirits of the dead conveying information about the non-visible side of things. During the seances those present are 'entertained by the dramatic prowess of a single person's repertoire of voices, sound effects and songs' (Feld 1982: 215) in an atmosphere provided by the effective interplay of light and shadow, the visual éclat of a feathered dancer's bird-like mimicries and movements, and the continuous background sound of a shaking rattle. People are moved to tears by the songs, and there is, writes Feld, a 'polyphony of weeping and song' (p. 215). 'Becoming a bird' is the Kaluli metaphor for the passage from life to death, and while death and loss are said to move women to weeping, song is intentionally constructed to move men to tears.

As well as the importance placed on sound in the form of birdsongs and the association of birds with deceased loved ones, the sound that emanates from drums is similarly respected as having powerful properties. The intention of ceremonial drumming is for listeners to reflect on a deeper reality and acknowledge that sound is always more than it appears to be.

The single-headed, conical, three-foot long drum is decorated, carved and painted so that it 'glistens'; all parts of the drum are attributed with human anatomical equivalences, the most important being the upper portion, which covers the living, breathing essence that is inside, thus continuing the notion that all things have both an 'outside' and an 'inside', or a visible and a non-visible aspect. The drum's 'voice', with its pulsing, throbbing and carrying qualities, is said to flow like water. The construction of a drum is complex and involves a magical means of imparting sonic pattern to the drum and infusing it with aesthetic power. Although drums are not considered secret or sacred, there is a certain amount of magic and secrecy associated with Kaluli drumming (Feld 1991: 83–4).

The most desired acoustic properties of the drum are an equal pulsation at the same pitch and consistency, and a throbbing quality with 'resonant carrying power' (Feld 1991: 87). Drumming is said to be most effective when the sound has 'hardened', that is, when it has begun to 'pulsate strongly'; and drummers are meant to feel the pulsing sensation in their upper arms and chest, as well as in the lower hands and fingers (p. 90). The drum pulse is regular and isometric, beating between 130 and 140 times per minute. Feld reports that the salient acoustic features of the drumming are the loud intensity and regularity of pulsation, the denseness of the sound as a continual overlapping throb, and the layering quality of the pitches, with clear overtone octaves and the inner fifth constantly shifting figure and ground (p. 84).

Following the Heartbeat in Australia

A physiological factor, such as the human pulse rate, appears to be used as an accurate time measurement device in some Aboriginal Australian performances (Ellis 1984: 161). Accompaniment beats tend to cluster around the average pulse rate of 60–75 per minute, or multiples of that rate. The common system of accompanying in pairs of beats is at the same tempo and rhythm of the double action of the pumping of the human heart, and as singers commented to Moyle, 'the accompaniment organises the songs for us' (Moyle 1986: 256, fn.).

The Pitjantjatjara in central Australia use a continuous stick-beating accompaniment known as *tukultjinganyi*, which is said to 'follow the heartbeat' (Ellis 1984: 161). The Pitjantjatjara say that while the breath controls the length of the phrase, the speed of singing and of beating is governed by listening to the heart. In the performance of songs that name (and therefore contain the power of) important geographical and sacred sites, the singing is accompanied by the large, strong beating of sticks (*timpil pulka*). The expression *inma pulka inkanyi*, or 'singing in a strongly accented style', describes the performance (p. 167).

While patterns of rhythmic segments differ, the beating is the same. Rhythmic accentuation is also a crucial factor in perception of time. Ellis writes that there is a complex process of overlaying patterns which affect a participant's awareness of the musical event, and which include all performance features related to accentuation and duration of central Australian songs. Each one is concerned with the manipulation of elements of time in some way, and often with the disorientation of the sense of everyday time (Ellis 1997: 63).

Ellis compares the 'flip' that is possible in reverse configuration diagrams (where a black and white figure drawing can be seen first in one sense if one concentrates on the black outline, then in another sense if one concentrates on the white outline) with the 'flip' that is possible in music. (This seems to reflect Feld's comments on the 'constantly shifting figure and ground' that occur during Kaluli drumming, as mentioned earlier.) In music, the background may become foreground and may not easily revert to background again. The combination of interlocking patterns in ceremonial performances provides a clue as to how changes in states of awareness, aimed at reaching into the concept of cosmic time (which underpins Aboriginal cosmology), is possible. Some Aboriginal music affects the perceived flow of time as it interrupts a recognized pattern and disorients the listener or the performer (Ellis 1984: 160):

> From the smallest element of the fixed duration of the short notes setting the song text, through the beating duration, the repeated rhythmic segments, rhythmic patterns, text presentations, to melody, small song and songline – each using its own time-scale, and each a series of intermittently emphasized patterns such that first one, then another occupies the centre of attention – a ceremony which combines past and future is unfolded.

In this way, the ceremonial performance of an Ancestor, and the mythological narrative that accompanies that performance, links past and future simultaneously with the present.

Ellis' work on the structure of Aboriginal music led her to make the observation that, far from being simple repetitive structures that may be memorized easily, knowledgeable Aboriginal singers play with a multi-layered system of finesse and intricacy of performance that Westerners can scarcely comprehend. Perhaps this incomprehension is partly attributable to the way music is viewed in the contemporary West.[2] While music has strong effects on the emotions, and some music is specifically associated with ethnicity and religion, it is rarely (if ever) totally involved with the mythological and religious significance of a ceremonial performance in quite the same way as it is in Aboriginal Australia.

The didjeridu is not present in all areas of Australia, but even in areas where it is found, music is primarily vocal and is built around short bursts of singing, the length governed by the physical endurance of the singer to maintain breath (Ellis 1985: 20). Nevertheless, as David Turner discovered, the didjeridu is more than just an instrument for producing sound, at least on Groote Eylandt (Australia).

Turner carried out anthropological fieldwork with Groote Eylandt people for many years, and studied didjeridu playing under the guidance of a Groote Eylandt man named Gula. Beginning with an interest in the work of Tim Wilson on Gregorian chant, Turner was interested in the notion of high and low frequency sounds. He noted that some sounds 'charge' the emotions, and other sounds 'discharge' the emotions. High frequency sounds 'charge' and 'pick one up', while low frequency sounds 'discharge' or make one tired. But the latter also cause the listener to lose touch with his or her body and enter into a kind of hypnosis. Gregorian chant sounds all 'charge' and are uttered in a characteristic slope which increases from low to high frequencies. Tibetan Buddhist chanting, on the other hand, charges and discharges at the same time. The effect of didjeridu playing, according to Turner, is like Tibetan chanting. It simultaneously 'charges' and 'discharges' and produces a paradoxical state of 'excited relaxation' (Turner 1997: 34).

Gula told Turner that playing the didjeridu makes you feel 'quick' (*amugwa*) and warm, as if you are walking along with a bounce in your step. But it also 'cools you down', like shade or shadow (*awarawalya*). That is, one feels both enlivened and becalmed at the same time. Just as the sound of the didjeridu is produced by breathing in and out at the same time (circular breathing), the effect of that sound is simultaneously dual: a meditative mind in an enlivened body. Gula said that the didjeridu is for (he put his hand to his solar plexus), and the song is for (he touched his head). That is, the didjeridu is for the heart and the song is for the mind. After about four hours of didjeridu playing, Turner felt light-headed, released of stress and 'energised'. When he played the music associated with Groote Eylandt mortuary ceremonies, he became 'very detached and peaceful' and saw how playing might 'calm the emotions and relieve the pain of grief' (Turner 1997: 62).

However, the didjeridu does much more than assuage grief. It is said to have considerable spiritual significance as it helps to transport the spirit of the dead person over to the 'other side' during mortuary ceremonies. In other words, when used in specific circumstances, and played in the appropriate manner, the didjeridu enables access to another reality (Turner 1997: 3). The didjeridu, at least in that part of the country, is considered to be a very personal instrument – it is one's breath, one's spirit and one's vibration (p. 69). When a new didjeridu is made, it is 'smoked' by holding it vertically over a fire and allowing the smoke to pass up through the air column. Turner's new didjeridu was smoked in this manner by Gula; then the mouth end was slapped to make an echoing sound, after which Gula chanted names of important places, invoking them to connect their spirit-matter, their songlines, to the instrument. The chant is said to call the spirits; the smoke to carry them through. Thus the didjeridu acts as a channel between this world and the next (p. 69). One of Turner's informants told him that care has to be taken when playing some tunes, even those that are not secret-sacred, as they can summon up spirit-substance that might run out of control if the instrument is not controlled properly (pp. 59–60).

Gula informed Turner that during a mortuary ceremony, tapping sticks sets the tempo for both the didjeridu and the song. They lead into a sequence of music, announcing to those present on the 'other side' that they, the singers and didjeridu players, are 'coming over'. The didjeridu player then summons up his own inner spirit and projects it via his didjeridu, and the lead songman follows with his own inner spirit. The singers and didjeridu players sit side by side, facing forward (in touch with their own 'shade') as they 'pick up' the melodic contours of the Creation Beings they sing and 'incarnate' them on this side (Turner 1997: 81–2).

Turner noted that most Groote Eylandt music was in the E flat range. This, together with the circular mode of breathing required to play the didjeridu, seemed to be important in leading to specific experiences. Having mastered the art of playing the instrument in the way taught to him by Gula, Turner says that he could 'access the Eternal', by means of 'insights, insounds, and visions'. By learning to play, or 'pull', the didjeridu, writes Turner, he gained an insider's insight into another world. As he became more adept at didjeridu playing, he began to feel vibrations deep inside himself, 'just below the navel', and this was accompanied by a feeling of detachment as if he were 'floating'. One night, after a 'particularly good' performance of didjeridu playing with others, Turner had the experience of 'floating above the landscape', and being aware of 'vividly outlined fields, trees and farms below' (Turner 1997: 38–9). The next section deals with the importance of sound in the form of song in Australia.

Songs in Aboriginal Australia

In Aboriginal Australia some songs are thought to be imbued with power in a magical sense: the power to enchant or to ensorcell, the power to summon lightning, to create fires or extinguish them, to make or stop rain, and so on. A well-enacted song performance even has the power to call the spirits into the presence of the song (Clunies-Ross et al. 1987: 5) (somewhat akin to the Kaluli discussed earlier). Such is the power of some songs that those which are closely associated with a recently deceased person are banned for a period of time after the death so that they do not attract the frightened and erratic spirit back into the presence of the living. In some regions of Australia (for example, in Western Arnhem Land), a songman can receive a new song composition through the medium of a dream.

In central Australia, Aranda songs have the power to call spirits into songs. When such a song is combined with dance during a ceremonial performance, the song calls in the spirits and the dance demonstrates to onlookers that they have arrived. Spirits can also be 'summoned' by being spoken to, or called forth through 'rhythmic foot stamping, clapping and throaty grunting', and valued performances are those where the performer seems to be controlled by other forces (Von Sturmer 1987: 72). However, rather than viewing the spirits as uniquely transcendent, it seems that the world of spirits and the human world are so closely interconnected in Aboriginal thought that the calling forth of spirit is linked with the calling forth of the inner spirit of the person who is linked with spirit through kinship ties.

The Yanyuwa (Aboriginal Australians who live in the Borroloola area of the Northern Territory) say that sometimes they 'find' songs via dreams, which they call 'dream state songs'. The Yanyuwa term, *almirr*, means 'to dream', but it is a dream of little consequence – anyone can have this type of dream. A term used to describe another type of dream is *almirrngantharra*, which means 'seeing into the dream', and refers to a dream which has some portent or other meaning. This kind of dream is regarded as important because of its prophetic content (it might signify death or a warning to someone); the possible meanings of this type of dream are shared and discussed with close kin and often its meaning may not be revealed for some months. The Yanyuwa call a third type of 'dream' *mawurrangantharra*, meaning 'seeing into the spirit world', and this is used to define an altered state of consciousness in which a succession of images and ideas present themselves in the mind. Mackinlay and Bradley (2003) (non-indigenous authors, hence their need to explain things in Western terms) equate it with the Western concept of 'lucid dreaming'. This latter kind of 'dream' pertains to 'dream state songs', whereby spiritual entities give knowledge to the 'dreamer'. This process of acquiring a song, which occurs while in the interstice between waking and dreaming, involves interaction between both the spirit and the human realms of existence, and the boundaries between the two are fluid.

The altered state is recognized by other Aborigines present and the person is spoken of as being 'deaf', and having 'left the world'. Ancestral spirits can appear in these kinds of states and convey special songs. New songs created through this process are significant because they help Yanyuwa people to maintain the relationship of humans to the spiritual world (Mackinlay and Bradley 2003: 2–24). The source of the musical stimuli is attributed to a spirit being and strongly associated with a supernatural source. Songs acquired in this manner, through *mawurrangantharra*, become part of the restricted sacred ceremonies and are regarded as very powerful (Mackinlay 2000). Similar ideas about song appear in other regions of Australia, but one has to be careful not to attribute region-specific beliefs to a pan-Aboriginal interpretation.

I now turn to the notion of vibrations, as this idea appears to be an important element which often accompanies sound to achieve an altered state of consciousness.

Vibrations and Binaural Beat

Pulsing, reverberating, vibrating and throbbing are all linked to the somatic effects of sound, particularly through percussion instruments. It is not surprising, then, that the effects of vibration, especially if employed with a regularly paced beat, will bring about sensations in listeners and musicians when employed in a highly charged atmosphere such as a religious ritual. Before moving on to further discussion of vibrations, it is important to note the 'binaural beat', as it so often occurs with percussion sound, and when binaural beat and the sensation of vibration occur together, they can have profound somatic effects.

The binaural beat is a sensory-information stimulus that provides potential consciousness-altering information to the reticular-thalamic activating system, which in turn alters arousal states, attention focus and level of awareness. The sensation of 'hearing' binaural beats occurs when two coherent sounds of nearly similar frequencies are presented, one to each ear, and the brain detects phase differences between these sounds. When presented with stereo headphones or speakers the brain integrates the two signals, producing a sensation of a third sound called the binaural beat (Atwater 2001: 1–5).

Binaural beats are easily generated at low frequencies (30 Hz) and have been associated with relaxed, meditative states. They are sometimes used as an aid to inducing sleep and in stress reduction.[3] Binaural beats in the alpha frequencies (8–12 Hz) have increased alpha brainwaves, and binaural beats in the beta frequencies (16–24 Hz) have been associated with reports of increased concentration or alertness, improved memory and more focused attention (Atwater 2001: 1–5).

The binaural beat can be used to enhance meditation, relaxation and pain management, and to reduce stress. Integrated with other sensory-information techniques, binaural beats can expand consciousness and enhance intuition, remote viewing, telepathy and out-of-body experiences. Felicitas Goodman's experimentation with shamanic drumming techniques (which often produce a binaural beat) revealed that rhythmic stimulation with either a drum or a rattle being beaten or shaken evenly, at 200–210 beats per minute, could lead listeners into altered states of consciousness in which linear time has no meaning (Goodman 1990: 225). Other researchers have commented on the fact that music can obliterate time. Levi-Strauss, for example, maintained that music could be used to disorient the listener's sense of linear time, and that once engaged in a musical composition, the listener was outside the limiting confines of time, entering into a kind of immortality (Levi-Strauss 1970: 15, fn.). Having digressed to discuss the binaural beat, I now return to vibrations.

In the late nineteenth century, Mrs Watts-Dunton Hughes conducted a series of experiments with her own invention: the eidophone. This instrument served as a concentrator of sound, and when someone spoke or sang into the instrument, the lycopodium powder placed on the edge of a plate near the instrument formed intricate patterns, demonstrating how sound vibrations affect surrounding matter. The long-continued sounding of one particular note tends to set up a sympathetic vibration or resonance in all the surrounding matter, and some vibrations are strong enough to break objects in the same vicinity (Butler 1970: 74–5).

Sound vibrations are mentioned as being important in many parts of the world. A Songhay magician/healer, according to Stoller and Olkes, says that although the meaning of words and songs are important, it is the sound vibrations that 'really matter' (1987: 87). Similarly, chanting the names of Krishna using the mantra: Hare Krsna, Hare Krsna, Krsna Krsna, Hare Hare, Hare Rama, Hare Rama, Rama Rama, Hare Hare (known as the Great Chanting for Deliverance), is believed to set up a 'transcendental vibration' that helps cleanse away misgivings of false consciousness and open up the possibility of spiritual understanding. The word Hare is the form of addressing the energy of the Lord, and the words Krsna and Rama are forms of addressing the Lord Himself. Krsna consciousness is said to be the original, natural energy of the living entity, and when devotees hear the transcendental vibration of the chant, this consciousness is revived. It is compared to associating with him personally and is regarded as supremely purifying. Through *kirtan* (a form of congregational chanting accompanied by percussion instruments and sometimes spontaneous dancing) the devotee associates with the Divine via sound vibration, and this can develop into a mood of spontaneous devotional rapture. Prabhupada claims that it is the simplest method of meditation to engender the experience of a transcendental ecstasy that comes through from the spiritual stratum (Bhaktivedanta 1980: 146).

Sanskrit mantras in the yogic traditions of meditation are words of power considered to be essential for the internal journey of self-knowledge. The resonance of the sound of the mantra first calms the mind so that stillness can be experienced, then repetition of the mantra 'take[s] one deeper into the resonance of syllables (external form) with activated energy centre or *chakra* (inner essence)' (Prattis 1997: 249). Ian Prattis writes that the sound resonance of the mantra operates as a total energy system; the syllables in a mantra act as 'a set of tonal frequencies that resonate with cellular templates and activate energy centres in the body, connecting and unifying them into a single integrated system' (p. 249). The aim in chanting is to move from chanting out loud to 'thinking the mantra quietly within', and progress to allowing the mantra to 'arise spontaneously from deep within one's being' (p. 249). Thus, chanting the mantra 'moves one progressively from external form to transcendental experience' (p. 249).

Western occultists[4] use a similar progression to the experience via Sanskrit mantras described by Prattis. One of Butler's techniques is to listen to a familiar voice reading something (poetry is suggested), then attempt to hear the sound of the poetry when the person is not reading it (Butler 1970: 69). Butler insists that audible perception can be enhanced by training in order to assist magical work. Another technique is to 'vibrate' names of 'power' (say, god names) when one is relaxed and breathing slowly and deeply. This can cause visual and audible images to arise, which can be used for purposes of communication between the conscious and superconscious levels of the person and lead to enhanced psychic abilities.[5]

In the practice of vibrating names, magicians advise that the voice must be made as 'vibrant' as possible. This can be attained by deliberately lowering voice tone while concentrating on a thought that is linked with the particular name, and employing at the same time a rhythm, or chant. Syncopation is an example of rhythm-and-break that has enormous value in the evocation of certain emotional states. Some sounds affect the subconscious and, if employed with other ritual aspects, such as incense, candlelight and ritual objects, they are effective in taking someone into a trance state. The ideal magical chant, says Butler, must appeal to the subconscious; it needs to be strongly rhythmical; and its reiteration must be made to rise and fall by change of key. The Gregorian chant (which was mentioned by David Turner earlier on) is said to be highly efficacious in magical work (Butler 1970: 78) and, like the Byzantine chants and songs of the Greek Orthodox and Russian Orthodox church choirs, can evoke strong feelings in Christians, such that they feel themselves to be in the presence of the Divine.

Discussion

At the heart of all the different religious and spiritual groups discussed in this chapter, certain elements are common: devotion and intense concentration or heightened awareness; focused thought on the activity (whether that is prayer, uplifting songs or playing or listening to music); the vibrations and sounds that affect body and mind; and the notion of the existence of 'other', whether a deity, another realm, a universal energy or similar idea.

Sound in the form of music can evoke deep emotions in all of us. Words have similar power to evoke emotional reactions and can even lead us to kill each other. No doubt the source of the classic magical words, 'abracadabra' and 'open Sesame', which led to the opening of the cave that contained the treasures of Ali Baba, was based on the idea of the power of words. In the story of Ali Baba and the Forty Thieves, it is the physical cave that is opened by the magical words. At the metaphysical level, the opening leads into the unconscious mind, or, as some would say, into another realm of existence. Intrinsic to both ideas is that powerful words/sounds have potency in themselves. There is clearly more to music than mere pleasure; as some cultures opine, sound can take us into other realities, help us to communicate with other beings, summon up 'demons' and evoke the gods.

The combination of thought and sound is a powerful mix. The term 'mantra' is a combination of the root *man* (to think) and *tra* (tool or tool-words). Thus, mantra is a 'tool for thinking', a 'thing which creates a mental picture'. The sound emitted by a mantra creates a mental picture. Thoughts as mental images that become realities is an old idea that is found in cultures as far apart as India and Alaska. Magic songs, spells or words and thoughts were used by the Copper Inuit (Alaska) to cure sickness and to provide good fortune for hunters (Merkur 1990: 50). In the Western esoteric system, thoughts, images and vibrations are said to produce 'tangible forms' that can become visible to those with psychic abilities (Besant and Leadbeater 1905). However, we are warned by Tibetan Buddhist, Govinda, against misinterpreting such ideas in a materialistic or mechanistic manner. The power and effect of something like a mantra depends on the 'spiritual attitude, the knowledge and the responsiveness of the individual'. The mantras, like magic songs, do not possess power on their own, but are only 'the means for concentrating already existing forces'. What is needed, writes Govinda, is 'self-discipline, concentration, inner experience, and insight' (Govinda 1973: 27).

There are common biological bases underlying altered states of consciousness, many of which destabilize the waking mode of consciousness. In achieving an altered state of consciousness, normal waking consciousness is disrupted, pushing psychological functions beyond their limits and disrupting subsystems by sensory overload or deprivation, manipulating the autonomic nervous system balance (Winkelman 2000: 115). This can be achieved in a number of ways, and in this chapter we have discussed those involving sound. Auditory driving, which includes drumming and other percussion instruments, as well as singing or chanting, can produce slow-wave EEG activity (alpha, theta and delta, especially 3–6 cycles per second (cps)), which can produce visual sensations, hallucinations and an array of emotional and abstract experiences (p. 148), such as those discussed in this chapter. Interestingly, not only is the sound-maker's brain activity altered, but sound can produce dominance in the alpha band for listeners (p. 148), which means that those in the audience can be affected by the same mechanisms to a lesser extent, especially if all concerned are culturally aware of the interpretations of the experience. The cortex is set into oscillation at the alpha frequency or slower, and singing, chanting and percussion procedures produce or enhance this state of dominance of slow-wave frequencies. Winkelman states that different altered states of consciousness found cross-culturally involve similar integrative brainwave patterns across the neuraxis (p. 114). Attenuation of the waking mode of consciousness allows the emergence of integrative symbolic and cognitive processes that are normally repressed by waking consciousness (p. 115).

Nevertheless, in case we become too complacent and leave the matter there, we have to take into account the meaning-value attached to the experiences that result from those altered states, and the ways they are modified and elaborated according to particular cultures and their own interpretive frameworks and epistemologies. While the West distinguishes between neurophysiology, psychology, psychiatry and religious beliefs, separating each in order to explain a phenomenon, most other cultures accept that the totality of these different aspects makes up the health and well-being of the whole person. As an example, the following excerpt from Janzen's work on the Tumbuka musical *ngoma* healers in Africa demonstrates that the healer is obviously taking whatever approach he thinks is going to help the patient, sometimes applying psychology, sometimes medicinal plants, sometimes belief. It is not so much the technique that is important, as the end product to heal the patient. As one healer recounted to Janzen (2000: 59):

> The aim of healing *ngomas* is to make the patient talk, to heighten emotions. If that fails, you go to the forest for roots, give them medicine. Either way, talking is important. The purpose of the drumming is to know the particular spirit, so it speaks out in the patient, so the healer knows how many, which, where they come from, what they want. When

the patient speaks, it's the spirit speaking. Spirit and person are one and the same. After medicine is taken, and *ngoma* is played, the patient must sing in increasing tempo, the song of the particular spirit. It's thus the patient who directs the healer on the type of treatment.

They say that the spirits like the music (certain music is preferred by particular spirits), so they may make themselves manifest by speaking through the sufferer, revealing what has to be done to help in the healing process.

Once the healer has established the type of spirit manifested he begins the corresponding type of music. Thus, the music enchants the sufferer so he can express himself better and reveal the spirit, and talking is critical to identifying the particular spirit that is in the person. The spirit and the person are said to be 'one and the same thing'. Some of the healers encountered by Janzen talk about spirits as being an aspect of the patient's psyche, as indicated in the above passage. While this aspect is considered plausible by the *ngoma* healers, it is only one aspect of many, including spirits. This is where the Tumbuka *ngoma* healer and the Western medical practitioner differ. The latter are not listening to the multiple possible ways of healing.

Sound is an incredibly powerful portal, and as Gouk states in no uncertain terms, if we are to understand the full meaning of music to other cultures, the scientific world needs 'to abandon prejudices and formulas, plunge in, and join the dance ourselves' (Gouk 2000: 23). Sound can be a vehicle for altering spiritual states, 'not only those of humans and animals, but also those of beings who lie beyond the visible realm' (p. 88). A neurophysiological approach is an exciting one, but it seems that we still have a lot to learn from other cultures which take more into account than what is happening to the body. The West's refusal to entertain the importance of the integration of all aspects of an experience results in a unidimensional approach to phenomena that is really rather limiting to further investigation.

> And more than once, my son,
> As I sat all alone,
> Revolving in myself the word that is the symbol of myself;
> The mortal limit of the self was loosed and passed into the
> Nameless,
> As a cloud melts into heaven.
>
> (Tennyson)[6]

The next chapter will focus on the technology of movement, especially in the form of dance, in order to open the portals.

–4–

Dance and Movement

To the Universe
belongs the dancer.
Whoever does not dance
does not know what happens.

Acts of John 95:16–17

The dance has long been recognized as having religious significance. In both the Old and New Testaments of the Bible, reports of visions, voices, ecstatic dancing and leaping occur frequently. As recorded in II Samuel 6, Saul travelled with ecstatic prophets, and 'David danced before the Lord with all his might'. In the Middle Ages there were dancing sects and dancing maniacs in Europe (Bourgignon 1972: 334), and in the nineteenth century a flourishing Christian sect was called the Shakers because of their ecstatic shaking during group dancing. The St Vincent Shakers in the West Indies maintained hours-long hymn singing and sermonizing, accompanied by handclapping and foot stamping at a precise tempo. While no music was involved in the services of the St Vincent Shakers, participants maintained unified motion, keeping simultaneous rhythm, while each person bobbed up and down, bent over at the waist, knees bent, until breathless from exertion. Once in trance, they gasped, groaned, sighed and shouted (p. 337).

Van der Leeuw (1963) remarked on the close connection between dance and religious feeling, commenting that it sets into motion powers that are 'holy'. Once engaged in the flow of dance, it is possible to lose oneself and become something else – as Ruth St. Denis discovered.

Choreographer, dancer, contemporary of Isadora Duncan and teacher of well-known modern dancers such as Martha Graham, Ruth St. Denis (1876–1968) was one of the first of the modern twentieth-century dancers to explore dance innovation. She claimed that during the last forty years of her life she was engaged in a 'deep private mysticism' via the medium of dance, which deepened her experience of biblical scriptures (Douglas-Klotz 1993: 109). In her autobiography (St. Denis 1939: 52), she talks about her 'call' to dance, and her special identification with the Egyptian mythological figure of Isis:

I identified in a flash with the figure of Isis. She became the expression of all the somber mystery and beauty of Egypt, and I knew that my destiny as a dancer had sprung alive in that moment. I would become a rhythmic and impersonal instrument of spiritual revelation rather than a person of comedy or tragedy. I had never before known such an inward shock of rapture.

After this first 'revelation', St. Denis increasingly regarded dance as important to the individual dancer's 'inner landscape'. Rather than focusing on the perfection of the technical execution of dance steps, she viewed dance as a particular way of expressing spirituality. As a dance educator, her own philosophy refused to entertain the dualism that separated body from mind and emotion, an idea prevalent during her times. As she said (cited in Douglas-Klotz 1989: 5):

We are not made of one substance and our bodies of another. The whole scheme of things in reality is not two, but One. On this hangs not only the whole law and prophets of the liberating philosophy of the new age but the very starting point and method of approach of the Divine Dance.

She pursued the merging of dance and the sacred well into her eighties, continuing to think that the key to sacred dance was inner development, and her own perform-ance was, as she expressed, the extension of her 'inner spiritual attitude and reality' (cited in Douglas-Klotz 1993: 113):

Dance is a living mantra. It is not a mere constant change of gesture and rhythm, calculated to intrigue the attention of the surface eye, but it is the very stuff and symbol of my inner creative life.

For her, dance expression was akin to revelation; the Scriptures could only be truly understood if they were played out through the body and dance needed to be returned to its sacred roots. She advocated the transformation of the Christian liturgy through the spiritual art of dance, and would have preferred to perform her dances in a temple or church rather than in a theatre. Her dance pupils were taught that they must first be inspired by a sacred theme or prayer, then gradually proceed to embody it, for the ultimate goal of dance performance was to change the consciousness of those watching in order that they appreciate the richness of their natural environment.

One wonders if Ruth St. Denis had read anything about Indian dance as her approach to dance mirrors that of some such forms, where the outstanding function of dance was to give 'symbolic expression to abstract religious ideas' (Gaston 1982: 6). Ian Prattis hypothesizes that some body postures create the shape of a symbol, and when breath is drawn with awareness into this created symbol it 'electrifies' the body because it has hit upon a corresponding symbolic structure deep in the unconscious (Prattis 1997: 160). From this perspective sacred dance is simply an extended choreography of symbols provided by the sequential postures of the body. The symbols so created act as a lens through which breath magnifies the whole effect of the body symbol on the unconscious symbols, thus producing a match between the external form (sacred dance) and the internal form (unconscious symbols). He suggests that this is why all traditions of sacred dance pay such meticulous attention to body posture and the precision of choreographic sequence, as well as to ritual preparation and breath control, and that all of this provides an entry point into the biggest mysteries of life.[1] The enactment of myth in sacred dance provides an opportunity, for the participants as well as the audience, to have a deep part of the psyche stirred and can lead to 'glimpses of eternity' (p. 162). Prattis also suggests that breath control, the precision and repetitiveness of dance steps, the symbols shaped by the body and the chants and music that accompany sacred dance are the 'drivers' that take audience and dancer alike into an experience of shared archetypal memory (p. 167).

Some forms of Indian dance recognized two aspects – *natya* (mime) and *nrtta* (pure dance), with an 'underlying template' known as *rasa* (Gaston 1982: 14). Anne-Marie Gaston writes that *rasa* awakens latent psychological states (*sthayi-bhavas*) in those 'beholding' the dance by the use of appropriate formalized imagery. The expression of certain *bhavas* by a dancer was considered an important way to worship God and was one of the reasons dance became a necessary and integral part of religious worship. The dancer sang the religious songs, externalizing her feelings with facial expressions, and danced using stylized movements. As well as stepping into the experience of *bhavas* herself, the dancer drew the audience into a different state, evoking an emotional response in those watching (p. 14). Another instance of the dance drawing participants into the spiritual experience of transformative gnosis can be found in that most famous and mystical Christian circle dance called the Hymn of the Dance, which appears in the Acts of John.

The Christian Hymn of the Dance

Anticipating his arrest in the garden of Gethsemene on the night before his death, Jesus gathered his followers and said to them, 'Before I am delivered to them, let us sing a hymn to the Father, and so go to meet what lies before (us)' (Acts of John 94:1). Having said this to his followers, Jesus then engaged them in what has been referred to by scholars as the 'Hymn of the Dance', but which might better be called a 'mystical chant'. He told them to form a circle around him, holding on to one another's hands, and then began to sing a 'hymn' (Acts of John 94:7–96:45), beginning 'Glory be to thee, Father', while the others circled round him, responding, 'Amen'. In Acts of John 95:24–27, Jesus is explicit that the way forward is through him:

95:24   I am a lamp to you
         who see me. Amen
95:25   I am a mirror to you
         who know me. Amen
95:26   I am a door to you
         who knock on me. Amen
95:27   I am a way to you
         the traveller. Amen

References to 'lamp', 'mirror', 'door' and 'way' are all means by which a place or places are revealed, and there is reference to going on a journey. In subsequent verses throughout the hymn, the physical dance and movement toward transformation occurs by means of conforming one's will to the dance leader. In Acts of John 96:28–40, Jesus says:

96:28   Now if you follow
         my dance,
96:29   see yourself
         in Me who am speaking
96:30   and when you have seen what I do,
         keep silence about my mysteries.
96:31   You who dance, consider
         what I do, for yours is
96:32   this passion of Man (humanity)
         which I am to suffer.
96:33   For you could by no means
         have understood what you suffer
96:34   unless to you, as Logos
         I had been sent by the Father
         […]
96:38   Who I am you shall know
         when I go forth.
96:39   What I now am seen to be,
         that I am not;
96:40   what I am you shall see
         when you come yourself.

This passage in the Acts of John is regarded by some to be the most mystical and magnificent passage in the entire Christian tradition. The dance itself is assumed by some to reflect an actual liturgical ritual practice that may have been in use in the Jewish community at Passover festivals. Barbara Bowe regards this dance as one which draws its participants into a transformative encounter with the divine realm, accomplished through their union with the Lord who stands in their midst. She writes (1999: 83):

As a performative text, the hymn both celebrates and enacts the mystery it proclaims, namely, the unity between the Lord as revealer, the One revealed 'on high' and the faithful recipients of the revelation who learn this mystery through the rhythm of this hymnic dance.

Bowe emphasizes the importance of the leader-response pattern of the hymn, as well as the antiphonal (alternative responses) echo that results from binding the voice of the leader with the voices of the respondents so that they merge into one voice. The antiphonal response format changes in 94:15 to a declaration of praise and thanks in the first person plural. Bowe suggests that a peculiar feature of the hymn remains constant throughout: there is a 'blurring of distinctions' between leader and chorus, an apparent loss of distinction in person between the singular leader in the centre and the chorus surrounding him. It is often difficult to decide exactly who is speaking.

The antiphonal 'Amen' continues at regular intervals and thereby *incorporates* (Bowe's emphasis) those in the outer circle into those mysteries being proclaimed. Bowe suggests that what is happening in the process of the dance, with its combination of movement and singing/chanting, is 'a kind of fusion of the one revealed, the revealer, and those who receive the revelation'. In lines 95:20 and 22, the dancers are urged to continue and to enter into the mourning and beating of breasts. Non-participants are not allowed in the dance hall, and all must join the dance or be left behind. To be included, they must *choose* to embrace its transformative movement (Bowe 1999: 93–6). Those who do not dance remain ignorant, or unaware.

The format and use of space in the circular dance physically and metaphorically forces the dancers to look *inward*, and, in the case of this particular dance, they are looking inward to Jesus – Jesus is in their centre, he is 'the way', and he is leading the invocations to the Father. So the link is from dancer to Jesus to God. Transformative gnosis happens *in the dance* (Bowe's emphasis, 1999: 97). Bowe suggests (p. 98) that the transformation which occurs is that the dancers become one with each other:

> By means of the dance, a unitive transformation seems to be taking place within those who make themselves one with its rhythm and proclamations. The three spheres of the participants in the circle, the Lord in the center, and the Father who dwells in the celestial realm are fused into a unity during the course of the hymn's movement.

In the final section of the hymn Jesus says (96:1), 'Now, if you follow my dance, see yourself in Me who am speaking'. Bowe sees this as a kind of 'mirror motif', a transformation, 'both at the level of knowing and of being', that happens as the dancers move with the rhythm of the dance. The dancers come into harmony with the revealer of knowledge through the rhythm of the dance. The dance is at the same time an 'act of union and *communion*', fusing the dancers with the leader. Bowe understands this hymnal dance as a celebration of the 'mystery of the union between the Lord as revealer, the Godhead, and those who dance their way into this mysterious divine presence' (1999: 100).

In a footnote, she suggests some similarities between the Hymn of the Dance and the Sufi whirling dance ceremony (Bowe 1999: 101, fn. 29). Both these dances are circular and have a leader in the centre with participants dancing in an outer circle, and both are designed to achieve a mysterious union with each other and with God. I now explore further Bowe's suggestion of similarities between this Hymn of the Dance and the Sufi tradition of the whirling dance, performed as the Sema ceremony.

The Sufi Dance: Meditation in Movement

A spiritual offshoot of Islam, the Mevlevi Order of Sufis, also known as the Whirling Dervishes, traces its origin to the thirteenth-century Ottoman Empire. The Order was named after its founder, Turkish mystic poet Jelaluddin Mevlana Rumi (1207–73). The practice of whirling, however, is thought to have its origins much earlier than the thirteenth century. It was already in use well before the time of Rumi, and may be linked with Central Asian spirituality and shamanism. The term 'Dervish' literally means 'doorway', or entrance from this material world to the spiritual heavenly world. The Sema ritual, in which whirling occurs, has been called the 'gate of secrets'; it is said to enable the dancers to pass beyond their usual existence into a knowledge of Truth. Spiritual manifestations and visions are common during the Sema.

The Sufi Sema ritual is the human being's spiritual journey to Perfection (*Kemal*) through intelligence, love and the abandonment of the ego. It is a physical, mental and spiritual act of surrender to the divine. The whirling dance is the physical act that makes it possible to unite the mind (as knowledge and thought), the heart (through the expression of feelings, poetry and music) and the body (by activating life). Basic to the notion of whirling is that all things in existence revolve, and these revolutions are natural and unconscious. One can participate intentionally and consciously in the shared revolution of other beings. Also, no matter in which direction one may face, one is always in the presence of God. Contemporary observers of the ritual have described it as a powerful ceremony that demands a shift in aesthetic sensibility.

The form of the ceremony consists of several parts. First, there is a eulogy to the Prophet who represents love, and this is followed by a drumbeat on the *kudum*, which symbolizes the divine command: 'Be'. The musical prelude is played on a reed flute, which symbolizes the divine breath that gives life to everything. The dance begins by the Sultan Veled Walk (*peshrev*), a circular procession around the ceremonial space, three times, to the accompaniment of *peshrev* music. The dancers (*semazens*) bow to each other during the procession ('essence to essence' and 'face to face'), to represent the salutation of soul to soul (Celebi, p. 2).

Four musical movements (*selams*), each with a distinct rhythm, beginning and close, are involved in the dance. The human being's birth to truth through feeling and mind is represented in the first *selam*; the second *selam* expresses the rapture of the human in front of God's greatness and omnipotence; the third *selam* is the rapture of self dissolving into love; and the fourth *selam* is the descent, or return from the spiritual journey. Having completed the journey, the individual is able to love and serve the whole of creation more easily, having experienced the bliss of divine love.

The third *selam* is an intense experience of annihilation of self, by way of elimination of ego, and a merging with the Beloved. This experience has been expressed poetically as: 'Together we fly through the heavens of Being to merge with our Creator' (Helminski, p. 2). To highlight the idea of going on a journey, at the beginning of the third *selam*, the sheikh may step forward to internally recite the prayer (p. 2):

> May Allah grant you total soundness,
> O travellers on the Way of Love,
> May the Beloved remove the veils from your eyes
> And reveal to you the secrets of your time and of the true centre.

With the right hand turned 'heavenward' to receive God's grace, and the left turned down to convey that grace to earth, the dancers twirl, counterclockwise, twenty to thirty times a minute, while silently repeating 'Allah, Allah', in a deliberate and finely executed movement. Each dancer moves with grace and ease in concert with the others: bodies straight, heads inclined slightly and their flowing white skirts describing a triangular pattern that is meant to be maintained throughout the ceremony. The movement is controlled, ordered and punctilious.

The goal of Sema is not to lose consciousness, but to realize submission to God. It is a 'meditation in movement' (Celebi, p. 2) where the mind is emptied of all distracting thoughts and focused on one's innermost centre, where one is closest to the Divine and can be filled with the presence of God. This is achieved through expanded awareness, love of God and feeling a connection through the dance leader (the sheikh in the centre of the circle who represents their link to Rumi). The *semazins* engage in an emptying of the self so that 'true reality' may enter; expressed poetically by another thirteenth-century Sufi master, Mahmud Shabistari, as 'sweeping out the house of the heart/mind' (Levenson and Khilwati 1999: 253). Ordinary consciousness, with its thoughts, emotions, sensations and memories, is swept aside in order to experience transcendental states of awareness and to receive 'the gift of enlightenment that is always present like the sun above thick clouds' (p. 252), a direct experience of the Reality or Truth, *al haqq*, or Allah. Whirling enables the participants to focus their attention through one-pointed concentration on the one Reality, and to lose themselves in it.

Comparisons

The Sema has been called the gate of secrets, and love for the Divine and all humanity is expressed as a bridge to divine love. The dancer is a traveller on a journey and the 'way' is through movement and contemplation of the Divine. In the Christian Hymn of the Dance, described earlier, Christ said he was a 'door' to those who knocked, a 'way' to the 'traveller'; by 'following the dance' one could come to understand the mysteries of which he spoke. The circular dance, with Christ in the centre as a focus of contemplation, is very similar to the spatial arrangement of the Sufi whirling dance. There is movement and journey throughout the hymn; physically, in the dance, and spiritually, transformation occurs by conforming to the will of the person in the centre. Similarly, the Sema ceremony of the Sufis is danced in a circle, with a sheikh in the centre, acting as spiritual director (and link to Rumi) so that the participant can be brought to a direct experience of the Reality or Truth. It is a Sufi way to transcend the self and open the 'gate' to union with the Divine.

Both the Hymn of the Dance and the Sema dance ceremony are journeys that can be made through movement, contemplation, will and an emotional longing for union with the Divine, in order to cross a barrier that prevents access to those who remain in a mundane state of ordinary consciousness. It is important to iterate that this kind of practice does not only depend on the dance movement; it is not acquired facilely and entails full immersion into the Sufi or Christian beliefs and practices. For many, it is the culmination of a life's work and not acquired in one evening. Without the inner development, the knowledge of the esoteric teachings, and the experience gained in the practices, both dances would be merely an exercise in movement without meaning.

While the Sufi Sema and the Christian Hymn of the Dance are meant to open the way for union with the Divine, or access to knowledge, this phenomenon is clearly evident in other cultures as well. In Minoan Crete as far back as the Bronze Age, sacred dances took place in natural settings of great beauty – in and around caves, near trees or, as depicted on the famous Isopata ring from Knossos, in a field of lilies. Although it is difficult now to assume the exact meaning of archaeological remnants, scholars suggest that the four female figures with upraised arms, depicted on the ring, are taking part in a circular dance to invoke a goddess (who also features in the scene). This is translated as a 'descending divinity', with the goddess responding to the invocation of the dancers through the power of the dance. Other artefacts of the times seem to confirm this proposition. Dancing grounds that were consecrated to different divine figures served as links between the world of mortals and the realm of the gods (Lonsdale 1993: 116).

Possession trance is thought by most scholars to be the core and essence of the Japanese Shinto shamanic dance called Kagura. A myth that recounts a shamanic rite in which the goddess Ame-no-uzume engages in a frenzied dance of possession is called 'Opening the Rock-Cave Door'. In the Shinto dance ritual, the *kami* (spirits) descended and entered the body of the shaman via hand-held objects called *torimono*, which served as channelling devices to enable the descent. The dance, accompanied by Kaguri music composed of drum, flute, cymbals and *kami* songs, was attributed with the power to summon the spirits, and was the most compelling part of the ritual. The dance itself exhibited two distinct parts: *mai*, which was danced in slow, circular movements to prepare the dancer to enter a trance state, and *odori*, which was the trance behaviour itself, when the dancer seemed to lose control, trembling, leaping and jumping with great gusto, because the dancer's body was possessed by the spirits (Averbuch 1998: 1–3).

Yet another example of dance that involves transition is the modern dance meditation that was inspired by Zen Buddhism. The purpose of Zen Buddhism is to attain enlightenment, to find the True 'I', and to end human suffering. Every action, it is said, can be performed in such a way as to move towards those goals, and for this new form of dance based on Zen principles, the basic techniques of meditation are expressed in the form of elegant and aesthetic dance movement. Exemplified in the fluid form of modern dance, beautifully performed and displayed in Lee and McCurdy's book (1985) *Zen Dance – Meditation in Movement*, mantra, dance and breath are employed to bring the dancer, through individual effort, closer to the goal of enlightenment. Each movement is a combination of dance technique and the dancer's intuitive mind, fused into a total self-expression, with the performer surrendering his/her mind and body as an offering to Buddha, with the appropriate 'power of heart'. The greatest hindrance to experiencing enlightenment is said to be discursive consciousness. In order to transcend the limits of the intellect and foster spiritual growth, the sound and vibration of the mantra is repeated so as to focus the dancer's energy, to rid the mind of idle chatter and allow the spirit to soar, unhampered.

The mantra employed in the Korean Zen dance recorded in Lee and McCurdy's book is 'Yimoko?' which means 'What am I?' or 'What is the True Self?' The dancer focuses on this question, which has the effect of heightening the intensity, power of concentration and centredness of the dance. As well as performing carefully executed, flowing movements and focusing the mind on 'Yimoko?', the dancer breathes in the area of the lower abdomen called the *tanjun* area (midway between the navel and the pubic bone), which is considered the centre of one's vital energy. *Tanjun* breathing involves expansion of the lower abdomen when inhaling, and the contraction of the lower abdomen area when exhaling, and the *tanjun* is experienced, not only as the centre of the body in motion, but as the body's point of contact with the energy of the universe. Thus, dance movement, breathing and focused meditation are all carried out with total concentration on the question, 'What is the True Self?' This form of dance is said to create a spiritual atmosphere of tranquillity, purity, centredness and balance, in a meditative state of mind, and to move with the rhythms of nature. The musical accompaniment represents the universe which accompanies human existence. The movements are simple and flowing, with much individual improvisation (Lee and McCurdy 1985: 104–7).

As well as dances that are performed to unite the dancer with the Divine or with spirits, dance and other movements and gestures are employed by many cultures, religious practices and even mainstream religious denominations, for the express purpose of physical or spiritual healing. Next I discuss the Pentecostal practice of 'healing in the spirit'.

Pentecostals

Christian Pentecostals value the religious experience over the word, and a fundamental belief is that an encounter with the Holy is not only possible, but to be encouraged, both as a communal spontaneous experience in public worship as well as in one's personal spirituality. Some of these religious expressions give rise to 'dancing in the Spirit', or 'being moved by the Spirit', an ecstatic swaying movement, characterized by raised arms and upward palms to express openness to God, vulnerability and receptivity. Lifted hands and bowed heads may also express feelings of penitence. In healing rites, one hand is placed on the person being prayed for (touching the one in need), while the other hand is lifted toward heaven, reaching out to God and offering oneself as a 'conduit for healing power' and an 'instrument for God's work' (Albrecht 1999: 190).

Swaying, dancing and singing form a kinaesthetic triad that demonstrates enthusiastic moving through the influence of the Spirit. Other actions, such as standing, kneeling, bowing, swaying, hopping, jumping and signing (similar to sign language) are also evidence of 'signs and wonders' that have their origin in the Divine. These movements are viewed as expressing the actions of God upon and through themselves. In some places, dance movements are choreographed and practised beforehand by a dance team in weekly rehearsals, but often the congregation joins in spontaneously during a service and dances with the team in 'free worship' (Albrecht 1999: 98). Sometimes 'dancing in the Spirit' leads dancers into a highly ecstatic state, as they sense the impulse of the Spirit and become moved irresistibly. Such enthusiasm has led to outsiders dubbing them 'holy rollers'.

To Dance or Not to Dance

While physical movement (including dance) is considered a serious way of accessing the Divine, some Christian denominations and sects through the centuries have explicitly forbidden dancing, viewing it as a licentious act. Even in 1988, at an ecumenical liturgy conference in which Catholics, Protestants and Jews assembled to discuss trends in liturgical practices, history and reform, the subject of dance was introduced by one of the speakers. It was suggested that there may be benefits in using dance in liturgy. However, when invited to take part in a dance demonstration where men and women were asked to hold hands, one of the clergymen objected. He found even the simple act of joining hands with women 'threateningly sexual', and 'felt vulnerable to emotions he believed were not acceptable in his leadership role' (Levine 1991: 334).

Three factors seem to complicate the practice of liturgical dance to those who view the practice negatively: first, dance has a sexual aspect as it focuses on the body; second, it might involve an individual rather than communal experience of God; and finally, it could be reduced to an entertainment device that might 'entice an audience with little taste for theology' (Levine 1991: 334). These three factors emphasize a restrained and more intellectual approach to religion; a dancer might be 'carried away' in the moment and so embarrass the clergy and the congregation.

The clergyman mentioned above would no doubt have been horrified had he attended the Sipsey River Association of the Primitive Baptist Church in west Alabama and north-east Mississippi of which Joy Baklanoff writes (1987). Founded in 1872, this church is an important religious organization in the black communities in which it is found. A major event that brings together almost the entire community is the foot-washing service, held in May and September each year. The goal of this service is possession trance, which is achieved by a combination of rhythmic sensory stimulation initiated by music, body movements, sermons and the consumption of alcohol. Under the guidance of church officers, specific cultural values are reinforced and the possession trance reflects the beliefs and expectations of the participants.

Baklanoff discusses the event as phases 1, 2 and 3, with anticipatory build-up through each phase that leads to a climactic point of the ritual where many, if not all, participants achieve an altered state of consciousness. The stages of the build-up depend on the sensory stimulation of the music, sermon-chants and body movements, as well as the drinking of alcoholic beverages. These phases can be compared with the build-up of emotions in many other Baptist or evangelical churches throughout the world. In the Sipsey River Baptist Church, it is probably better articulated, more intense, more expressly stated and is a particularly black community event.

Baklanoff calls the slow progression and build-up in phase 1 the 'Warm-up'. Once members of the congregation are inside the church, a deacon signals the opening of the ceremony by lowering, then raising his head; he then begins with a popular hymn and another deacon offers a prayer. Celebrants join in and there follows a continual pattern of singing hymns for about five to ten minutes, interspersed with three- to five-minute prayers. A rhythmic pattern is set up throughout the sermon, and there is a melodic dimension to prayer. For more information on the harmony, tone and rhythm, the reader should refer to Baklanoff. Suffice to say that there is a repetitive and continual pattern of movement, singing, humming and leader-response calls, 'with an occasional ecstatic groan or scream' that steadily increases in volume.

During the Warm-up phase, participants sing and move their arms in time to the music. This is done in a ring-dance style, in a circular movement, first one way, holding each other's hands, then moving in the opposite direction. At the same time, everyone moves closer together toward the centre of the circle, so that as the song progresses the circle becomes tighter. The congregation fills up as people drift in, and by the end of the first hour, the church is filled, donations are collected and phase 2 begins.

The second phase consists of the church elder's sermon, which can last as long as two hours. He begins in a normal speaking voice, breaking into a chant after about thirty minutes, with the tempo increasing and gradually reaching a crescendo. There are usually only three sermons preached, but there can sometimes be as many as six. Following the last sermon there is a fifty-minute break for refreshments before phase 3 begins.

Phase 3 begins with Communion, then the elder instructs the male officers to fill large basins with water while he explains the biblical basis for foot washing.[2] While the elder is speaking, the singing and fellowship intensifies. Elders wash one another's feet and then everyone else in the congregation sets about foot washing in same-gender pairs. All the while, singing continues, with random bursts of hymn singing from the leaders.

During the foot-washing section of the ceremony, about half the female particip-ants and a few men go into possession trance, called 'groaning' as the trancers make groaning sounds. This is all done according to informal rules about who can begin 'groaning' and in what order. The possession trance described by Baklanoff (1987: 399) is worth describing in detail:

> Certain organized, recognizable cues such as cries or body motions, which are unique to the individual, signal the onset of the PT [possession trance] to the other participants. The PT usually begins with the enunciation of short, repetitive phrases or with the execution of certain body movements, which build up to a climactic peak. The PT movements include holding both hands up in the air shaking them in opposition with the torso. There is also opposition between the pelvis and thorax as the participant moves in a twisting motion. During the PT facial expressions range from tortured to ecstatic.

Those possessed say things like, 'I'm dying', 'I feel so good', 'I'm as free as I can be', 'I'm alright now'. This continues up to the point of climax , which is marked by trembling and animal-like cries, and the person may fall to the floor. When the possession trances cease, one particular song is sung, 'I've Been to the Water'. The words of this song reinforce the significance of foot washing and mark the conclusion of the sacred portion of the ceremony. Phase 4 is the feasting and socializing.

Baklanoff notes that during the foot washing there is an anticipatory build-up toward the climactic point of the ritual: possession trance. The stages of this build-up depend on the sensory stimulation of the music, sermon-chants and body movements, as well as the drinking of alcoholic beverages.

As can be seen yet again, many spiritual experiences are intensely emotional. Christians often talk of a 'longing' to know God, and Sufis emphasize the importance of 'heart'. Yet the missionary urge, in post-Enlightenment times, was to 'spread the

Word' of God to 'savages' in 'God-forsaken places', and eradicate anything they considered to be uncivilized and primitive; dance and emotive displays of religious fervour were regarded as uncivilized. However, examples from all over the world show that religious ecstasy is most frequently preceded by intense emotion, which is often expressed in dance and song. The next example, from Africa, illustrates the human expression of emotion and its subsequent healing benefits, through dance.

The !Kung and *!Kia*

The *!kia*-healing dance of the Kalahari Bushmen in south-west Africa is performed regularly, by both men and women, sometimes twice a week. It is designed to alter consciousness and take people into trance (*!kia*) in order to activate *n/um* (energy), which the !Kung believe is necessary to maintain health and promote personal growth.[3] They say that transcendence must be brought into ordinary life, and ordinary life into transcendence, if personal growth is to occur. All !Kung people can experience *!kia*; it is not the domain of any religious specialist (Katz 1976: 283).

The !Kung say that *n/um* resides in the pit of the stomach, and through energetic dancing and rapid, shallow breathing, it rises up the spine to a point at the base of the skull, at which time trance occurs, often making the tranced person tremble and become hot. It then enters every part of the body, producing a tingling sensation at the base of the spine. Considered a very powerful energy, *n/um* can be transferred from one person to another and can be put into a patient to combat illness. During the healing ritual, many of the participants go into *!kia*, to various degrees, and an atmosphere develops in which individual experiences of trance can have a contagious effect on others.

The *!kia* healing ritual usually lasts from dusk to dawn, during which time songs, rhythmic clapping of hands and dancing produce a highly charged physical and emotional state that can be experienced as fear, exhilaration or fervour. People undergo body tremors, heavy breathing and a change in consciousness to the extent that extraordinary physical feats are reported, such as walking on fire, seeing with X-ray vision and over great distances, as well as the power to heal the sick (Katz 1976: 287).

!Kia has a transformational and transcendent aspect; consciousness is altered to the degree that a sense of self, time and space are significantly changed and there is a feeling of ascent, of 'bursting open' or 'opening up', so that something more important can come out (Katz 1976: 288). One of Richard Katz's informants expresses this (pp. 286–7) as follows:

> You dance, dance, dance, dance. The *n/um* lifts you in your belly and lifts you in your back, and then you start to shiver. *N/um* makes you tremble; it's hot. Your eyes are open but you don't look around; you hold your eyes still and look straight ahead. But when

you get into *!Kia*, you're looking around because you see everything, because you see what's troubling everybody ...

The !Kung say that the *!kia* ritual is very intense, both physically and emotionally, and experiences can vary from fear to exhilaration. *!Kia* has a transformational and transcendent aspect, and participants say that they become more themselves, what Katz describes as feeling one's 'more essential self'. One's state of consciousness is altered to the degree that senses of self, time and space are altered significantly.

Two predisposing factors that increase the likelihood of becoming a master of *n/um* are emotion and fantasy. The !Kung say that the experience of intense emotions is good preparation for the deeply emotional *!kia* experience, and since fantasy is an excellent preparation for contacting and accepting an altered state, those who have a rich fantasy life are more likely to become masters of *n/um*. *!Kia* is regarded with awe and is greatly feared as an experience, a fact which only serves to enhance the emotional state that follows. The *n/um* masters that Katz conferred with during his fieldwork repeatedly referred to the pain and fear experienced at the onset of *!kia*. They are frightened of losing themselves and not 'coming back', as the following quote (Katz 1976: 288) demonstrates:

> In !kia your heart stops, you're dead, your thoughts are nothing, you breathe with difficulty. You see things, n/um things; you see ghosts killing people, you smell burning, rotten flesh; then you heal, you pull sickness out. You heal, heal, heal, heal ... then you live. Then your eyeballs clear and then you see people clearly.

The !Kung work within a spiritual and ideological framework that allows them to express transcendence in an atmosphere of support and immersion in their own culture. Katz comments that if transcendence is pursued without cultural supports, any experience quickly dissipates and there is very little effect on a person's daily behaviour (Katz 1976: 301). (This may be open to debate and contemporary Western 'doofers' might argue this point. But doofs, which consist of all-night dancing, also involve entheogens, and so will be covered in chapter 7.)

Discussion

Opening up to a spiritual experience through dance or movement appears to involve preparing the body for a somatic experience that will allow unity with the divine, awaken an energy that is within the body or open the body to allow something else (such as a spirit) to enter. Dance or dance movement often begins with a measured, controlled and meticulously executed performance, is repetitive and is accompanied by music to evoke the emotions and prepare participants for what is to follow. Even seemingly chaotic and spontaneous dance movements are regulated and follow a certain format. Often (but not always) the dance is circular in nature; either the group dances in a circle, or the individual spins in a circular motion, as evidenced in the Sufi Whirling Dervishes. Rotational movement and particularly frequent or prolonged whirling and turning affect balance and equilibrium, and facilitate dissociation.

In all the aforementioned examples, the participants are totally involved in the event, and are fully enculturated, cognizant that there will be an expected pattern or format to the dance event, and acknowledging that certain behaviour is appropriate. A common pattern is the slow build-up (what Baklanoff calls the 'Warm-up' phase), followed by a seemingly spontaneous, less controlled and sometimes frenzied phase. It is in the latter stage that the dancers feel a 'bursting open' or 'opening up', when the body is susceptible to something either going out of the body (a kind of power or energy) or coming into the body (spirit). There may be a change in perceptions: of time, of identity or of physical sensations such as pain/no pain. Possession trance is intimately connected to dance, but dance or movement is also highly relevant to other altered states that assist in healing, or in feelings of oneness with the Divine. It would seem that there is a breaking down of normal strain and tension that allows the rigid body to relax and enter a kind of abandoned 'flow' experience (Csikszentmihalyi and Csikszentmihalyi 1988). These authors noted that one can enter flow when one steps outside normal everyday activities to engage with an activity that completely captivates the attention (such as rock climbing, when the climber is intensely focused on the climb). In the flow experience, there is total focused involvement, the sense of being outside everyday reality, a sense of serenity and timelessness; one is neither bored nor overly stressed, and is not concerned about what others think. When the dancer engages with the dance in this way, s/he can enter 'flow', transcend the ordinary and enter into communion with something other than the mundane.

The next chapter will pursue some of the ideas contained in this chapter by exploring the significance of touch (including pain) to the religious experience and whether this is another type of portal.

–5–

Tactile Portals

Negotiating the Demands of the Flesh

> The primary form of sense is touch, which belongs to all animals. Just as the power
> of self-nutrition can be isolated from touch and sensation generally, so touch can
> be isolated from all other forms of sense. (By the power of self-nutrition we mean
> that departmental power of the soul which is common to plants and animals: all
> animals whatsoever are observed to have the sense of touch.) ... soul is the source of
> these phenomena and is characterized by them, viz. by the powers of self-nutrition,
> sensation, thinking, and motivity.
>
> Aristotle[1]

The skin is the outer surface of the human body, the protective veil between inside
and outside; and it is the medium through which touch is felt. It can be stroked in
tenderness or subjected to great acts of cruelty. What is done to the skin reflects
cultural and subcultural ideologies: the skin can be tattooed, scarified, painted,
pierced and branded to communicate identity and ideology. The sense of touch can
convey 'bodily knowledge' (Howes 2005b: 28), and healing by touch is thought
to be both spiritually and physically efficacious; some alternative healers say that
they can 'feel' illness in a person's body merely by touch, and in some shamanic
societies, an illness is 'sucked out' of a sick person's body. Hands can touch not
just the physical body, but may tap into unseen forces. The purpose of Ayurvedic
massage, for example, is to improve the flow of the life force (*prana*) throughout the
body (Govindan 2005) in order to strengthen both mind and body; and the energy
field around the body can be manipulated by the skilful healer.

Tactile communication between certain people (a man and a menstruating
woman; between castes in India) can be considered polluting and necessitate
purification rites, while the laying on of hands or the handling of venomous
snakes can be proof of belief by the faithful, and the handling of sacred objects,
such as holy books, or sacred *churinga* (sacred boards) in Aboriginal Australia,
are acts of reverence and belief. Touch can also convey certain secret knowledge,
as in the Masonic handshake. The kiss can demonstrate love and affection
between people, or devotion and obeisance (kissing the Pope's ring), or respect
(the final farewell kiss of the living to the dead). All these tactile demonstrations
draw on haptic dynamics.

In Tibetan Buddhism, liberation through touch includes tactile contact with certain birds, animals and living humans, as well as objects that somehow have been connected with people considered holy (walls of grottoes in which enlightened people once meditated, imprints of their feet and hands, relics), and non-sentient objects, such as monuments and paintings, that are associated with miracles, walls of grottoes in which enlightened people once meditated, and holy books. In most, if not all cultures, touching or the placing of hands on the body is considered to be a highly effective method of healing the sick, and healers invariably speak of receiving healing energy or assistance through other-than-human means. For example, when the Arctic Circle Inupiat shamans (both men and women) use their healing abilities, they say that the spirits and ancestors work through them. They also say that this assistance can help them to communicate with the dead, find lost people and objects, and change the weather. The Inupiat taught anthropologist Edith Turner how to detect sickness with her own hands, through sense perception of the fingers, and from them she learnt that it is possible to feel 'sick tissues'. Through a 'certain awareness in the human consciousness' and an opening up of feelings, she writes, there is a link between the healer and the sufferer, and the channels to the sick person are opened (Turner 1996: 76). She found that spirit perception and spirit experience comes in flashes, is elusive and is 'a very intimate thing, very much concerned with the human body'. One can, she says, 'develop the sense' and the ability to see or feel, with the hands, but no dogmatic statements can be made about these experiences, and they fail categorization as one is dealing with 'elusive imponderables' (1996: 229).

Touch, as Aristotle proclaimed, is the 'root' sense, without which life is not possible (cited in Harvey 2002: 4–5). Aristotle argued that although the tactile feeling seemed to be a property of the flesh itself, it was 'deeper than skin', indeed that the real organ of touch was situated 'further inward'. Touch, he declared, was analogous to thought; further, that without a sense of touch it was impossible to have any other sensation, for every body possessing a soul has the faculty of touch. Not only does touch heal the sick – and this notion is repeated through many epochs and across cultures – but the flesh can be stimulated or deprived of tactile contact, and both means have been utilized, intentionally or unintentionally, as an avenue through which to project beyond the body, into the realm of spirit. Indeed, far from escaping the demands of the flesh, which is the main purpose behind practices such as celibacy and self-inflicted somatic punishments, bodily transcendence often takes place through bodily sensations, even when the flesh is denied tactile stimulation. This chapter emphasizes the idea of the flesh most significantly.

The touch, the kiss, the handshake and the embrace 'bridge the gap between soul and body'; touch lies at the core of the Christian mystery (Ryan and Ryan 1992: 331). Jesus laid hands on those he healed (Luke 4:40) and people could be healed by merely touching Christ's garments (Luke 8:43–8):

As he went, the people pressed round him. And a woman who had had a flow of blood for twelve years and could not be healed by any one, came up behind him, and touched the fringe of his garment; and immediately her flow of blood ceased. And Jesus said, 'Who was it that touched me?' When all denied it, Peter said, 'Master, the multitudes surround you and press upon you!' But Jesus said, 'Some one touched me; for I perceive that power has gone forth from me.' And when the woman saw that she was not hidden, she came trembling, and falling down before him declared in the presence of all the people why she had touched him, and how she had been immediately healed. And he said to her, 'Daughter, your faith has made you well; go in peace'.

This statement attributed to Jesus is an intriguing one as it appears to be saying that healing power resides in the body and can be brought forth by the touch of others. Jesus only perceived that someone had touched him because of the sense he had of power issuing forth from his body, as if it were an almost tangible substance. This notion is reiterated in Mark 5:25–34.

Extraordinary miracles were attributed to the hands of Paul, working through God; diseases were cured and evil spirits departed from a sufferer's body (Acts 19:11–12). The relics of saints and other holy people are sometimes kept in amulets and worn close to the skin as good luck pieces or for the purported efficacy of their healing properties. Some Christians still believe in the efficacy of touching certain holy places or relics (such as the rock at Lourdes where the Virgin Mary is said to have appeared), and this is a deeply moving experience for many. Western Christian theologians, in general, are loath to acknowledge sensual contact with such objects as a holy act or a means of achieving salvation, but the faithful still recall that through the hands of the apostles many 'signs and wonders' occurred. Thousands still throng to Christian faith-healing services today, to be 'slain by the Spirit' and healed by the miracle of God working through human touch.

Like the Inupiat healers in the Arctic Circle, Mick Fazeldean, an Aboriginal healer in Australia, heals people by concentration, meditation and touch. Although he does not understand how his healing powers work, he says that when he first sees a patient, he looks at them and says a small prayer, at which time, 'there is a power just like electricity that comes through from the switchboard on the other side' (Hume 2002: 66). As he places his hands on a sick person's body, he feels a 'kind of electricity' and that 'electricity comes from down deep' (Fazeldean 1987: 102). If the patient does not improve within about thirty minutes, he does the procedure again, by moving into what he calls 'different levels of the mind', taking the patient 'up to another floor in my mind' (p. 102):

I try to get to that other level to work first and work on it just with the mind. Then the appropriate power will come down strongly the moment I go on to touch the body concerned ... an electricity goes through and takes away from the body whatever is causing the pain. Electricity – that is the word that comes closest to explaining the workings of my healing.

Immediately after such a healing he might have a spinning sensation in his head. During some of the healings he feels that something is being extracted from the patient's body (which he describes as 'like bones'), even though he does not see any physical object coming out of the patient. Compare this to Edith Turner's (1994: 71–95) account of the Ndembu healing ritual, and of her seeing something coming out of the body at the moment when healing took place, as well as her ability to feel 'sick tissues' (above).

The sense of touch is important in other areas of Aboriginal Australian life, and I now give a brief background to Aboriginal epistemology in order to pursue its importance.

Aboriginal Australians

In Aboriginal Australia there are various names for a fundamental cosmological and epistemological principle which has been translated into English as the Dreaming. The Dreaming is not the dreams that one has at night (though this is one way that it can be accessed), but rather an all-encompassing timelessness, a sense of place and space, as well as law and a moral code, that was set down for living Aborigines to follow during the creative period when the Dreaming Ancestors emerged from beneath the ground. During this time, the Ancestors travelled across the earth, giving form to the formless, and leaving tangible expressions of themselves (their essence) in the land. Where the Ancestors bled, ochre deposits were created; where they dug in the ground, water flowed and springs formed; where they cut down trees, valleys were formed (Hume 2002: 25). It is to these Ancestors that living Aborigines refer when they speak about their connection to the land and to everything that exists, both sentient and non-sentient. All knowledge and wisdom is derived through the Dreaming, and the focus is on ancestral presence in the land – on place and space, or 'geosophy' (Swain 1993: 25). When the Ancestors completed their travels, they went back into the ground, and it is there they stay until they are 'brought up' again by the living. This can be done through ceremony, dance, art, songs and stories.

The dominant belief, despite regional differences, is that there is a pervading Ancestral essence, power or life force that emanates from the spiritual realm and which is imbued in the land. Tapping into that essence is done in a number of ways, which involve all the senses in order to 'call up' Ancestral presence. Ancestral designs are painted in sand, rocks, bark and ceremonial objects, as well as on bodies; stories of Ancestral journeys are sung and danced; artwork is touched and stroked; and the Ancestors are called up from beneath the earth itself by the dancing feet of the performers. Raising dust when dancing is vitally important in dance, since 'the feet penetrate the ground to raise the Ancestors' (Watson 2003: 229). The land itself is compared to a living, sentient, conscious body, which relates to living Aboriginal people. The surface of the earth, like the skin of the human body, can be painted with

Ancestral designs that act as an avenue for Ancestral presence. Indeed, the skin of the body and the 'skin' (surface) of the land are equivalent. When an Ancestral design is painted on the living skin of the body, the design that was on the Ancestor's body is put onto the living human body and, in essence, the person becomes contained within the Ancestor. The skin is also the medium through which the spirit leaves the body at death (Morphy 1991). Visual and tactile familiarity with the land and the tactile sensing involved in mingling human hands in the soft materials of the ground in public sand demonstrates a state of openness to the environment (Watson 2003: 293).

Terms employed for sand drawing and painting on canvas 'cluster around ideas of touching, poking and piercing' (Watson 2003: 52). Cradling and running the hands along sacred objects, such as sacred boards, is equivalent to touching the Ancestor itself; it is 'a physical quality and tactile, entirely different from the visual sensation in eyesight' (Bardon 1979: 22).[2] When a traditional healer looks 'piercingly' in the eyes of a patient, and when a storyteller pokes the surface of the earth in sand drawing, these are both suggestive of entering a different realm of matter or experience. Both are closely linked with penetrating the surface of the earth to enter the realm of the Ancestral beings, a realm which is 'located geographically beneath the surface of the ground, but experientially beneath the surface of waking reality' (Watson 2003: 107).

Giving the specific example of the Kutjungka (central Australia) women's ceremonies, Christine Watson writes that 'striking the ground is an important part of a two-way communication process' between Kutjungka people and the conscious spiritual powers they say are present within the earth (Watson 2003: 107). The action of striking, whether in sand drawing or in ceremonial dancing, impacts on the sentient land, setting up vibrations in it, and calls on Ancestral presences within the country to witness what is happening. One of the ways for humans to give the country power is to sing the song cycles pertaining to that part of their country; another is to wash the sweat from their bodies into the waters. Similarly, emotions can be shared between country and humans; if a person feels sad, the country will feel sad too.

As in other Aboriginal societies, Kutjungka people experience Ancestral beings and other spirit beings as active in the world. These spirit beings are perceptible to spiritually sensitive humans in their waking consciousness or dream states, and are capable of communicating important information to humans. Sometimes Ancestral spirits visit the living in their dreams to show them body painting designs, dances, songs or healing rituals. Kutjungka women use terms describing the way an object is 'touched, stroked, beaten or penetrated' (Watson 2003: 239) to name their image-making practices, and these terms are fundamental to the conceptualization of their ontology and world view.

Ancestors are also said to be in a painting that 'shimmers'.[3] Techniques of fine cross-hatching and dots help to convey the notion of shimmering and luminosity.

Desert Aboriginal painters have described multiple lines or multiple lines of dotting as representing the sound passage, songs or power of the Ancestors. Paintings that exhibit a luminous quality, producing a surface that appears to vibrate, elevates that surface from ordinary to extraordinary. Similarly, luminosity can also transform the living body of a ritual performer, or the surface of a non-sentient object, from mundane to supramundane, denoting Ancestral presence (Morphy 1989: 21–40; Morphy 1991). 'Shimmering' conveys well the vibrancy and aliveness of paintings that demonstrate this quality. Image-making is not simply visual, but 'integrally involves the sense of touch as well as sonic and bodily elements' (Watson 2003: 50). Often people sing the song cycles pertaining to the Ancestral story (sonic manifestations of the Ancestor) while they are engaged in the image-making of that story. This is not done for paintings that are destined for the commercial art market, because it would 'call up' Ancestral presence and would not be appropriate.[4]

Kutjungka women, writes Watson (2003: 198), attain transformative spiritual experiences through participation in specific women's ceremonies:

> During these ceremonies the women's bodies are penetrated by the sacred sounds of the song cycles, telling of the power and deeds of the Ancestral women, instilling within their bodies the possibility of attaining similar spiritual power. The women's bodies are opened, too, by the process of inscribing special body painting designs with the flesh of the breasts and upper arms. In this process, women's torsos are penetrated by a volley of sound from the song cycle, while the forms made by the Ancestors as they metamorphosed into the fleshly features of their country are ingrained within the flesh of their own bodies. In this way, Ancestors and sites in country penetrate the bodies of living women.

At the close of a ceremony, the women move into a tight circle to signify the re-entry of Ancestral beings into the ground from whence they came.

To reiterate, the purpose of much ritual is to 'look after country' by maintaining a balanced physical and spiritual environment in a complex relationship between people and land. (This is why the hotly debated issue of land rights in Australia is so important to Aboriginal people.) 'Looking after country' entails and incorporates human bodily sensory awareness and connection with the sentient living country itself.

Another important and highly effective method of accessing portals through tactile means is through bodily pain. The use of physical pain, sometimes intense physical pain, to attain religious ecstasy or a transcendent spiritual experience is a fairly universal practice, and acts of suffering, indeed extreme acts of penitence in some epochs and cultures, have been a mark of the true believer.

Portals of Pain

> In his hands I saw a long golden spear and at the end of the iron tip I seemed to
> see a point of fire. With this he appeared to pierce my heart several times so that it
> penetrated to my entrails. When he drew the spear out, I thought he was drawing the
> entrails out with it, leaving me completely afire with a great love for God. The pain
> was so sharp that it made me utter several moans; and so excessive was the sweetness
> of this intense pain that I wished never to lose it.
>
> St Teresa of Avila, *Vida* XXIX

Some forms of pain infliction, such as tattooing and flagellation, have been employed
in many cultures as negative sanctions on people who have breached rules of socially
acceptable behaviour or transgressed cultural mores. Body modification that involves
pain dates back as far as 10,000–15,000 years before the Christian era (Comphausen
1997: 5). Often, physical pain is endured either voluntarily or involuntarily to mark
a rite of passage, to obtain membership into a particular subgroup or as an indication
of one's strength and courage. The anthropological literature abounds with reports
of physical pain involved in rituals that mark passage from childhood to adulthood.
Circumcision, subincision, deep scarification, clitoridectomy, tooth avulsion,
chopping finger joints, slashing and gouging the flesh are just some of the many
ways that people across the world have inflicted pain upon themselves and others.

As well as the functional use of pain as an indelible and important marker in rites
of passage, the use of pain to reach heights of ecstasy is well documented, especially
among medieval Christian saints and mystics. Modern mystics, such as Simone
Weil, also recognize the important place of painful bodily experiences in devotional
life. Weil believes that our understanding of the supernatural is deepened through our
encounters with bodily pain (Weil 1952); pain completely captivates our attention.
Through focusing intently on the crucifixion, the mystic's own intense pain can
be channelled into experiencing Christ's pain in order to identify completely with
Christ; the sense of self is then temporarily obliterated in the process. In Europe in
the Middle Ages, the connection between pain and mystical encounters with Christ
was almost institutionalized.

The focus of Christian religious devotion in the twelfth century was on a glorified
Christ, but this emphasis shifted to a suffering Christ by the fourteenth century, a
shift which had perceptible outcomes for religious piety. Fourteenth-century church
walls vividly depicted a Christ who suffered death on the cross, and fascination with
the humanity of Jesus increased (Ross 1993). Indeed, the image of the suffering
Jesus functioned as the primary scriptural symbol to demonstrate the depth of God's
love for humanity. Immeasurable love was coupled with immeasurable pain. To
understand this concept, it was necessary to undergo the experience of pain: to feel
and experience as Christ had felt and experienced.

Inflicting pain on a sinful body through corporal punishment was considered a means to spiritual perfection and union with Christ (Flynn 1996: 257). Mystics such as St Teresa of Avila (cited above) and Catherine of Siena (b.1347) approached their pietism with the same attitude as that expressed by Hadewijch, the thirteenth-century Flemish Beguine who said, 'desire to suffer in order to ascend' (Flynn 1996: 257). Sequestered in small cells or cell-like rooms, the aspiring ascetic underwent sleep deprivation, extreme forms of fasting and self-inflicted torture. Some knelt on iron spikes (p. 258), wore metal chains fastened around the waist so tightly that they pinched and broke the skin (p. 257), bound their arms and bodies tightly with penitential horsehair garments (called *cilicia*) (p. 258) or vines of thorns (Lester 1995: 196), or methodically engaged in self-flagellation (Bynum 1987: 246–50). Hedwig of Silesia scourged herself, Blessed Clare of Rimini had herself bound to a pillar and whipped on Good Friday, and Blessed Charles of Blois wrapped knotted cords around his chest (Vauchez 1977: 197, 374, 365), while Christina of Spoleto perforated her own foot with a nail (Bynum 1987: 391). Some lived on nothing but the sacraments, some consumed the pus excreted from the wounds of their patients, and many engaged in self-flagellation with ropes or chains. Catherine of Siena flagellated herself with an iron chain three times a day, each beating lasting for one and a half hours, until blood ran from her shoulders to her feet (Bell 1985: 43). She also limited her sleep to only thirty minutes every forty-eight hours (Flynn 1996: 257). Dominican Benvenuta Bojani (b.1255) used a rock as a pillow, deprived herself of sleep and, if she felt her eyes growing heavy during prayer, poured vinegar into them to force herself to stay awake. She flogged herself with an iron chain three times nightly, and on one occasion, St Dominic appeared in her vision and 'ordered her to consult with Father Conrad [her confessor] about what she was doing' (Bell 1985: 127–30).

Although extreme asceticism resulted in a debilitating physical condition, it seems that it had the effect of elevating the spirits. Reports of paranormal phenomena such as levitation, body elongation and stigmata were not uncommon (Lester 1995: 196), likewise trance, ecstatic nosebleeds (Bynum 1992: 165), catatonic seizures, bodily rigidity and, for the few, stigmatic wounds. Such bleak austerity and systematic physical afflictions were designed to prepare the soul for divine encounters, revelations, visions or a sense of 'fusion with the crucified body of Christ' (Bynum 1987: 208–9).

Some pious men of these times saw visions and described their own affective experiences of God; however, women's religiosity was explicitly somatic and visionary. Indeed, the sensual and erotic aspects of women's religious experiences were ridiculed by German mystic David of Augsburg (d.1272) as 'erotic ticklings', and many were 'a bit suspicious of such piety' (Bynum 1992: 169).

The suffering body of Jesus Christ on the cross evoked strong images for the pious. Their own prolonged physical suffering was preceded or accompanied by hours of penitential prayer, focused concentration on images and total immersion and belief in the Christian faith. The Roman Catholic saint, Ignatius of Loyola (b.1491) made explicit references to all the senses, including that of bodily penance through chastisement of the flesh. Calling it 'sensible pain' that could be sought through wearing haircloth, cords or chains of iron, by scourging or wounding oneself, or by other kinds of austerities such as sleep and food deprivation, he nevertheless cautioned that although penance through pain should be felt by the flesh, it should not penetrate to the bones. It may give pain, but not cause infirmity. He therefore advised penitents to scourge themselves with small cords, which cause pain, but not to excess (Longridge 1919: 74). St Ignatius wrote a series of Spiritual Exercises that incorporated the use of all the senses, along with prayer, meditation and contemplation, in order to 'seek and to find the divine will' with a view to the 'salvation of one's soul' (p. 27). Stemming from his own experiences in 1521, the idea of these Spiritual Exercises is to help the 'exercitant' to discover the will of God in relation to the their own future, and to give the person energy and courage to find that will. Over four weeks of twenty-one specific meditations, designed to be carried out while in retreat, the practitioner addresses what St Ignatius called the three major divisions of the spiritual life: the purgative, illuminative and unitive (p. 10). Each of the exercises is designed with a definite end in view, to 'praise, reverence and serve God' and to save the soul of the practitioner. Multi-sensorial methods are involved in these highly experiential exercises. One must have the right intentions and perform the right actions with regard to 'outward bodily posture', to be able to 'see with the eye of the imagination the corporeal place' of one's object of meditation (for example, the temple or mountain where Jesus Christ may have stood). In a Spiritual Exercise that focuses on hell, one is advised 'to see with the eyes of the imagination' great fires and bodies on fire; to hear the 'wailings, the groans, the cries, the blasphemies against Christ'; to 'smell the smoke, the brimstone, the filth, and the corruption'; to 'taste bitter things, such as tears, sadness, and the worm of conscience'; and to 'feel with the sense of touch how the fires touch and burn the souls'. Always, prior to any exercise, there is a preparatory prayer, and at the heart of all the exercises is the notion that the 'deep sense of love and mercy of God is never forgotten' (p. 58). The senses, it seems, are all involved in the journey to understanding God. He said, of the body: 'When I turn to look at myself what a sight do I behold! All my corruption and bodily foulness, the result of a nature infected and vitiated by original sin'. St Ignatius died in 1556, and his Spiritual Exercises have had a significant impact on the Western spiritual tradition since that time.

The sanctifying potential of tortured flesh was also recognized by John of the Cross (d.1591), Bernard of Laredo (d.1540) and Francis of Osuna (d.1542), each of whom wrote about their own personal insights on pain (Flynn 1996: 260). Far from escaping the demands of the flesh, divine transcendence took place through bodily sensations. Pain created a mystical understanding of the divine suffering (Italian mystic Angela of Foligno (d.1309), cited in Bynum 1992:170):

Once, when I was at Vespers and was contemplating the Crucifix … suddenly my soul was lifted into love, and all the members of my body felt a very great joy. And I saw and felt that Christ, within me, embraced my soul with that arm by which he was crucified … and I felt such great security that I could not doubt it was God … So I rejoice when I see that hand which he holds out with the signs of the nails, saying to me: 'Behold what I bore for you.'

Paradoxically, while denying other, more pleasurable bodily sensations, pain was particularly emphasized and permeated the practices of the mystics. St Teresa valued her pain, viewing it as a form of bodily and psychic purification, emptying and purging the soul of all sins. Unbearable physical sensations indicated that the hand of God was tearing from the soul its worldly inclinations and measured the validity of the mystical experience. St Teresa relates that during rapture, 'when the immortal soul was being carried away by God from the material world, the body acknowledged its flight'. Both physical and psychic pain reached an 'unbearable' climax at the moment when the soul reached its reunion with God, and became the true testimony of the soul's arrival. From St Teresa's account, mystical union was a mixture of agony and ecstasy, a bitter-sweet sharp, intense pain, but one that she 'wished never to lose' (Flynn 1996: 273).

Saint Maria Maddalena de' Pazzi (b.1587) took the long, thorn-covered stalks of orange trees and tied them tightly around her head to imitate Christ's crown of thorns, sometimes leaving it on her head for an entire night. On different occasions she had herself tied to a post with her hands bound behind her back, or would lay on the ground so that members of the congregation could step on her body. She also slept on straw, walked barefoot in winter and dripped hot candle-wax on her own body. While some forms of self-mutilation were intended to imitate Christ's pain, others were ways of testing and fighting bodily temptation (Puccini 1970: 9, 50, 38, 140–1). As well as these self-inflicted tests of endurance, Maria Maddalena was sometimes subjected to pains and injuries said to be inflicted on her by devils: being thrown down stairs and beaten or bitten by them, causing her extreme pain (p. 78). Such behaviour today would be attributed to the hysterics of a religious fanatic and the result of a mental disorder. Even the Church, while recognizing that piety was closely associated with acts of penance, struggled for some centuries to distinguish between mystical experience and various forms of mental disorder ('insanity'), such as hysteria and epilepsy (Mazzoni 1996).

The employment of pain as a portal can be found in many other cultures and religions besides those I have already cited (Crapanzano 1973; James 1982; Laski 1961; Murphy 1992).[5] Sufi Dervish trance induction is sometimes brought about through the use of skewers, hot irons, ingestion of broken glass, piercing and bloodletting in some of the North African Sufi orders. One of the most well-known examples of North American indigenous uses of spiritual pain is the Sun Dance,[6] performed throughout the Plains tribes. The religious aspects of the

Sun Dance focused on the acquisition of supernatural power to assist in healing and health, and to dispel evil influences. The principal goal was to reconnect participants to the energy and power manifest in the sun at its most potent time of the year, the summer solstice (Lincoln 1994: 5). Another goal was the quest for power and success in hunting and warfare. In early times, piercing was part of a warrior's training and the ritual was a chance to display courage and endurance. Sun Dances drew large crowds of dancers, singers, drummers and spectators, and lasted for several days, with dancing, fasting, mutilation and self-mortification lasting up to four days and nights. Dancers had to abstain from alcohol and peyote. A contemporary Oglala Sioux man describes his experience of the Sun Dance (Lewis 1990: 103):

> The experience of the Sun Dance I can't describe. It's like being hypnotized. As I go up and down [dancing] it's as if the sun were dancing. It is a good feeling. It is all preparation, planning, fasting, being ready. It is not easy. My throat is dry and I am tired. I don't sleep before; I cannot sleep. I am thinking and planning how it will be. There is sacrifice, pain, death, and dying, and coming back again to the real world. You can tell if the Sun Dance leader is a real leader. If there is rain or great wind he is not proper for it. The Sun Dance is for the generations coming... Someday I want to have a real Sun Dance ... no metal, no glass, no cars. My first Sun Dance was in the hills, way off there.

Participants could choose to dance in a number of ways: one was to gaze at the sun from dawn to dusk; another involved having wooden skewers inserted into their breasts and either tied to rawhide ropes secured halfway up the sacred pole, being suspended about one foot off the ground or having the skewers attached with thongs to one or more buffalo skull/s that must be dragged along the dance area (Olsen 1994: 245). The sacred pole, which formed the centre of the dance, acted as the vertical connection, or *axis mundi*, between this world and the next (Lincoln 1994).

To Bruce Lincoln's account of the Sun Dance, Jilek adds that the dancers first purified themselves in the sweat lodge; then, after the passing of the peace pipe, they entered the arena in a procession, led by the Sun Dance chief (whom he calls the 'shaman-director'), the person who traditionally determines the course of the ritual procedures (Jilek 1989: 173). The dance event was accompanied by the rhythmic chanting and drumming of teams of singer-drummers. The intensive drumming, carried out in a highly charged atmosphere of intense excitement (whistle blowing, men yelling war whoops and the beating of willow wands by women in the audience), aids the vision-seeking Sun Dancer to enter an altered state of consciousness. After vigorous dancing with quickening tempo for an hour or more, dancers finally receive a vision and are 'seized by a jolt of power', at which time they are lifted from their feet and thrown to the ground, where the 'power-filled body lies motionless during the soul's archetypal shamanic journey' (p. 175). Dancers who took the vow to dance with pierced flesh were tied to the centre pole by a thong that the chief inserted in their chests. Holding on to a protective staff, they danced until 'breaking the flesh' (p. 174).

The physical connection of torturous tools to willing flesh in order to achieve an altered state is also used extensively in some Hindu sects. The Kavadi (or Kavandi) of India and Malaysia publicly celebrate their religious beliefs through a demonstration of voluntary suffering one day a year, when they have hooks attached to heavy weights inserted into their flesh in order to attract the attention of the Divine and have their prayers answered (Hullet 1981). Some Sanskrit terms for pain make explicit the connection between pain, knowledge and breaking down barriers. The term *vedana* is related to the causative form of the verb 'to know' and refers to making something known through torture. Another term, *ruja*, originates in the root *ruj* ('to shatter into pieces' or 'break open') (Glucklich 1998: 392).

The Hindu Thaipusam festival,[7] held every year in Singapore during the full moon of the tenth month of the Tamil calendar (January or February), involves devotees in extreme physical acts of devotion. Held in honour of Subramaniam,[8] the purpose of the festival is to honour vows and pledges that have been made to the deity in return for his help (curing the devotee or a sick relative, making an infertile woman pregnant, passing exams, or for good fortune, a better life or help in finding a spouse). On this occasion devotees carry ornate *kavadis* to fulfil vows physically. *Kavadi* is a physical burden which has to be carried by the devotee during the three-kilometre pilgrimage from Sri Sriniva Perumal Temple to the Chettiar Hindu Temple.

The *kavadi* itself usually consists of two semicircular strips of wood or metal, with cross-pieces that support the structure on the shoulders of the bearer, or it might be tied on the ends of a pole and carried over the shoulders. It is often decorated with peacock feathers, palm leaves and flowers, and has two brass pots filled with fresh milk tied to it, along with other decorations. Some *kavadi* weigh up to thirty kilos and are attached to the devotee via spikes, skewers or needles attached to fish hooks. Other parts of the body, especially the cheeks, tongue and forehead, are spiked with silver needles, long metal spikes and fish hooks, often topped by a trident, which is the emblem of Siva. Some might also wear sandals studded with iron nails, or attach limes or small metal pots to the thighs, upper arms and other parts of the body with fish hooks. Not all *kavadi*, however, require such extreme physical endurance; some devotees may simply carry on their heads a brass jug of milk, or small altars with offerings.

For forty-eight days prior to the two-day Thaipusam festival, the devotees purge themselves of all physical and mental impurities. They abstain from meat and alcohol, cigarettes, sexual intercourse and any contact with menstruating women; they refrain from impure thoughts, do not shave or cut their hair, and do not use utensils which others have touched. There must have been no recent deaths in the family; otherwise the pollution of death will cling to them. They are allowed only one vegetarian meal a day, and for the twenty-four hours before they carry the *kavadi*, they must maintain a complete fast. On the night before the two-day pilgrimage, they sleep overnight on the floor of a temple so as not to be contaminated by beds. All these physical prerequisites, as well as religious exaltation, music, incense and an emotionally charged atmosphere throughout the whole proceedings, produce in the devotee a state of ecstasy, such that little or no physical pain is said to be experienced and no blood shed. Krishna Vadya, a priest at the temple in Malaysia which conducts the annual ritual, says, 'the belief in Lord Murugan is what prevents the pain and the bleeding'.[9]

During the procession, musicians accompany the *kavadi*-bearers, playing the *molam*, or hand drum, and other instruments, and relatives and family chant prayers, offer emotional support and burn incense (often the air is thick with smoke from the incense). At peak moments, such as during the insertion and, later, extraction of the needles and spikes in the body, and to help a devotee enter a state of trance, relatives and friends shout prayers to the deity loudly into his ear and show their emotional bonds to him in tactile ways: grasping him on the arms and shoulders while the needles are being inserted, and continuing their emotional support during the whole process. Some of the supporters are so affected by the event that they go into trance themselves. Removal of the spikes and needles is just as painful as their insertion and has to be done carefully, with the same amount of support from others as was given for their insertion. As the needles are removed, sacred ash and limes are applied to the wounds, helping to stop the flow of blood.

Asked why they carried *kavadi*, Stewart Wavell's (1967) respondents gave as reasons for demonstrating their gratitude to the deity the recovery from illness of one of their family members, or recovery from some misfortune. Wavell also asked if it was worth it, and received the following responses: 'I walked with God'; 'there is no pain, only gratitude and love, and afterwards you feel so peaceful'. A young student said: 'When I think of that journey, all I remember is flames around me, cool flames that did not burn; and the needles in my body did not seem like real needles at all – they were like needles without points, like needles of eternity'.[10] Many devotees reported sensations of weightlessness, pure consciousness, feelings of an upward movement or that they did not exist. As well, they felt detached from the external environment, or had feelings of cosmic unity and depersonalization. Most devotees said they felt little or no pain during piercing, and reported sensations of timelessness and ineffable feelings of rejuvenation.[11]

The senses are all called on during this highly emotionally charged event, with the loud music, the beating of drums, the chanting and whirling of the devotees, the ringing of bells and the scent of incense, all performed as the devotees make their way along the densely packed route, flanked by excited onlookers. But the emphasis on physical pain, induced by torturous implements such as elaborate, spiked metal cages that surround the upper torso and head of the devotee, point to pain as the sensorial focus par excellence of the Kavadi ceremony.

The devotional displays of piercing the flesh that are associated with the indigenous North American Sun Dance and the Hindu Kavadi ceremonies are imitated by Western 'modern primitives', such as Fakir Musafar. Musafar first coined the term 'modern primitives' in 1979 to describe himself and those interested in the personal exploration and experimentation of the body through what he calls 'body play', which includes extremely tight corsetry, as well as tattooing and piercing. He draws upon ideas and practices from any available source, without regard to the cultural and socio-political contexts. For Musafar, the experience that is the result of pain-inducing practices is more important than the cultural context, and he is eager to try them all.

Modern Primitives and Sadomasochism

Fakir refers to himself as 'shaman', 'artist', 'master piercer' and 'body modifier'.[12] As a child he was fascinated with tribal cultures and wanted to emulate some of the practices he saw or heard about in order to experience at first hand what they would feel like. He is known as the father of the modern primitive movement, and, in addition to extensive tattooing, branding and piercing on his own body, he offers courses of instruction at workshops licensed by the State of California to anyone who wants to learn his techniques and explore the limits of physical pain in order to reach a spiritual experience. He tells his students: 'If it protrudes, pierce it; if it doesn't, don't' (video: *The Human Canvas*). He says that his workshops appeal to people who are ready to accept pain, go beyond it and explore where this will take them. His self-published book, *Spirit + Flesh*, only available online from his website, illustrates physical experiences such as bondage, sensory deprivation, tattooing, piercing, fetishes, body rituals and modifications from the period 1948 to 2002.[13]

In the video, *The Human Canvas* (televised on SBS, Australia on 5 August 2000), Fakir talks about pain 'transforming the body' in order to attain 'a higher state of being' and experience 'a greater reality'. In his own enactment of the Sun Dance, he professed that something 'wonderful' occurred that resembled a near-death experience:

> Something happened ... my body was floating upward and I looked up and saw this great white light above me. It was the most marvellous thing. I didn't want to come back into my body but it said, 'you still have work to do. If you don't go back you will be dead'. I struggled and came back down into my body.

In his one-day, intensive, body-piercing workshops, Fakir offers his students an 'energy pull ritual' through which to explore 'ecstatic' states by means of gradually increasing tension on bodily piercings in order to increase the level of pain experienced. In the first part of these sessions, Fakir explains how the practitioner can 'travel to inner space and unseen worlds', through a combination of receiving piercings in the upper chest area, rhythmic breathing (for pain control) and live drumming.[14] One person (Cléo) who has gone through this ritual writes:

> I have done this ritual five times now. Every time it has been a different journey. The whole exploration for me is about altered state, energy, fire (yes it can be really hot) and visions … It is a personal dance of ecstatic fire, bright or soft.[15]

Other experiences are said to include an instant 'high', experiencing group energy, connecting intimately with others present, feeling one's chi energy, assuaging grief and sexual energy.

While indigenous practitioners of pain are engaging in culturally entrenched practices that highlight their beliefs, and are performed within particular cultural, social and political contexts, modern primitives are searching for a kind of generic experience of bodily pain that will take them beyond the body and into altered states.

I diverge for a moment here to discuss briefly the issue of cultural appropriation as it is an important one, especially with regard to religious practices. New Age cultural 'borrowing' seems to be 'everywhere and nowhere', as Pink (2000: 114) has observed, and much has been written on the commodification of indigenous culture. Many people engaged in New Age practices that appropriate cultural items (to date, Native Americans have been the most often targeted in this regard, with 'dream catchers', pseudo sweat lodges, 'vision quests' and the search for one's 'totem animal'). On the other hand, many of the alternative health practices are based on Eastern cultural practices, and not only have they been beneficial to the health of many people, but they have also highlighted the intrinsic value of other ways of healing besides the Western medical model.

Some of the criticisms of the New Age as a sociocultural agent that actively appropriates indigenous culture (Marcus 1991; Grossman and Cuthbert 1998) might well be levelled at some aspects of the New Age – especially where there is blatant commercialization, but in other cases, indigenous entrepreneurs or spiritual healers are equally involved in New Age practices, and some embrace a synthesis without even knowing that a synthesis has occurred. One only has to travel to religious sites throughout the world to remark on the commercialization from within a culture by members of that culture (the sale of holy water from Lourdes; the sale of holy relics at markets in Thailand; the sale of various paraphernalia at religious sites throughout India, and so on). Many Westerners practice yoga for the benefits derived from the physical postures, breathing and meditation, without necessarily delving into the spiritual aspects of yoga traditions (although they may do this as well), and its very popularity with Westerners has led to an increase in respect toward Indian traditions like yoga by many middle-class Indians.[16] Nevertheless, the ways in which yoga has been exploited in the West for commercial purposes is abhorred by many people in India. Yoga originated from classical yoga texts, including the writings of the Indian sage Patanjali. While traditional yoga practitioners might look kindly at Westerners' attempts to practise yoga for their own well-being, when foreigners claim patents and copyrights on poses and techniques that derive from classical Indian yoga treatises, India's heritage is, rightly, viewed as at risk. Some fitness instructors in the West are engaging in yoga piracy, and the Indian Government has established a task force to look into the exploitation of traditional knowledge and intellectual property theft. It seems that yoga in the United States alone has become a multibillion dollar business, especially when famous celebrities such as Madonna become adherents. Some individuals in the West are claiming intellectual ownership of yoga postures and have copyrighted sequences of poses that have been taken straight out of classical Indian yoga texts which have existed in India for thousands of years (Orr 2005: 1–2).

Gross commercialization of cultural practices goes beyond the boundaries of cultural diffusion, but to patent traditional practices and claim them as the property of specific groups or individuals is blatant exploitation. Where the boundary line becomes rather blurry is when innocent individuals who desire to learn about another culture's beliefs and practices (such as yoga) respectfully follow a Western version of those beliefs and practices, either singly or in groups, and/or when a person from the other culture does the teaching in the West for profit. I raise this question here without pursuing it (this is not the reason for writing this book), to highlight the fact that while gross commercialization is to be abhorred (and it seems that in the yoga case mentioned above it was the push for copyright and patenting of yoga postures that was the final straw), there are many subtleties involved in the use and abuse of cultural items. Cultural diffusion and cultural appropriation are complex issues that will become increasingly important in the future.

As increasing numbers of Westerners are searching for the kinds of experiences that are brought about by specific cultural practices (and shamanism is often investigated in this search), either through imitating cultural practices that involve pain, tattooing, vision quests, sweat lodges, the use of entheogens (to be discussed in a later chapter) or Eastern meditation techniques and postures, the question of whether or not the actual experiences are the same might also be an interesting area for further anthropological investigation. Anthropologists and indigenous people at present are engaged in discussions about the political and ethical aspects of cultural appropriation, but so far have not launched into the question of whether or not the experiences per se might be similar, nor just how culturally specific they may be.

Like the 'modern primitives', some contemporary sadomasochistic (S/M, or the 'leather community') ritual acts borrow heavily from other cultures in order to explore the pursuit of pain. Although the principal goal of sadomasochism is to attain erotic pleasure through pain and humility, it seems that a secondary spin-off from these practices is a shift in consciousness and a sense of transcendence when practitioners push themselves beyond normal limits of endurance.

While those studying S/M practices usually focus on perversion and power relations, practitioners themselves are more likely to explicitly address the religious parallels of experience. Performance artist Aña Wojak, who inserts lead-weighted hooks into various parts of her body, and has her clitoris pierced, writes (Australian Museum 2000: 46):

> These performances explore the spirituality of pain, where the body is the medium in a ritualised setting. It's about transcendence, releasing pain, embracing fears, releasing fears, embracing pain, balancing control and surrender to focus on the energy spiralling out from a still inner place.

Mira Zussman's article shifts the focus regarding sadomasochism (S/M) from the psychodynamics of perversion and power relations between participants to altered states of consciousness achieved in consensual S/M, bondage and fetish play (Zussman 1998). She proposes that there is an affinity between S/M and ecstatic religious practices.

From a study that she made in the S/M communities in California, she discusses this notion, as well as the evocation of fundamentally different states of consciousness in the types of practices. For example, practitioners say that altered states in consensual bondage and fetish play differ significantly in heterosexual and homosexual play. She recorded references to experiences that included feeling a 'cosmic energy', 'entranced state', 'cathartic release', 'liberation', 'euphoria' and even a 'white light'. Most of her informants compared 'leather sexuality' to the trance and ritual acts of shamanic, aboriginal and Western religious ritual (Zussman 1998: 34). Sometimes the distinction between pain and pleasure is blurred; intensification of excitement appears to negate the pain-pleasure barrier. Participants reported feeling 'totally alive', and 'being carried off to a different dimension' that is more real than ordinary reality (pp. 31–2).

Zussman writes that the masochist seeks out pain and sometimes humiliation, while the submissive seeks out bondage, servitude, pain or instruction in order to derive pleasure. What is central in bondage and fetish play is a certain degree of entrancement. Although suffering and humiliation in 'play' are sought-out experiences, there are also reports of feelings of transcendence that may be described as leaving the body, or intense euphoria. Whether a submissive has 'left his or her body in bliss' or 'withdrawn in terror' is a moot point, as the response by the submissive to the acts upon his/her body are apparently the same (Zussman 1998: 22–3; Califia 1988: 46).

When preparations for an S/M 'scene' are deliberately and meticulously carried out (described as 'being mindful'), they can give rise to 'a kind of hypnotic state of consciousness' (Zussman 1998: 26). The hypnotic and erotic process of rope-binding (leather, latex, lace, rope or chains), constriction (tight lacing and restrictive costuming) and immobilization can lead the submissive person into another state of consciousness while accessing multiple senses. It is not sensory deprivation that is experienced, but rather a heightened sense of awareness, with increased sensitivity to tactile stimulation.

At first glance it might seem questionable (and, to some, offensive) to include medieval pious religious people, and traditional Hindu and indigenous religious practices in the same discussion with contemporary pain/pleasure seekers, and indeed there are many differences between the two groups. But in the act of causing pain to the body, there are also commonalities. The pursuit of ecstatic union with Christ through imitating Christ's physical suffering on the cross, and the resulting spiritual pleasure this arouses, are the main goals of the medieval mystic. For the 'modern primitives', of whom Fakir Musafar is an outstanding example, painful pursuits that would be regarded as extreme acts of self-torture to most of us, allow them to attain a not dissimilar experience. Both use pain as the medium for ecstatic pleasure, one for explicitly religious purposes, and the other as experiments in a self-focused foray into altered states of consciousness.

There are, however, gentler ways of attaining ecstatic pleasure, that for most people might be a more palatable and enjoyable passage to ecstasy.

Tactile Bodies: Body to Body, and Flesh to Flesh

Sex, whether abstaining from or engaging with, is recognized as a very powerful force.[17] Universally, religions have something to say about sex and how it figures in their beliefs and practices. Many contemplative orders insist on celibacy for the entirety of their followers' lives. Some religious groups advocate sexual intercourse only for the procreation of children. The rarer religious groups engage in some form of sexual regime in order to access divine realms; or sexual climax might figure prominently in trance activity. Many groups have strong rules about whom one may have sexual intercourse with (homosexuality is often abhorred), and/or the physical condition of the woman (not menstruating, for example) when intercourse is contemplated, as well as means for ensuring fidelity between couples (chastity belts).

Engagement and Abstention

Erotic Engagement

Christian saint, Teresa of Avila spoke of achieving 'spiritual marriage' with Christ, and described her most sublime experiences as unfolding in three stages: union, rapture and the climactic 'wound of love'. The seventh-century Muslim Sufi poet of Basra, Rabi'al-'Adawiyya, expressed her passionate devotion to the Prophet

Muhammad in many ardent poems using conjugal imagery. In Christian Sri Lanka, female pilgrims are reported to experience orgasm as they are exorcized at a local shrine where they rub their genitals on the holy cross, and, at the climax, claim they are penetrated by Christ himself (Stirrat 1977; Gombrich and Obeyesekere 1988).

In North African saints' cults, associated with the former slave populations and known as 'black brotherhoods', ecstatic female dancers explicitly compare their feelings after experiencing trance to those of sexual intercourse (Crapanzano 1973, cited in Lewis 2003); and in Vodou, which originated in Africa and is now very strong in Haiti, an erotic physical relationship with a *loa* (spirits elevated to divine status) can occur when the person is in a trance state; the *loa* are said to 'ride' or 'mount' the possessed person.

When a deity is perceived as an external quasi-physical being, and deity worship becomes more personal and intimate, it is only a small step for that relationship to turn into an erotic one. This seems to have occurred with many of the medieval mystics, especially during the periods of romantic and courtly love proclaimed in music, song and poetry. In more contemporary times, with the charismatic offshoot known as the Toronto Blessing, a small group of women seem to have experienced a similar outpouring of love, with similar physical manifestations – as researcher Martyn Percy (2005) discovered.

The Toronto Blessing is the name for a phenomenon associated with the Toronto Airport Christian Fellowship, which began in 1994 along the lines of a funda-mentalist revivalist tradition. Experiences of participants included the declaration of miracles, professed healings, speaking in tongues and an emphasis on deliverance, all typical for this kind of tradition. The Toronto Blessing was a little different to other similar groups of the times in that it reported an unusually high number of people being 'slain in the Spirit', and the physical outcomes were more excessive than usual – people would laugh uncontrollably, writhe on the floor and/or make animal-like noises such as barking, growling or groaning. From 1994, Toronto became a pilgrimage site, with an estimated two million people having made the pilgrimage; many reported major changes in their lives after their experiences in Toronto. It was rumoured that, among other happenings, tooth cavities were miraculously filled with gold and 'dustings' of gold appeared on the hair and shoulders of the faithful (though evidence of this remains uncorroborated). The entire experience, it seems, was very cathartic, and the effect of the 'blessing' on worshippers provided them with 'individual spiritual renewal' and feelings of empowerment (Percy 2005: 78).

Martin Percy first visited the source of this charismatic Christian group in Toronto in 1996, at which time he noted an abundance of appeals to the romantic nature of God and the desire for intimacy and oneness with God, played out in a grammar of paternalism and quasi-erotic intimacy (Percy 2005: 78). When he returned in 2002, he noted that numbers had waned considerably, but that services and prayer meetings were still lively and the earlier emphasis on the personal and intimate nature of one's relationship with the Lord had taken an interesting turn. The overwhelming amount of romantic metaphors that had permeated worship, teaching and testimony during his earlier visit had become more explicit and intense. The structure and grammar of worship, he writes, made overt use of sexual analogies drawn from biblical and Christian tradition, but were given a more erotically explicit slant. 'Worship means', explained one of the leaders in the Toronto Blessing '"to kiss towards", – to come into His tender presence; so let Jesus *respond* to your loving ...' (p. 79). Worship services moved through three stages: wooing or courting Jesus; 'mystical foreplay' (often accompanied by use of musical instruments such as guitar or piano being 'delicately stroked' or touched); and relational consummation. The encounter with Jesus was understood in specifically romantic terms. Songs of intimacy and passion were articulated in CDs and tapes that advertised praise songs with titles like 'Intimate Bride', 'Warrior Bride' and 'Passionate Bride', billed as 'songs of intimacy and passion for soaking in God's presence' (p. 80). The covers of CDs, tapes and books were illustrated with pictures such as a bride embracing or encountering Jesus, or a young woman in full bridal regalia holding a large sword, thus actualizing and individualizing the notion of romantic love for Jesus. Other collections of songs included 'How Big is He', 'I Can Feel the Touch', 'Take Me' and 'Soaking in Glory' (p. 80). Thus, the focus was on women's relationship to Jesus.

At the daily morning prayer meetings that Percy attended, 95 per cent of the attendees were women in their late middle age (average age of 57), and the meetings were led by women, for women. These seemed to take on an implicit erotic tone. The women were advised to set aside a 'tastefully decorated' room somewhere at home where they could relax ('resting with Jesus') in order to combat stress. They were sometimes counselled to 'reach out your hand so you can sense the fragrance of the Lord. This is a place of peace, and it feels like *velvet...*' The resource centre stocked fragrant oils and scented candles to enhance these 'tastefully decorated' rooms for relaxation.

This phenomenon of romantic and erotic devotion is not unlike that of medieval mystic women such as Cistercian nuns, the Beguines and others who experienced mystical union as oneness with Jesus as man. For a long time an important symbol for the expression of mystical life during these times was ecstatic love, and its accompanying feelings of devotion, longing, forlornness, companionship and union (Borchert 1994: 208). A woodcut miniature *c.*1430 (Badische Landesbibliothek, Karlsruhe, illustrated in Borchert 1994: 208) depicts a woman seated on a bench while a haloed Christ stands before her, gazing into her eyes while playing a string instrument. The ecstatic experience of romantic and erotic love was so intense that some women became ill and confined to their beds for years. One woman was reported as regularly experiencing up to twenty-five 'ecstasies' a day (p. 209). Prolonged weeping and 'spiritual inebriation' became so intense that another woman lost her voice for days. Catherine of Genoa (1447–1510) constantly entered states of ecstasy bordering on madness (Buber 1985: 108):

I am so plunged and submerged in the source of his [God's] infinite love, as if I were quite under the sea and could not touch, see, feel anything on any side except Water. I am so submerged in the sweet fire of love that I cannot grasp anything except the whole of love, which melts all the marrow of my soul and body. And sometimes I feel as if my body were made entirely of some yielding substance …

The mysticism of much of the Middle Ages was influenced by the notions of romance and courtly chivalry, played out in music and poetry. The physical manifestation of such ecstasy is portrayed beautifully by the Italian artist and sculptor, Bernini, in his sculpture of St Teresa of Avila (1514–82), with head back, eyes partially closed and mouth open. Bernini portrays her as the epitome of ecstatic mysticism. Realistic sexual imagery was also used to represent union with God and to convey the individual's total involvement and experience of intense joy.

Clearly, religion and the body impact on each other and there is something transcendent about sexual union; something that has been recognized (and often misinterpreted) through time and across different religions. The Greek historian Herodotus (*c*.485–425 BCE) wrote that every Babylonian woman had to go once in her lifetime to the temple of Ishtar and offer herself for a fee to any man who desired her; she subsequently placed the fee on the temple altar. The temple of Aphrodite Porne at Corinth was said to house 1,000 women who temporarily embodied the goddess they served while performing sex. At the same time their male sexual partners were elevated into a divine state, a reflection of the *hieros gamos*, or sacred marriage (Bishop 1996).

Ritualized sex has been part of fertility rites that ensure the continual maintenance of the cosmos, and of plants and animals, and has been used in fertility magic as a form of sympathetic magic. Through orgiastic and ritual outlets, sexual intercourse has been institutionalized in some cultures and historical epochs. A virginal maiden might be impregnated by the Divine, or mythical figures might conjoin with humans to produce offspring that are half-human, half-beast. Some contemporary UFO religious groups talk of aliens from another planet landing on earth to impregnate humans with their seed, thus continuing the idea of a supernatural coupling with mortals to produce wholly other beings that have the appearance of humans; and contemporary Wiccans incorporate the notion of *hieros gamos* into the Great Rite, which can be carried out either literally or symbolically, as part of an advanced initiation rite.

The Power of the Erotic

The nature of the Tungus shaman's relation with his spirit guide is one of being bound to the spirit by marriage. Both Zolla (1986) and Hamayon (1996) discuss the centrality of the marital alliance as well as the sexual imagery in much shamanic discourse. Hamayon describes some of the activities in a shaman seance as miming the act of rutting or coupling with the animal spirit partner, and the trance is a kind of spiritual sexual climax. In similar shamanic rituals in Nepal, Mastromattei (1988) reports that orgasmic seizures occur, and Devereux (1974) claims that some mediumistic performances reported in Western extrasensory perception contexts involve the medium having an actual orgasm.

There is also mention of union with the Divine through physical means in Hasidism. Ba'al Shem Tov, the founder of Hasidism, is said to have written that performing physical activities such as eating, drinking and sexual intercourse are a means to union with God. The pleasure of the union of man and woman (only man and woman unions are mentioned) through sexual orgasm, he wrote, gives pleasure to God himself. Contemplating and adoring God through carnality was known as *avodah ba-gaszmiut*, divine service through materiality. The Hasidic idea was that the physical can lead to the spiritual; materiality is the 'ladder towards the invisible', or a portal to the invisible realms (Tokarska-Bakir 2000: 69).

Both physiological and symbolic sex have been seen as a bridge between human and divine, a physiological path to personal transcendence. The union with God may be couched in terms of sexual unity, sexual bliss or dissolving the sense of self to merge with the 'Beloved'. The flow of reproductive energy is viewed by some as associated with the flow of the creative energy of the universe.

The erotic dimensions of love are often confused with the pornographic and viewed as suspect, if not anathema to the spirit of spiritual transcendence, union with God or enlightenment. In an influential book published in 1932, *Agape and Eros*, Swedish theologian Anders Nygren distinguished between self-giving love (agapaic love), the epitome of which is God's self-giving love, and *eros*, which he defined as selfish and carnal, seeking its own fulfilment. For Nygren, the message was that one should strive for *agape* and deny *eros*. Paul Ricoeur (cited in Nelson and Longfellow 1994: 72), on the other hand, defends the erotic as being part of the enigma of sexuality, and when *eros* is accompanied by tenderness and fidelity, it can result in spiritual fulfilment. Similarly, Manning Nash (cited in Lewis 2003: 35) suggests that erotic love is often a template for religious meaning as it provides an expression of self-transcendence.

Nevertheless, contrary to popular (erroneous) Western opinion, in all these religions, sexual practices are, in fact, very marginal to the overall beliefs and practices. Indeed, they may be put into practice rarely, if at all, and are just one of the means of expression of transcendence. These excerpts only serve to point out that religion and sexual intimacy are connected, and many religions contain some references to transcendence through erotic engagement of some sort. Unfortunately, in most religions, *eros* has come to take on connotations of negativity, and the transcendent aspects of the sexual act are denied their place, or knowledge of such practices are only divulged to advanced practitioners – no doubt because of how easy it is for people to degrade the spiritual purpose of the practice and focus on the titillating aspects, without regard for the context and true intention.

Sexual Abstention and Tactile Deprivation

Depriving oneself of the somatic pleasures of sensuality is often viewed as the true mark of a holy person, and in many monastic orders, celibacy is strictly adhered to, at least in principle. In the Roman Catholic Church, celibacy is defined as 'the renunciation of marriage implicitly or explicitly made, for the more perfect observance of chastity, by all those who receive the Sacrament of Orders in any of the higher grades'. Any transgression to the vow of chastity is not only a grievous sin, but is sacrilege. The rule of celibacy is in some measure utilitarian, in that the unmarried priest is able to devote his entire life to the service of God and his parishioners; without wife and children, he is not distracted in his loyalties or in his obligations to God. But the pragmatics of celibacy is not the only reason for the Church's rule on unmarried priests. From its earliest period, the Church was personified as the Virgin Bride and as the pure Body of Christ, or as the Virgin Mother; a virgin Church should be served by a virgin priesthood. The priestly character of Christ's Church was 'imparted by the Holy Ghost in the Divinely-instituted Sacrament of the Orders'. Although virginity and marriage are both considered holy, virginity possesses a 'higher sanctity and clearer spiritual intuition'. This is the mystical reason for the Church's stand on celibacy. Those who handle the 'sacred mysteries' should observe the law of continence, in order that purity is maintained by those who handle 'the vessels of the Lord'.[18] The pure object cannot be touched by the impure object.

St John of the Cross, a Carmelite mystic of Spain, wrote instructions to novices on how to access direct contact with the Divine through the immortal soul by way of isolating the 'pure core of the transcendent spirit from the mind, and its sensory apparatus'. In writings such as *Subida del Monte Carmelo* (Ascent of Mount Carmel, 1578–80), *Noche oscura* (Dark Night of the Soul, 1579) and *Cántico espiritual* (Spiritual Canticle, 1578–83), he describes the effects of sensory deprivation. His own experiences of sensory deprivation were the result of a nine-month stint in 'a tiny cell, deprived of sunlight and ventilation', his unwashed clothes soaked with the 'stench of his own urine, faeces and blood from flagellation wounds' (Flynn 1996: 268). Prolonged fasting, flagellation and sleep deprivation, along with blocking out light and sound, touch and taste, were all designed to cure the soul of bodily pleasures. The next step then was to eliminate the will, the memory, understanding and reason in order to move beyond self-consciousness and be free of earthly preoccupations. In order to 'pass the threshold of eternity' one needed to 'eradicate the flow of meandering thoughts' and cross into 'total oblivion' (p. 270).

The writings of St John of the Cross attest to the experience of sickness so intense that all appetite for food and sensory and motor activity ceases. In his *Subida del Monte Carmel*, he advises the reader to 'close the eyes in prayer, shutting out light so that the visual faculty remains in total darkness'. Then sounds are to be blocked out, and the 'sensual qualities of food that satisfy the palate and olfactory organ' are to be denied, followed by the elimination of the 'pleasures received from touch'. The body is mortified through prolonged and excessive fasting, flagellation and sleep deprivation. These austerities sometimes lasted weeks and even months.

Personal denial, he wrote, meant rejection of reason as well; suspension of all feeling, plus suspension of the intellect, was the way to allow God to speak. Rational reflection was equally as detrimental to knowledge of God as were the senses. He sought instead to 'enter into the sightless, soundless, odorless order of things by suspending human reason entirely' (Flynn 1996: 269–70). He used language that revolved around the image of a void and the contemplation of 'emptiness'.[19]

Discussion

It seems there is a fine line between sensory stimulation and sensory deprivation, and they may be competing constructions of the same practice. Extreme pain inflicted on the body can result in heights of ecstasy and pleasure, and isolation and deprivation of bodily touch might have the same result as overstimulation.

Pain perception and pain tolerance thresholds differ from one person to another, and activities in the central nervous system, such as memories of an experience, may intervene between stimulus and sensation and invalidate any simple physical explanation. Also, distraction of attention away from pain (such as visualization, focused attention on a pleasant memory, absorption in an exciting activity such as sport) can diminish or abolish the pain. Pain experience and response is complex and involves virtually all parts of the brain, including cortical activities that underlie past experience, attention and other cognitive determinants of pain (Melxack and Wall 1991: 145). Pain is also influenced by cultural and social factors. A parent who gives too much attention to their child's minor cuts and bruises elicits a higher negative response from the child with regard to pain than a parent who shows little sympathy. Pain (and pleasure) is a highly subjective somatic sensation, which is often expressed in culturally appropriate ways. There are cognitive, affective, motivational and sociocultural aspects to pain information that are transmitted through pathways from the brain, which can forestall, ameliorate or enhance pain (Skevington 1995: 23).

There is also a fine line between pain and pleasure, as indicated in the experiential accounts recounted in this chapter, and there is physiological evidence to indicate that pain itself elicits analgesia; the body can activate its own form of pain relief in response to painful stimuli. The research of scientists Robert Gear, K.O. Aley and Jon Levine (1999) indicates that (at least in rats) the mesolimbic system of reward responds to aversive as well as to positive stimuli. Exposure to a painful stimulus – as well as exposure to drugs of abuse – stimulates the same reward circuit, say Gear et al. These findings were also discovered independently by other researchers, who similarly provide data supporting the notion that 'there may be a shared neural system for evaluation of aversive and rewarding stimuli' (Becerra et al. 2001: 927).

The reward pathway is a neural network in the middle of the brain that prompts good feelings in response to certain behaviours, such as relieving hunger, quenching thirst or having sex; it thus reinforces these evolutionarily important drives.

In the study conducted by Gear et al. it was found that the reward pathway activates pain relief through the release of both opioids (a morphine-like drug produced by the body) and dopamine (a chemical messenger whose effects can be mimicked by amphetamine and cocaine). Their research indicates that, rather than being associated only with positive experiences, the release of dopamine in the nucleus accumbens is also associated with negative experiences. Since the system of reward responds to aversive as well as to positive stimuli, it is possible that by activating the nucleus accumbens, a painful stimulus might be experienced as rewarding. This may sometimes occur in self-injurious behaviours.

From this type of research, one can deduce that religious acts of devotion that involve self-injurious behaviours, causing pain to the body in a variety of culturally or religiously specific ways, undoubtedly activate the nucleus accumbens. It is possible that such stimulation can take someone through pain and into a state of pleasure. Bodily pain can actually result in bodily pleasure. However, while Western science usually takes the approach that religious phenomena can therefore be reduced to rational, scientifically verifiable data, traditional societies (and religious devotees) do not. This is not to say that other cultures do not make distinctions between behaviour that is inspired by religious or mystical means and behaviour that can be attributed to more mundane explanations. As a case in point, the Abelan tribe of New Guinea makes distinctions between states that are attributed to spiritual intervention and states that are not; and the Tungus reindeer herders of Siberia, where trembling and certain gestures sometimes signify possession by spirits, recognize that at other times they may merely indicate fear (Lewis 2003: 27). Western science might do well to reserve reductionist explanations and look cross-culturally to other ways of thinking and knowing. When researchers start asking the appropriate questions of people whose beliefs and practices have hitherto been ignored as 'folk superstitions' and the beliefs of 'savages', new avenues of thought can be pursued.

The next chapter pursues a more 'tasteful' topic – that of employing the mouth and nose to pass through oral and nasal portals.

–6–

Olfactory and Gustatory Portals

> I have often noticed that [scents] cause changes in me, and act on my spirits according to their qualities; which makes me agree with the theory that the introduction of incense and perfume into churches, so ancient and widespread a practice among all nations and religions, was for the purpose of raising our spirits, and of exciting and purifying our senses, the better to fit us for contemplation.
>
> Michel de Montaigne, 1580[1]

De Montaigne's insights into the qualities of 'scents' to cause changes in our sensibilities as far as contemplation is concerned has long been recognized and employed in various world religions, and embraced with fervour in the twentieth century with the advent of the New Age and its abundant commercial stocks of incense sticks, fragrant oil burners, massage oils and the emergence of aromatherapy. With the modern West's principally ocularcentric focus as the main sense of perception, the history of smell and taste in the West has resulted in 'olfactory blandness' (Hall 1969: 45) and an 'odour-denying attitude' (Howes 1991b: 144), in comparison, that is, to sight and sound.[2] The senses of smell and taste are usually mentioned only peripherally as being of consequence to accessing altered states, and often viewed as a non-essential (albeit pleasing addition) to the major methods of sight, sound and movement. This does not mean that they have not been considered important, but merely that the person reporting the events has not paid them much attention or has failed to recognize their significance.

Some non-Western cultures and religions are not so inattentive to olfactics (the study of sense of smell), and some could be said to contain osmologies (classificatory systems based on smell). Songhay spirit possession, writes Paul Stoller, is full of fragrance as well as movement. Certain kinds of perfumes are preferred by particular families of spirits, and incenses, consisting of an array of aromatic roots and resins, are burned to attract and please the spirits (Stoller 1995: 3). Aromatic shrines that offer scents to the gods are to be found in many places throughout the world: copal incense is used in Mexico, sandalwood (among other aromatics) is prevalent in Hindu temples, burning sweet grass is used by many Native Americans (Classen, Howes and Synnot 1994: 131), and there are many other examples. The Ongee of the Andaman Islands (Bay of Bengal), for example, order their world according to smell. The Ongee regard odour as the vital force of the universe, as well as the basis of personal and social identity. In order for the cosmos to remain harmonious, both individual and social olfactory equilibrium needs to be maintained. Living beings are thought to be composed of smell; bones are solid smell, and an inner spirit is said to reside in the bones of the living. When one is asleep, this internal spirit gathers all the odours that the person has emitted during the day and returns them to the body, enabling life to continue. Death is explained as the permanent loss of one's personal body odour, and spirits, called *tomya*, can kill people by absorbing their odours (Classen 1993: 127). Spirits can smell, but not see, so smells can be masked by painting the body with thick clay, a method that is used also to stop odours from escaping the body, which can lead to illness (Classen 1993: 129–30; 2005: 153–4). Spirits can be contacted via the medium of smell (such communication is called *mineyalange*, which means 'to remember') or kept at bay and confused through the use of a smokescreen. If a person wishes to undertake a visit to the spirit world (a dangerous journey which is taken by men during their initiation rites), it is done by hanging baskets of rotten pig meat on trees, and by dispersing bodily odours to the winds. The men's wives assist them in this journey by massaging their bodies before they embark, and on their return the women massage their smells back into the men's bodies. Once they become light enough to travel with the spirits, men[3] can learn spirit ways and how to appease them. Those who regularly allow the spirits to absorb their smell and carry them away are called *torale* (shaman) by the Ongee – persons who gain knowledge from their spirit journeys that benefits the whole community.

In Tibetan Buddhism, where liberation through all the senses is highlighted, soteriological practices, such as tasting relics, drinking and eating sacred food, smelling (and touching) sacred substances, circumambulating stupas, are some of the things that lead one on the path of liberation. Indeed, they guarantee liberation (Tokarska-Bakir 2000: 69).[4] As well as long hours of repetitive prayer, chanting and mantras (of which one of the purposes is to destroy discursive consciousness), carnal contact with objects which in themselves are considered able to liberate, as well as eating and drinking certain foods or liquids (for example, water that has been used to wash a venerated monument), are considered practices that are equally important as understanding texts in an intellectual way.

One of the five 'swiftly liberating' skilful means of liberation through the senses, according to Thondup Tulku, is ambrosia: substances which liberate by tasting.[5] Nectar, pills and pellets that have been blessed, after careful preparation with herbs and special ingredients, allow for liberation through taste. *Dam rdzas* is a substance which is 'noble and wondrous in its origin', and can take the form of pills and pellets prepared by saints from herbs and special ingredients, which are often given away after having been blessed (Tokarska-Bakir 2000: 78). When some of the great teachers of Tibetan Buddhism die, small spherical relics called *Ring bsrel* are said to emerge from their ashes; or they can emerge from sacred places such as stupas, or from some Buddha statues. These pellets bridge the line between the animate and inanimate worlds, and are brought forth through the devotion of disciples.

Pellets coming from very holy people can set free a person who tastes them within their subsequent seven lives. One of the descendants of Organ Lingpa, upon tasting the flesh of a highly esteemed corpse, was supposed to have been overcome with such religious zeal that he rose in the air about fifteen inches above the ground, and travelled to various countries 'through the air' (Tokarska-Bakir 2000: 80). When a recently deceased person is in the liminal or intermediate state between life and the next incarnation, beings called *Dri za* that feed on smells are said to hover over the corpse. One way of deterring them is to place an amulet on to the corpse's back, throat, head and heart.

The neglect of the sense of smell has not always been so prevalent in the West. In the ancient world, the Greeks were connoisseurs of fragrance, and employed it copiously for aesthetic purposes, bathing in rich Egyptian unguent, rubbing the jaws and breasts with thick palm oil, covering the arms with extract of mint, spreading marjoram on eyebrows and hair, and placing the essence of ground thyme on the knees and neck (Classen 1993: 17). They also let scent-drenched doves fly about the room in order to shower guests in fragrant perfume (p. 17). Religious rituals in the ancient world also incorporated different fragrances; incense was used to attract and unite humans and gods, and altars were laden with scents that were believed to give great joy to the gods. Greek gods were noted for their sensitive noses and for their own powerful smells (Evans 2002: 193). In Egypt, incense was used to purify a dead king from odours escaping from his corpse and to protect him from evil. It was also used to establish contact with the gods, who were thought to be present in the smoke of the incense. In order for the dead king to reach the divine abodes of the gods, the dense smoke provided a 'stairway' for the king to ascend to the sky to be with the gods (Nielsen 1986: 9). The smoke facilitated both human movement from earth to heaven, and divine movement from heaven to earth:

> The fire is laid, the fire shines;
> The incense is laid on the fire, the incense shines.
> Your perfume comes to me, O Incense;
> May my perfume come to you, O Incense.
> Your perfume comes to me, you gods;
> May my perfume come to you, you gods.
> May I be with you, you gods;
> May you be with me, you gods.[6]

In ancient Mesopotamia, a rich variety of aromatic substances was available for purchase, and these were used for a number of purposes, such as medicine, offerings, perfumes and divination. In times of personal trouble, people would visit a diviner, who made himself pleasing to the gods in order to perform the divining ritual. Such rites might contain resins or incenses composed of tamarisk, cypress, cedar and various aromatic oils thought to please the gods. An old Babylonian text contains a diviner purifying himself:

O, Shamash! I am placing in my mouth pure cedar (resin),
I am wrapping it for you in the locks of my hair;
I am placing for you in my lap compact cedar (resin),
I washed my mouth and my hands;
I wrapped pure cedar (resin) in the locks of my hair,
I envelop for you compact cedar (resin).
Being now clean to the assembly of the gods, I shall draw near for judgement …[7]

The use of incense in the magical rites of ancient Mesopotamia is mentioned repeatedly in the ancient texts. Frankincense appears to be particularly popular, and was thought to carry prayers to the gods. Scents were a nearly universal component of ancient religious rituals in the Mediterranean area, and were associated with all that was sacred, heavenly or divine. The gods had their own particular fragrances and were discerned through the senses of smell and taste just as much as through the oral and visual senses. Aphrodite, for example, was associated with the scent of roses. Unpleasant odours, on the other hand, repelled the gods (Classen 1993: 19). The early Church Fathers connected these beliefs with pagan idolatry and sensuality, and subsequently banned perfumes, advocating the repression of smell altogether. Origen declared that demons fed on the smell of incense smoke, and Athenagoras declared that, as God Himself was perfect fragrance, He did not need the fragrance of flowers and incense (Classen 1993: 19).

From its inception, until late in the fourth century, Christianity excluded incense from its worship and devotional practices – the only religion of the ancient Mediterranean to do so. However, St Ephrem, a Syrian theologian (*c*.306–73 CE), insisted that incense could intensify human understanding about God. Ephrem's attitude to 'scents' was a turning point in Christian worship and prayer, as the use of incense appeared for the first time; Christian appreciation for the significance of sacred smells began to deepen accordingly. During the fifth century, incense usage became normative for all Christian ritual, public and private, and Christian writers regularly described the use of incense as part of an olfactory dialogue in which human and divine approached each other through scent (Harvey 1998: 112–14).

Ephrem believed that religious experience could be both cognitive and sensory, which is more in keeping with Tibetan Buddhism (mentioned earlier). Indeed, the sanctified human body could receive knowledge of God through its own physicality. The hymns of Ephrem disclose that eating and smelling are closely related experiences. When the 'Bread of Life' is eaten, Christ pervades the whole of the believer's being. When inhaled as the Fragrance of Life, Christ penetrates throughout the believer. Ephrem's olfactory imagery is about encountering God through sensory experience (Harvey 1998: 100–11).

Food, or abstinence from food, was at the heart of religious practice for European medieval women saints, who willingly engaged in penitential asceticism. Sometimes called 'dry eating' (Bynum 1987: 38), they might take only bread, salt and water, preparing themselves for Christ's body and blood in the form of the Eucharist, or abstain from eating altogether. Often the main devotional emphasis was on partaking only of holy food (the Eucharist) which they substituted for ordinary food. Fasting and illness were seen as preparation for mystical union and for being fed by Christ. After consuming an unconsecrated host, Mary of Oignies vomited it out, washing her mouth to rid herself of the taste (p. 117). Ida of Léau, who experienced frequent fits and trances, felt no hunger on days when she had taken the Eucharist. Many women were considered insane because of their Eucharistic cravings. The reception of the Eucharist was frequently the moment when these women received ecstatic union with Christ, and the 'sweetness of ecstasy' (p. 117). Indeed, Ida 'received her Lord as food between her lips' (p. 118). So intense was the belief that fasting was a way of attaining ecstatic union with Christ, that many women reached a point where they were unable to eat normally – the mere smell and sight of food could cause them nausea and pain (p. 119). When their male religious superiors tried to put a stop to the women's extreme fasting by denying them the Eucharist, they reported vivid experiences of being nursed from Christ's breast. An extreme act that was rewarded with a mystical vision of Christ allowing her to drink from his wound, was experienced by Catherine of Siena after she had drunk pus from a leper's wounds (Bell 1985: 25). The women equated their penitential acts, self-starvation and illness with Christ's suffering on the cross. Bynum writes that women's visions occurred most frequently in a Eucharistic context, and that their relationship to the holy food was often tied up with the bypassing of ecclesiastical control. If they were denied the Eucharist, many of them simply received it in a vision, or the host might fly down from heaven to give it to them, thus challenging the priestly role. Abstinence and Eucharistic ecstasy were referred to by the women as *imitatio Christi* – or fusion with the body of Christ (Bynum 1987: 246).

Divinity was characterized by sweet scents, and fragrances of extraordinary beauty revealed divine presence. God was understood to pour forth the powerful aroma of divinity, the rich perfume signifying holy presence and blessing upon the faithful.

The Sweet Odour of Sanctity

Sanctity is said to have its own distinct aroma, an ancient idea. In classical myth-ology, the gods of Greece and Rome were said to 'exhale the sweet scent of ambrosia', the food and perfume of the deities (Classen 1998: 44). Odours infusing and being emitted from the body formed part of an 'olfactory theology' (p. 53) in Europe in the Middle Ages, which dichotomized the good and the bad with corresponding labels of beauteous fragrances and foul stenches. The presence and memory of the Divine was conveyed in a language of scent. The flesh of Christ, with its 'penetrating delights', brought 'marvellous rest and peace'. People spoke of Christ as 'the heavenly physician' who purified human flesh with 'His sacred touch', and whose 'divine aroma' produced an aromatic ecstasy (Camporesi 1989: 223). In general, women were more closely aligned with the senses of taste, touch and smell, being associated with animal senses, intuition, emotion, sensuality and nurturing, while men were aligned with sight, hearing and higher spiritual senses, as well as rationality and logic. Classen considers the ways in which the various sensory characteristics were attributed to women and to men, and contrasts the 'dominating male gaze' with the 'nurturing female touch' (1998: 6).

Christians believed that those who lived in a state of grace would be infused with the breath of God, a divine fragrance which indicated God's presence (Classen 1998: 36). The bodies of the holy supposedly emitted a sweet odour that signified the presence of the Holy Spirit. Conversely, great sinners could be recognized by their foul odour. Stigmata, parts of the body that spontaneously exuded blood in imitation of Christ's suffering on the cross, were said to emit a fine fragrance, but the self-inflicted wounds of the penitent were sometimes described as having a 'holy stench' (p. 50). Witches, believed to have the inverse qualities of the saints, emitted foul, poisonous odours, and touching a witch was thought to inflame men with sinful desire (p. 80). Well known for their expertise in herbs and potions, they were said to have a keen olfactory sense, and a strong ability to cure as well as to harm, using odoriferous substances.

The sweet odour of sanctity occurred on or after the death of a saint, and it was said that the coffin of St Francis Xavier, upon being opened up four months after his death (in the sixteenth century), emitted a sweet smell from his curiously incorrupt corpse (Classen 1998: 37). Similarly, just prior to and after the death of Teresa of Avila, Spain (b.1515), a supernatural fragrance diffused her body. The odour of sanctity at the death of a saint was believed to be due to the sweet smell of the soul leaving the body. Conversely, when the Holy Spirit entered the Virgin Mary, she was penetrated by a 'sweet odour' (p. 55).

Lydwine of Schiedam, Holland (b.1380), was taken by her guardian angel on a journey through 'spicy heavenly realms' and 'fragrant paradisiacal meadows', and during one of her raptures she was garlanded with an aromatic veil of flowers by the Virgin Mary (Classen 1998: 37). In seventh-century England, a man who experienced near-death (indeed he was presumed to be dead) reported that he had journeyed through divine realms to 'a very broad and pleasant plain, full of such a fragrance of growing flowers that the marvellous sweetness of the scent quickly dispelled the foul stench of the gloomy furnace which had hung around' him (p. 46). Encounters during such journeys were not always pleasant for everyone. Teresa of Avila professed to have been alternatively tormented by the Devil and pierced by the love of God during her own mystical raptures; and of an unwilling visit to hell, she wrote: 'The entrance seemed like a long narrow lane ... and on the ground there was a filthy mud which reeked of pestilential odours' (p. 39).

Through scent, boundaries could be crossed. Ephrem wrote: 'When the blessed Apostles were gathered together the place shook and the scent of Paradise having recognized its home poured forth its perfumes ...' (Harvey 1998: 115). Thus, smell allowed for the intermingling of human and divine in a communion of being, rather than separate entities. It was also thought that the scent of Christ mingled in the fragrance of the rising incense. Ephrem's Hymns speak of Paradise as 'that treasure of perfumes/that storehouse of scents', 'all fragrant', a place where 'scents are most wonderful' (p. 115).

In mid-fifth-century Europe, incense and roses were assigned new spiritual values. With the Crusades, the West discovered the spices and perfumes of the East, which began the medieval passion for pungent flavours and odours (Classen 1998: 20).

In the pre-modern West, odours were thought to have an important role in health and illness, both causing and curing disease. The rose's scent was thought to be not only aesthetically pleasing, but to have curative powers (Classen 1993). An Enlightened Europe focused on the mind over matter, and knowledge derived solely from 'mind' devalued sensory knowledge; yet the Hebrew Bible abounds in olfactory imagery, and the role of smell is sometimes referred to synonymously with that of knowledge (Ritchie 2000: 59). Smells – both foul and fragrant – evoke memories and draw on knowledge that may be long-forgotten. As olfactory signals are transmitted, via minuscule, hair-like cilia at the ends of the olfactory neurons, into the limbic region of the brain, the core of emotions and memory, it is not surprising that de Montaigne (quoted at the beginning of this chapter) noted that scents 'cause changes' in us. An aroma, such as a particular brand of perfume, suntan lotion, incense, and so on, can trigger the memory of an event that happened long ago, especially if it is a smell that is not experienced on a daily basis.

The dualism of mind/body in the religious (particularly Christian) arena led to covering up the naked state of the body itself (for example, the missionary horror of naked indigenous bodies) and to repugnance of bodily odour. The contemporary West's embarrassment about 'foul' odours – particularly of the bodily kind – probably stems from Europe's urban putridness in the not-so-distant past. In mid-eighteenth-century Europe, the stench in cities was overpowering:

> The streets stank of manure, the courtyards of urine, the stairwells stank of mouldering wood and rat droppings ... the unaired parlours stank of stale dust, the bedrooms of greasy sheets ... People stank of sweat and unwashed clothes; from their mouths came the stench of rotting teeth ... and from their bodies came the stench of rancid cheese and sour milk and tumorous disease ... (Suskind 1986: 3)

It is no wonder that perfumed gardens were highly prized, that many of the castles throughout Europe had extensive herbal gardens not far from the buildings themselves, and that the stench of decay/death, saintliness/purity were at opposite ends of a continuum.

The Foul and the Fragrant

In general, there is a universal notion that pleasant aromas or fragrant scents (however culturally defined) are associated with or can attract good spirits/the Divine/ the Holy. Conversely, malodorous scents are a sign of, or attract, bad spirits, evil, the devil, and so on. Francesca de Ponziani (Frances of Rome, b.1440) experienced a demonic vision in which the devil brought a corpse into her bed; all who came into contact with her at that time could smell the odour of death on her clothes and skin, and the smell permeated her house (Bell 1985: 139). Seductresses and witches are often associated with bad odours. Witches were said to be consumed with impure ardours and to exhale a stench – not just from the mouth, but from the entire body – and to infect those who approached them. Mary Douglas has written extensively on the dangers associated with liminal creatures, and the notion of the pollution and danger of those that do not fall into easy categorization (Douglas 1975). A witch was considered to be something other than a good woman, and not quite human. A decaying corpse is also a liminal being – not quite one thing or the other – and the smell emanating from the putrefaction of a corpse is sometimes viewed as dangerous in itself: it is 'matter out of place' (p. 50). Smell, as Gell points out, always escapes; it is 'distinguished by formlessness, indefinability and lack of clear articulation' (1977: 27). Howes (1987: 410) suggests that there is a connection between olfaction and transition from one category to another (for example, from a familiar, albeit dead, person to the category of ancestor), and that smells are most noticeable at boundaries or liminal states, such as crisis rites, or rites of passage. Once the odour of death and decay dissipates, the anomaly of liminality ceases to be.

The Christian idea of pits of hell and the presence of the devil is often linked with the smell of sulphur, which smells like rotten eggs. It seems that bad odours are associated with rotting flesh, disease and death, which might explain the apparent universal 'principle' that foul smells lead to death, which is mostly feared, and the (contagious) essence of a thing remains in its smell. Bodily orifices are vulnerable to entry by smells: witches might enter the soul of a person through the nose, and in some cultures, where sorcery abounds, a hole in the nasal septum is inserted with a bone so that bad spirits may not enter.[8] The Warao of Eastern Venezuela say that a live fish has no bad odour, but when pulled out of the water its life essence fails and fetid air seeks it out (Classen, Howes and Synnott 1994: 146). Good odour disappears with the life essence, leaving a putrid carcass in its place.

Breathing in foul odours is regarded as rendering oneself vulnerable to invasion by spirits, and censing a possessed person is thought to encourage spirits to make themselves and their demands known.[9] Curiously, while a person may be rendered vulnerable to possession through breathing a foul odour, once the spirit is in the host body, it can be transformed into fragrance through the intercession of the spirit.[10] Pungent smells like garlic are effective for keeping away unwanted spirits, vampires and the like, while the odour of ginger is used to stimulate dreams and produce prophetic vision (Classen et al. 1994: 155).

A dirty, smelly body is said by some Muslims to be vulnerable to evil, and dung heaps to be full of spiritually dangerous evil jinn; breaking wind is a heinous act inside a mosque as it is closely associated with harmful spirits and might harm or kill any angels abiding there. In contrast, the scented person is surrounded by angels, and fragrant scents, such as incense or rose or orange water, purify the body of evil influences and ally one with the forces of good (Classen et al. 1994: 130).

In Christianized Kenya, 'Chief Sniffers', known as *jucheckos*, stand at the entrance of the church, at a distance of two to eight feet, and sniff the air in front of each person before they enter, in order to discern whether their intentions are good or evil. The inner state of the person is believed to be revealed through their smell more than through any other sense. *Jucheckos* can detect both the intentions of the individual and any 'evil object' they may have on them (Ritchie 2000: 64).

Scents to Open up Boundaries

Shamans, sorcerers and diviners are said to establish communication with spirits through perfumes (Rasmussen 1999: 55–73). We have already seen evidence of this in the divining practices of ancient Mesopotamia. Some aromas are considered so strong that they are only appropriate for possession rituals because they 'activate spirits' and cause possession (p. 68). Some possessions are instigated through censing to the accompaniment of drumming.[11] The lighting of fragrant incense is sometimes a precursor to a ritual that invokes spirits, or sweetens the air for more reverent action with a sacred place.

The idea of scents opening up boundaries between humans and spirits, enabling ease of communication, appears to be universally pervasive, especially in the context of transition rituals/rites of passage. The liminal nature of transition rites, especially funeral rites, makes the ambiguous nature of scents (coming from a tangible product and becoming an intangible product, such as fragrance or smoke) an appropriate accompaniment to ritual activities. In cultures where bodies cannot be kept too long, perfumes in the form of incense or flowers not only cover up the smell of decaying flesh and help to dispel evil influences, but also they attract good spirits/angels that assist the spirit or soul on its journey. The ephemeral nature of smoke that floats upward and outward, and scent that permeates the air around it, evokes images of the soul on its spiritual journey (Forty 1999: 68).[12] Smoke is also used in some places to mask body odour, especially in funeral rites, where the spirit of the newly deceased might take revenge on the living, and seek them out by their smell or seek out the living in order to steal their life-smell (Morphy 1984).[13]

Conversely, the Ongee shaman allows the spirits to 'suck up his smell' so that he can lose his own odour temporarily and become more like the spirits in order to gain important knowledge (Classen et al. 1994: 134). Similarly, the Chewong of the Malay Peninsular interact with the spirits through odours. The Chewong shaman feeds good spirits with an incense of fragrant wood, blowing the smoke in four directions and praying for divine protection. The smoke is thought to carry the shaman's words up to the spirit world. The Chewong shamans also hold ritual seances to spirit guides known as the leaf-people, who wear flowers and sweet-smelling leaves in their hair. Their presence is perceptible by their fragrance, which is said to be so beautiful that the Chewong women 'often cry out of sheer emotion when they smell it' (p. 131).

In some cases, particular spirits can be associated with specific aromas. In the Afro-Brazilian spirit possession cult Batuque, which is dedicated to the *jurema* spirits, the leaves of the sacred jurema tree are burnt as incense. Jurema leaves, bark and flowers are also made into a tea, which is then placed in a bowl under the altar for the spirits to drink. As soon as the participants in the ceremony smell the smoke of the jurema leaves, they are prepared for the arrival of the *jurema* spirits. The incense sets the stage for opening up boundaries so that the spirits may enter into the world of the living. The thick, fragrant smoke is said to have cleansing or purifying properties, and makes an area 'fit for the presence of the spirits'. It also helps to induce a trance-like state in the participants, which is further aided by intense rhythmic drumming and dancing. Once in possession of the bodies of their followers, the *jurema* offer advice to those who seek it and perform rites of curing (Classen et al. 1994: 132).

Odoriferous substances (usually associated with pleasant scents such as ginger, mint, frankincense) are employed almost universally to communicate with the gods or to pierce deep into the mysteries. The fragrance of sweet grass burned during a Dakota (Western Plains, North America) rite of purification and ultimate unity, or oneness, was to 'make the four-leggeds, the wingeds, the star peoples of the heavens and all things, as relatives' (Lee, cited in Howes, 1991b: 131). The burning sweet grass itself becomes the vehicle for a transformation in consciousness, as it induces visions of unity and relatedness.

During the closing ritual of the Jewish Havdalah (which literally means 'division'), fragrant spices are said to move the sacred back to the profane (Howes 1991b: 129). In the Roman Catholic Mass, the actual moment of transubstantiation (when the bread and wine are transformed into Christ's body and blood) is marked traditionally by the tinkling of bells and the censing of the bread and wine with burning balsam. The bread and wine undergo a metamorphosis; they are changed into other substances entirely.

Gell suggests that 'the sense of smell is the liminal sense par excellence, constitutive of and at the same time operative across all of the boundaries we draw between different realms and categories of experience' (1977: 27). Smells, burning substances and the smoke produced are aids for communication between humans and non-humans, as well as purification and markers of transformation. They usually accompany other technologies in religious rituals and can sometimes indicate the presence of the non-human.

As nasal passages are essential for the breath of life to enter the body, and at death are the ultimate passage between life and death, breathing techniques are also employed as a means of moving into trance states, sometimes by stopping the breath in order to simulate the death experience.

The Breath

Sometimes the term for breath is the same as that for life force, energy or soul/spirit. About the breath, Vietnamese Zen master, Thich Nhat Hanh (cited in Prattis 1997: 159) says:

> Our breath is the bridge from our body to our mind, the element which reconciles our body and mind and which makes possible one-ness of body and mind. Breath is ... the tool which can bring them both together, illuminating both and bringing peace and calm.

Breath control has been recognized as another vehicle to move individuals into a state of spiritual awareness that they would not otherwise experience. In the spiritual schools of Vipassana and Zen meditation, breathing is cited as a means to enlightenment, realization or full awareness. Thich Nhat Hanh says that there are sixteen different methods of inhaling and exhaling, and when used in combination with the Four Foundations of Mindfulness, they are the essence of the Full Awareness of Breathing Sutra. Breathing is a 'means of awakening and maintaining full attention in order to look carefully, long and deeply, see the nature of all things, and arrive at liberation' (Douglas-Klotz 1997: 66). Various yoga texts affirm that the awareness of breathing is a doorway to enlightenment, especially when combined with bodily postures. Attention to the yogic four phases of breathing – inhalation, pause, exhalation, pause – can lead to deeper ranges of sensation than those of normal breathing patterns. The yogic system of *pranayama* (breath control) is used intentionally to experience an elevated state of spiritual consciousness that is different from everyday waking consciousness. The Buddha addressed the significance of breath in the *Anapanasati sutra* (Discourse on the Mindfulness of Breathing), which advises followers to breathe in and out while being sensitively aware of the entire body. It is said that by developing and frequently practising breathing mindfulness, one can achieve great benefits.

The pranayama, or science of breath, is followed in other esoteric schools, such as the Sufi movement, and is similar to that of the Hindus.[14] The early-twentieth-century Indian Sufi teacher and interpreter, Hazrat Inayat Khan (1991: 135) describes how the awareness of breathing can unify the various essences (*lata'if*) of the body and link them to the Divine:

Breath is the very life in beings, and what holds all the particles of the body together is the power of the breath, and when this power becomes less then the will loses its control over the body. As the power of the sun holds all the planets so the power of the breath holds every organ … Breath is a channel through which all the expression of the innermost life can be given. Breath is an electric current that runs between the everlasting life and the mortal frame.

Sufi *mureeds* (spiritual disciples or followers of Islamic Sufism) practise a series of purification breaths (Inayat Khan 1994: 108). Using combinations of the nose and mouth, the *mureed* concentrates on the pure energy of the *prana* (or subtle magnetism of the universe), while at the same time visualizing a colour and an element. The breathing exercises include extension of exhalation, fineness of inhalation and the ability to direct the breath mentally. They involve awakening the *jelal* (Arabic for dignity, grandeur, the masculine or active principle) as well as the *jemal* (Arabic for beauty, elegance, the feminine or receptive principle), or responsive influence, and include combining breath with thought. Teachings on this subject include advice as to breaths that are appropriate for going to sleep, dealing with difficult situations, creative work and meditation (pp. 106–18). The eventual goal of such breathing practices is to focus the mind in preparation for direct contact with the Divine.

When conscious attention is paid to breathing, accompanied by other methods of attaining trance, a very powerful transformation can occur. Ian Prattis points out that symbols, mantras, sacred posture, dance, mandalas and other forms of focus are used at different levels of meditative entrainment, and the key to all this is the conscious use of breath and symbolic focus (Prattis 1997: 159). When he employed focused attention on breath control in his meditations, it had dramatic effects. For example, when he was practising t'ai chi with great attention to posture, precision in movement and body-breath coordination, he felt movements deep inside, which he described as 'affecting the cellular level' of his body. This in turn produced profuse sweating, trembling and shaking, as energy moved from the cellular level into the physical. Experimenting with different breathing techniques, Prattis (p. 155) found that deep breathing took him into a state of mental calm, and short explosive breaths produced:

…a sort of portal or gate that I could feel myself going through. I also felt light headed and dizzy. The death breaths however, really did the trick. On the inbreath and retention I would feel stable, on a particular plateau of experience. On the outbreath and holding emptiness for as long as I could, my limbs and body would shake and tremble. There would also be periods of profuse sweating and extreme cold particularly in my hands and feet. Then on the last gasp of holding emptiness I would take an inbreath. The trembling and shaking would stop, and while holding the fullness of inbreath for a count of twelve I would experience a deep clarity.

The trick, he said, was to move the mind into the *perception* that this was the last breath one would take, and so enter a death-like state.

Rapid, shallow breathing is used by the Kalahari Bushmen (Africa) to raise *n/um* (energy) from the base of the spine to the top of the head. One man described it to Katz (1976: 59) as follows:

> Rapid shallow breathing, that's what draws *n/um* ... then *n/um* enters every part of your body, right to the tip of your feet and even your hair ... in your backbone you feel a pointed something, and it works its way up. Then the base of your spine is tingling, tingling, tingling, tingling ... and then it makes your thoughts nothing in your head.

Once this is achieved, the person is in a very intense emotional and physical state, and is able to enter a higher phase of consciousness, at which time s/he may perform healing cures, handle fire, walk on fire, have X-ray vision or see over great distances.

Breaking the normal rhythm of breathing in one way or another, when engaged in other spiritual activities, can change one's consciousness. It can lead to increased self-awareness, self-knowledge and altered states.

Discussion

While food, or denial of food, and smell are important in aiding the transition through portals, they are rarely used without other sensory modes. Breathing, also, is a strong facilitator and one whose technological importance is often sidestepped or not emphasized in the West.

Earlier on in this chapter I referred to spirits being contacted via the medium of smell among the Ongee of the Andaman Islands; they refer to this as *mineyalange*, which means 'to remember'. The experience of scents evoking memories that can take us back to early childhood is commonplace to us all. The Ongee explicitly realize a connection between breath, smell, spirit and memory. In a study carried out by neuroscientists Richerson and Bekkers (2004), it was found that there is a connection between memory and the neural network responsible for breathing. Some synapses in the brain, they say, 'undergo long-term changes in their strength in response to activity' (p. 25). Such changes are labelled 'synaptic plasticity'. While previous studies recognized that the hippocampus area of the brain displays synaptic plasticity, and this is linked to memory, Richerson and Bekkers were surprised to discover that synaptic plasticity is also to be found in the neural network responsible for breathing. Indeed, the respiratory system 'learns' – that is, 'its output is altered in response to prior experience' (p. 25). Three short episodes of hypoxia (lack of oxygen to the body and its vital organs, which occurs often at high altitudes) can induce a form of respiratory memory called long-term facilitation (LTF). In experiments with animals, it was found that short, repeated episodes of hypoxia used to induce LTF in animals are similar to the hypoxic episodes that occur during sleep in people with sleep apnoea, and such episodes also occur in normal people exercising at high altitudes. LTF, write Richerson and Bekkers, 'leads to a prolonged increase in lung ventilation that counteracts any future episodes of hypoxia' (p. 26).

So, teaching people better breathing techniques prior to the onset of illness might help to alleviate disorders such as sleep apnoea, emphysema or even cervical spinal cord injury. As patients with neuromuscular diseases or cervical spinal cord injuries often need mechanical ventilation in order to breathe properly, patients suffering from breathing disorders might some time in the future learn how to 'enhance their respiratory output' if the capacity of the respiratory network to remember were harnessed. Those practitioners who are well versed in breathing techniques in order to enter a trance state might prove to be a rich source for scientific investigations into hypoxia.

Meditation has been practised in non-Western cultures for thousands of years, yet scientific research on meditation is quite recent. Meditative techniques usually focus on the breath in order to produce tranquillity of mind, and control of the breath is particularly important in yogic exercises. The combination of breath, posture and meditation has all sorts of positive effects on the mind and body; for instance, increased mental alertness and reduction in stress, anxiety neurosis, bronchial asthma, thyrotoxicosis migraine and rheumatic disorders (Dhar 1999: 1). Certain breathing exercises alone can produce a decrease in blood sugar and serum cholesterol and a rise in the serum protein level (Dhar 1999: 1; Roth and Creaser 1997: 2151). Integration of yogic practices, breathing exercises and meditation, when practised regularly, can promote tranquillity of mind (its purpose) and increase resistance to stress. What we breathe in through our nasal passages, and how we breathe, has both spiritual and practical effects, on our bodies and our minds.

The next chapter explores another, sometimes more immediate, sometimes dangerous, way of bursting through the portals, either positively or negatively: through the ingestion of drugs.

—7—

Entheogens as Portals

I believe that drugs are a catalyst; they break down the barriers and open the doors, but it's the people that make the magic happen.

Dan[1]

If drugs could help God Realization, then drugs would be more powerful than God. How can we accept that? Drugs are chemical substances, which are material. How can something material help one realize God, who is all-spiritual? It is impossible. What one experiences from taking drugs is simply a kind of intoxication or hallucination; it is not God Realization.

Srila Prabhupada

Some authors (Huston Smith, Gordon Wasson, Alan Watts and Mary Barnard) suggest that most religions arise from psychoactive substances; indeed, Mary Barnard proposes that they all do (see Smith 2000: 19). Did Karl Marx get it wrong? Should he have said, 'opium is the religion of the people'? If the aim is to destroy discursiveness in order to enter into altered states of consciousness, and with the body reacting involuntarily to the effects of drugs, it is important to discuss the connection between drugs, religion and altered states. In this chapter I discuss 'drugs', their use for religious purposes, the importance of 'set', 'setting' and emotions, and, finally, I discuss briefly entheotourism.

The ingestion of perception-altering substances is commonly acknowledged cross-culturally as a way to journey into the non-material world of spirit. The non-drug portalling devices (drumming, dancing, chanting, and so on) that have been discussed in previous chapters often accompany the use of entheogens; or, rather, all these modalities act in concert with one another.

Drug, Medicine or Entheogen?

The term 'drug', which means a substance taken to alter one's physical or mental state, is now a heavily laden one that implies, for many people, street drugs, drug abuse and degradation. 'Prescription' tacked on the front of 'drugs' lessens the negative implications, but might still make some people uneasy if they associate it with mental illness; while the term 'psychedelics' is usually associated with the 1960s era of hippie culture. 'Psychoactive substances' is a fairly neutral term that states its meaning clearly: substances that activate the psyche or help expand consciousness. Some writers now distinguish between the negatively laden 'drugs', preferring, instead, to use the more descriptive term, 'entheogens', which is, literally, 'generating the god within'. People using such substances in their spiritual quest say that this more aptly describes their reason for taking them. In shamanic circles, the term 'medicine' is used more often. Whichever term is employed, the reason for taking such substances is usually to move the individual into another state of consciousness, or to interpenetrate another dimension or realm of existence.

In many indigenous cultures, plants are used pedagogically – to guide people between seen and unseen worlds. Shamans are the people, par excellence, who are versed in the ways of psychoactive substances; they are the journeyers between the worlds, the healers and psychologists for the communities in which they live. The Rigveda contains references to many deities, of whom Soma is one of three most prominent (along with Indra and Agni). In the first, and earliest, of the four Vedas, Soma is described as a God, a plant and a beverage that was pressed or extracted from the soma plant. The juice of soma occupied prime place in the ritual ceremonies of the Yajurveda and Sama chants of the Samaveda. The active ingredient of the psychoactive plant soma is ephedrine, which stimulates the metabolism, raises blood pressure and is a powerful stimulant. It may have inspired the mythology and rituals of the earliest followers of the Rigveda,[2] as soma and its influence are mentioned often in these writings. A thirteenth-century BCE poem or hymn suggests that soma has magical properties that enable the partaker to be lifted up 'like currents of wind', 'like swift horses bolting with a chariot', making one: 'huge, huge! Flying to the clouds' (Staal 2001: 752). The effects of drinking soma, it seems, include 'delight, intoxication, and inspiration' (p. 752). Accompanying the drinking of soma, chanting, recitation and breath techniques formed essential parts of a twelve-day ritual that was observed by Staal in Kerala, India, in the early 1980s.

Staal suggests that the effects of some psychoactive substances are similar to those of breathing in chant and recitation, including silent utterances that developed into meditation (Staal 2001: 745–78). Whatever its origins, soma is a psychoactive plant that, Staal suggests, was regarded as a god, inspired a mythology and became a ritual (p. 759). Beliefs and rituals often survive after the use of a psychoactive plant has almost disappeared, and the origins of early mystical experiences induced by entheogens might then enter the realm of myth or a founder's revelations of deity.

Ayahuasca/Yagé

Some South American shamans use ayahuasca to alter perception. Also known as huasca, yagé, caapi and vine, ayahuasca is a Quechuan term that refers to the main ingredient (*Banisteriopsis caapi*), which is both the jungle vine that contains psychoactives, and the medicinal/divinatory brew made from it. The brew is a traditional South American preparation that often combines several other plant species, among them tobacco, brugmansia and datura. In other places, ayahuasca is prepared with a wide variety of ingredients, including pure chemicals (when it is sometimes called 'pharmahuasca'). Along with inducing vomiting, it produces complex and colourful visual and mind-changing entheogenic effects, and is also reported to have healing properties, hence its use by shamans. Depending on individual variation, and whether or not food has been taken beforehand, effects begin twenty to sixty minutes after ingestion, and can last from two to six hours.[3]

Some common visuals from the ayahuasca brew consist of geometrical patterns and colours, aerial voyages, landscapes, cities, towers, parks, forests, seeing or being attacked by beasts of prey, snake-like plants, brilliant lights, other-than-human beings and gods. Phantasmagoric and supernatural beings are highly prevalent, as are divine beings, palaces and temples, landscapes, objects of art and magic, forests, serpents, extraterrestrials and spaceships, royal figures, flowers and non-natural animals, as well as felines and serpents, and ancient civilizations. Emotions can range from bliss, elation and awe, to horror and immense fear, but many experiences are dominated by sensations of love, and individuals repeatedly feel that they touch on the 'true essence of their own personality' (Shanon 2002: 63).

Bodily effects (in addition to vomiting and visuals) include the sensation of physical change, and the auditory, olfactory and tactile senses are affected. Light is a central feature in the visuals and is often coupled with powerful spiritual experiences. A common phenomenon when one is coming out of the experience is to see lines of light, 'like spider webs connecting everything', which was described by one of Shanon's informants as 'lines of the Divine presence without which the world could not be' (Shanon 2002: 83).

Two contemporary churches that use ayahuasca as a religious sacrament are the Santo Daime and the Uniao do Vegetal, both originating in Brazil, but now found in other parts of the world. These two churches synthesize shamanic beliefs and practices with Christian elements. Members of the Santo Daime Church use the ayahuasca drink to 'get in touch with their own "divine light"' (Saunders et al. 2000: 54). It is said that the spirit of the ayahuasca vine is the teacher; it gives 'strength'; and the leaf gives 'light', or the capacity for visions' (p. 54). Another ayahuasca-based spiritual community is the Gnostisismo Revolutionario de la Concienca de Krishna, based in Colombia, which incorporates Gnosticism into the Indian spiritual tradition of Krishna. As its name implies, it is both politically motivated, campaigning for the human rights of the jungle campesinos, and environmentally driven, initiating ecological projects in the area. Known as yajé in this community, ayahuasca is looked upon as teacher and spirit guide, assisting the drinker to heal, divine and gain inner knowledge (Saunders et al. 2000: 69).

Throughout indigenous communities in the Amazon, ayahuasca continues to be employed for medicinal purposes: the curandero (healer) drinks the brew in order to discover a patient's problem and make a diagnosis. 'Power songs' are chanted by the curandero throughout the session, interspersed by the 'blowing of tobacco, the sucking of the negative energies of the disease, the beating with a bunch of leaves, and the spraying of perfumes and scents' (Shanon 2002: 26). Interestingly, a French European-trained medical doctor, Jacques Mabit, combines his Western medical training with the use of ayahuasca in order to treat drug addicts at the Takiwasi rehabilitation centre in the upper Peruvian Amazon region (p. 27). One heroin addict at the Takiwasi centre compared his own use of street heroin with the way ayahuasca was being used to rehabilitate addicts (Saunders et al. 2000: 139):

> You don't respect the rules when you are drugging yourself as the preparation of the drugs is done without any tradition. It's done by people who want to make business, not to cure people. You do it to relieve yourself or because you want to destroy yourself. The worlds you access through heroin are not the same worlds that you access through ayahuasca.

Also called yagé among the Barasana Amerindians living in the north-west Amazonia on the frontier between Brazil and Colombia, ayahuasca, made from the macerated bark of *Banisteriopsis caapi* vine, is employed in ritual dances, along with coca. Both coca and yagé help the Barasana to learn and concentrate on the dancing and chanting in their rituals, and facilitate communication with their ancestors and their fellow men. Coca (made from powdered coca leaves), tobacco, beer and yagé are all employed by the adult men in their rituals. Coca itself 'signals capacity to engage in communication with other human and spirit beings in the outside world' (Saunders et al. 2000: 5). As well as being used at work during the day, it is drunk in the men's conversation circle at night, and during ritual dances, when it is often taken with yagé, tobacco and beer. They say that coca gives them energy, elevating their mood and helping them to concentrate, and the hallucinogenic yagé makes it more potent. A large gourd of beer is sometimes served as a chaser each time yagé is consumed, to help swallow the yagé and 'keep it down' (Hugh-Jones 1996: 47).

Among the Desana branch of the Tukano Indians of eastern Colombia, all who partake of yagé are aware of its physical effects, as well as the stages that are encountered after ingesting it. After carefully ministering yagé, the shaman guides ingestors through the known phases of the experience as part of a community ritual. For example, when the person feels and hears a violent current of air and undergoes the sensation of being pulled along by a strong wind, the shaman knows that he[4] is making the ascent to the Milky Way, and if the person can communicate with the winds, he can follow the Milky Way to Ahpikondia (Paradise) (Reichel-Dolmatoff 1969: 335).

These experiences of personal contact with the supernatural serve to confirm and consolidate Desana religious beliefs. They view existence in this world as a dream, a reflection of the reality which exists in the 'other dimension' (Classen 1993: 133). With the aid of the ritual leader/shaman, the individual is guided through some amazing and sometimes terrifying visions (snakes that wrap themselves around the body, snakes that jump and menacing jaguars, for example). In a controlled sensory setting, and with the use of hallucinogens, the shamans say that their main task is to manipulate the senses in order to make people 'see, and act accordingly ... hear and act accordingly ... smell and act accordingly and ... dream and act accordingly' (p. 133).

The Desana's world is multi-sensorial: energies, colour, odour, temperature and flavour all form part of Desana cosmology. A certain sound might be associated with a colour, temperature and odour, and thought to convey a particular message to the brain by its vibrations (Classen 1993: 133). The myth associated with the *Banisteriopsis caapi* vine is that the vine was born when the Sun impregnated a woman with his light through her eye. The resulting child was the vine itself, and it was made of such a brilliant light that it overwhelmed mere men. The Desana believe that the cosmos is animated by colour; life is created through the Sun 'mixing and matching colour energies' (p. 131). Individuals receive colour energies when they are born, and these energies return to the Sun when they die. If they have conducted their life morally, they will awaken to the reality of the other world. Changes in the body's colour (which can be detected by the shaman passing a rock crystal over the patient's body) alert the shaman to any physical illness, which can be cured by invoking the 'chromatic energies' within the crystal. Although women are not permitted to take hallucinogens to experience visions, men take them on almost all ritual occasions.

Experimentation in the West

When Michael Harner lived with the Jivaro (South America) in the late 1960s, and first drank the brew from the *Banisteriopsis caapi* vine they prepared, he found himself in a world beyond his wildest dreams. He met bird-headed people and dragon-like creatures who explained that they were the true gods of this world. With the help of spirits he flew through the 'far reaches of the Galaxy'. The senses, wrote Harner, become 'deranged'; there is little or no control over bodily movements (convulsions may be experienced); and frightening and extraordinary visions are seen (Harner 1973: xiii). He recognized common themes among *Banisteriopsis* users: the sensation of light, seeing predatory animals such as jaguars and snakes, a sense of contact with the supernatural, visions of distant people or places, seeing a recent event or being capable of divination.

Harner popularized shamanism in the Western world, but he was by no means the first person to write about his experiences with mind-expanding drugs. When Aldous Huxley took mescalin in 1953, and wrote about his experiences in both *The Doors of Perception* and *Heaven and Hell* (1954), he equated the mescalin experience with what Catholic theologians call 'a gratuitous grace', one that is invaluable:

> To be shaken out of the ruts of ordinary perception, to be shown for a few timeless hours the inner and outer world, not as they appear to an animal obsessed with survival or to a human being obsessed with words and notions, but as they are apprehended, directly and unconditionally, by Mind at Large ... is of inestimable value to anyone.

Huxley experimented with several drugs, including peyote, which is the common name for the cactus *Lophophora williamsii,* a bitter-tasting mescalin that may be eaten directly as buttons or powder, made into a paste or drunk as a tea. The Huichol tribe in Mexico traditionally use the sacred cactus in ceremonies, and the hunt for the cactus forms part of the sacred quests. In North America, the Native American Church uses the peyote cactus for peyote ceremonies and vision quests (Saunders et al. 2000: 77). One forty-year-old male who took peyote in the context of a formal peyote ceremony at the Native American Church in North America, describes why he did so (p. 77):

> By taking these plants, I was able to return to the origin of my intention. I wanted to feel life in its abundance, feel the beauty of nature, feel the love in my heart, feel the deep peace of the spirit ... feel the Creator within me and all around me.

A personal sense of self, boundaries and structure, as well as preparation of self and the environment or setting, are all necessary before embarking on a psychoactive journey if one is not to be negatively affected. Two aspects which appear to be crucially important to experiences in altered states of consciousness (especially when the experience is instigated by the ingestion of psychoactives) are 'set' and 'setting'.

'Set' and 'Setting'

> I came to the conclusion that certain psychedelics could be beneficial in the spiritual quest as a starter, an occasional support, or a deepening agent. However, I'm convinced that one must have an inclination in that direction to start with. I believe firmly that psychedelics will only bring to the surface what lies dormant. If there is confusion, fear and guilt, you'll experience the proverbial 'bum trip'.
>
> Werner (a Zen Buddhist monk and teacher in his early seventies,
> who occasionally took Ecstasy), cited in Saunders et al., 2000

Researchers of psychedelic substances refer to a user's attitudes, preparations, preoccupations and feelings toward a particular drug and toward other people in attendance at a psychedelic session as 'set', and to the complex group of things in the immediate surroundings when one is taking a drug: time of day, weather, sounds or music and other environmental factors as 'setting'.[5] These two terms are equally useful when discussing experiences that are not drug-induced, but occur as a result of the factors which have been discussed in each of the chapters in this book. Perceptions are vulnerable to environmental stimuli (setting), which can cause radical changes to apprehension and comprehension.

As well as 'set' and 'setting', Benny Shanon adds two other pertinent terms which may relate to either set or setting, and which he calls 'factors' and 'variables' (Shanon 2002: 306). The more general factors are the personality of the drinker (Shanon speaks specifically of drinking ayahuasca, but much of what he writes is appropriate for any entheogenic substance) and the sociocultural framework in which the drinker partakes. The 'variables' can be localized in specific moments in a session. Shanon emphasizes that an individual's personality and general constitution have a strong effect on the experience. He talks about the importance of being 'psychologically solid', that is, having a balanced frame of mind, without any major underlying psychological problems, as well as being physically 'purged' so that the body is in a healthy state. Speaking only of drinking the ayahuasca brew, he writes that paying attention to one's state of mind and diet several days prior to consumption seems to bring about more positive images and experiences than partaking while in a psychologically disturbed or physically 'impure' state. Although there is a non-personal aspect to experiences (and this is demonstrated by very similar experiences and 'stages' of experiences in ayahuasca-taking that appear to be common to most people), the individual's character does have a strong impact. Shanon points out that a religiously inclined person is more likely to have visions of a religious nature, an adventure-minded person may have fantastic voyages, a playful person may have ludic-like experiences, and so on. The more relaxed the person is, the higher is the likelihood of having a 'good session'; if afraid, menacing figures might be encountered (pp. 308, 314). This all seems to indicate that our subjectivity is projected on to objective images that are, in a sense, in and of themselves, or 'free-standing'.

Music is also important to the drinker of ayahuasca, and can have a strong influence on the experience. In the Brazilian Church of Santo Daime (mentioned earlier), for example, hymns form the basis for and can define what is experienced. Even the progression of the music follows a particular pattern that fits with the anticipated feelings of, first, anxiety and supplication, then energy and drive, and, finally, singing that conveys feelings of bliss and euphoria. Singing to the music provides an active outlet for people who find sitting still a problem during the drinking of ayahuasca, and because the accompanying songs and music are heard by all, the person acting out does not disturb others. Singing is also a great outlet for emotions.

A Strong Desire for a Spiritual Experience

A 'sincere yearning for a spiritual experience', suggest Saunders et al. (2000: 193), is the ideal state of mind, which makes for a very positive 'set'. To diverge from the discussion of ayahuasca for a moment, I give as an example of 'sincere yearning' that of an Australian occult artist of the mid-twentieth century, Rosaleen Norton. When Rosaleen Norton decided to embark on the first of many forays into alternate realities, she consciously provided herself with the right setting for her experiment, which, together with her 'sincere yearning', yielded experiences and images that she subsequently conveyed in her art.[6] She became known as the infamous 'witch of Kings Cross' (Sydney, Australia), and her journeys while in trance-like states resulted in esoteric artwork that shocked a very conservative Australian public in the 1950s. A controversial and highly criticized figure, her artwork displayed supernatural beings and characters that were half-human, half-animal, and almost always highly erotic. She is cited here because her own description aptly demonstrates the importance of set and setting in assisting her experiences (Drury 1988: 30):

> I decided to experiment in self-induced trance; the idea being to induce an abnormal state of consciousness and manifest the results, if any, in drawing. My aim was to delve down into the subconscious and, if possible, through and beyond it.
>
> I had a feeling (intuitional rather than intellectual) that somewhere in the depths of the unconscious, the individual would contain, in essence, the accumulated knowledge of mankind: just as his physical body manifests the aggregate of racial experience in the form of instinct or automatic reaction to stimulus.
>
> In order to contact this hypothetical source, I decided to apply psychic stimulus to the subconscious: stimulus that the conscious reasoning mind might reject, yet which would appeal to buried instincts as old as man, and would (I hoped) cause psychic 'automatic reflexes'. Consequently, I collected together a variety of things such as aromatic leaves, wine, a lighted fire, a mummified hoof, etc. ... all potent stimuli to the part of the unconscious that I wished to invoke. I darkened the room, and focusing my eyes upon the hoof I crushed the pungent leaves, drank some wine, and tried to clear my mind of all conscious thought. This was a beginning (and I made many other experiments which were progressively successful).

To reiterate, the environment in which trance can occur (setting) and the quality of a person's consciousness, their values, emotions and expectations (set), greatly influence the kind of experiences an individual can have. The same setting, however, can invoke either positive or negative experiences to people of different 'sets', that is, the quality of a person's consciousness, their values, emotions and expectations, can alter the experience quite radically. Stafford (1992: 25) suggests that a 'good set', in an environment considered by the person to be safe and nurturing, can produce positive experiences, but the reverse can be true for someone with a 'bad set'.

With most of the portalling devices used in earlier chapters, there is a slow build-up to the experience. Because drugs provide a quick route to a change in perception, their very speed can cause problems. Common factors in many of the experiences discussed throughout this book are: a dissolving of the ego and a paradigm shift in perception. If this occurs suddenly with the aid of drugs, and the trip is powerful, the experience can be terrifying (Saunders et al. 2000: 42). Experienced users of entheogens insist that careful preparation beforehand, a good 'set' in an appropriate 'setting', and proper integration of the experience afterwards are key factors in turning difficult situations into valuable experiences. However, they do not always ensure a 'good trip'.

Nicholas Saunders gives an example of what he thought was the perfect setting for him. In 1996 (p. 23) he wrote of his peak experience using LSD in such a setting:

> After my first psychedelic trip, I had an even more profound experience on LSD. The setting was perfect: I was with Anja out in the country in a beautiful secluded place on a perfect summer's day. We had made love and were in love, felt calm, relaxed and open to one another. At one point I felt that I was able to let go completely, like never before, and the result was to allow my 'essence' to flow out and to rejoin its source. It was like 'coming home' but far more so. It was incredibly 'right' and joyful and I wept with joy.

Saunders interviewed a Buddhist monk, whom he calls Otto, about his experiences with both LSD[7] and Ecstasy,[8] and about his opinions on the 'ideal situation' for a beginner. According to Otto, the ideal situation for a beginner is in the company of a trusted, more experienced friend, in an environment that is 'conducive', that is, in a setting that is relevant to the beginner's own spiritual practice. For some, this may be singing, praying, painting, meditating or sitting in a cathedral; for others, walking alone in the mountains. He also advised that the beginner must be prepared to accept that not every attempt is positive (Saunders et al. 2000: 106–7). This was the case with some of the participants in the Good Friday Experiment that was undertaken in the 1960s by Walter Pahnke, a physician and Christian minister with interests in mysticism, to assess whether psychedelic drugs induced religious experiences. Pahnke used LSD in his experiment at a time when LSD was not regarded as an illegal drug. The experiment was carried out in a 'conducive' setting (a Christian church, with all the participants being Christian), and, while some of the participants reported positive, 'mystical' experiences, one referred to his experience as 'a psychotic episode', and another had such a bad reaction that he had to be given tranquillizers (see Doblin 1991). The case reinforces the idea that 'set' plays a crucial role in experience. In Pahnke's enthusiasm to report positive aspects of the experiment, he omitted, or underemphasized, the difficult psychological struggles experienced by most of the people involved.

As emotions form part of the 'set' of a person, one's emotional state prior to an experience, whether drug-induced or not, contributes significantly to the experience. So too does the extent to which one is absorbed in preparations for, and the activity itself.

Emotions, Absorption and 'Flow'

The importance of a high level of emotion has been overlooked by many researchers, yet it opens the individual to the type of experience s/he may encounter. Neuro-physiologist Antonio Damasio, in two of his books, *Descartes' Error* (1994) and *The Feeling of What Happens* (1999), carefully and painstakingly points out that emotion is not only important, but necessary to reason. Emotion, it seems, is also a highly significant variable in any spiritual experience.

Absorption in an activity which enables one to enter into a receptive state of consciousness is considered by both Irwin (1985) and Nelson (1991) to be the critical capacity for the occurrence of what Nelson calls a 'praeternatural' (mystical and paranormal) experience. Irwin suggests that there need to be at least two factors present for the occurrence of a praeternatural experience: circumstances *conducive* to absorptive behaviour, and *motivation to engage* in absorptive behaviour. Peter Nelson adds another factor to this formulation: the absorptive activity occurs against a background of either negative and/or positive 'affective charge', and provides a doorway to alternate worlds, or altered states of consciousness. In addition, person-ality factors play a part in an individual's 'readiness' for an experience (Nelson 1991).[9] The notions of 'set', 'setting', emotion and absorption are all involved in helping to open the door.

Comparable to Nelson's idea of absorption is Czikszentmihalyi's (1975) notion of 'flow'. In the flow experience one has the sensation of acting with total involvement, and there is little distinction between self and the environment. The person still has control, but is completely absorbed in whatever activity s/he is engaged in. There is also little distinction between past, present and future, or between object and subject; rather, there is the sensation of a unified flowing from one moment to the next, and object and subject dissolve into one. Czikszentmihalyi gives rock climbing as a perfect example of such engagement – the climber becomes so immersed in the climb that s/he seems to merge with the rock face itself. The mystical union of the individual with their god, and the absorption of drummer with drum, in trance, are other examples. The combination of affect and absorption can be applied to hypo-arousal (meditation, prayer) and hyper-arousal (chanting, trance dancing), which are both employed in religious activities universally. The Whirling Dervishes become increasingly absorbed in the trance-dancing through long hours of repetitive dancing, and this is accompanied by a high affect level (focusing on their love of God). Emotive arousal is also generated in contemplatives who are 'lost' in meditation or prayer, by increasingly heightened sensitivity to inner awareness. Both exercises may result in an experience of ontic shift, where a person feels a highly significant 'reality shift', that is, 'a sense that they are no longer dealing with the world as it is ordinarily known' (Howell 1989: 86).

A contemporary Western example, perhaps, is the 'trance-like tribal rituals' of the technoshamans and the participants in a rave, which will be touched on in the next section, along with their close cousin, clubbing.

Clubbing, Raves, Technoshamans and Doofs[10]

Absorption in long hours of dance, combined with music and drugs (Ecstasy, cocaine, amphetamine, marijuana, alcohol and, to a lesser degree, LSD), forms the fundamental reason for the contemporary Western phenomenon of 'clubbing', described by Phil Jackson as essentially being about 'having fun' (2004: 3, 56). People go to 'party, dress-up, take drugs, dance and have sex' – an unabashedly hedonistic bodily experience that does not pretend to be anything else. Clubbing is profoundly 'visceral and corporeal', and its participants engage in 'a writhing, rhythmic and chemical realm of social encounters, virulent beats and seductive desires' (p. 2). Clubbing can vary from 'trance clubs to hip-hop venues, dress-up gigs and fetish clubs, queer clubs and straight clubs, Asian clubs, techno nights, house clubs, drum 'n' bass gigs, soul nights, funk nights, tranny clubs, free parties and saucy sexual soirees'; all of which is built on, 'shifting social, sensual and emotional states', suggests Jackson (p. 3).

Jackson writes that clubbers are acting out against the 'sober, sanitized and rational body' that permeates mainstream Protestant British culture and its disdain of pleasure. This attitude, he proffers, has become Britain's habitus, in that Protestant moral attitudes are so entrenched that they have become 'generative principles of distinct and distinctive practices' (Bourdieu 1977), or templates for the way people lead their lives. Clubbing, according to Jackson, generates an alternative body of knowing and behaving, which restructures the former habitus, replacing it with the pursuit of pleasure for pleasure's sake. While this is an 'unintended consequence of the drugs, the dancing and the crowds' (Jackson 2004: 5), clubbing is 'a conspiracy of pleasure' (p. 6), taking the body to unparalleled delights of the flesh.

The dance floor itself is where the social dynamics of heightened emotions, dancing and drugs create a communal energy that is sensual and much sought-after by clubbers. The 'pounding of the bass' and the 'rapid-fire riffs of the drums' (described as being 'tangible' and 'akin to being touched') (Jackson 2004: 29), pull each of the dancers 'deeper into the succulence of the beat' (p. 18). Clubbers talk of the erotic nature of the all-night dance/drug experience when: 'Your heart soars, your spine tingles, you are infected by a beat that unleashes a profound emotional and utterly physical response' (p. 27). 'If I believed in God', writes Jackson (p. 28), then that God would take the form of a bass beat. One of Jackson's clubbers (p. 32) expressed the club dance as:

> ...a collective experience in the same way as the hypnotic-type, voodoo, drumming ceremonies. It's the nearest contemporary Western people can get to those quasi-trance experiences and time does funny things to you and you get this feeling of pure energy. Energy in yourself and feeding off everyone else's energy and feeding off the music, the rhythm of the night.

The dance, the music and the drugs are said to work together as a triptych: the music affects the dancing, the drugs affect the music and the dancing alters the way people feel the drugs and the music. The downside of all this, admit the clubbers, is sleep deprivation and exhaustion, feelings of disconnection from the mundane world and, in the worst case scenario, suffering from drug addiction or overdosing. A partygoer himself over many years, Jackson has witnessed the splintering of clubs from what he calls large-scale raves to smaller social settings, and the gradual commercialization of the scene.

The clubbing that Jackson writes about is a British phenomenon. The doof, which started out as an overseas import to Australia in the form of the rave, is an Australian phenomenon. While the British club scene stays inside urban buildings, the Australian climate and vast space has moved the potential clubber/raver outside and into the natural surroundings of the Australian bush; it has evolved from being purely sensual hedonism to (unexpectedly) something more akin to nature spirituality. When the dance party relocated from urban buildings and out into nature, the dance became, for some, a means of moving through the portal. But first, let us see where it came from.

Alternatively referred to as dance parties, dance culture, bush parties or doofs, raves are part of a Western youth subculture that began in the 1980s. Ravers dance all night to the pulsing beat and sensory bombardment of the sounds and visions of digital technology. They usually attract large numbers of people and are often held in abandoned inner-city warehouses or out in the country. The aim is essentially one of pleasure, communitas, and usually involves the use of psychedelics, especially Ecstasy.

Although many young people attend raves for hedonistic pleasure and temporary escape from reality (for example, the clubbers), others report the therapeutic effects of raves, and some even talk of meaningful spiritual experiences after nights of dancing to electronic music from dusk to dawn (Hutson 2000). While the intention of some ravers is no doubt simply one of pleasure, along with an excuse for using drugs such as Ecstasy in a 'safe' environment, some refer to the rave in different terms, giving it meaning that verges on the religious. One of Scott Hutson's informants, for example, said that the rave was her 'church', that other ravers were the 'congregation' and that after every rave she 'walk[s] out having seen [her] soul and its place in eternity'. The

DJ who is responsible for selecting and playing the music is sometimes referred to as the 'high priest', and the drug Ecstasy as 'holy sacrament' (p. 39).

Not all ravers view the rave in spiritual terms, but those who do interpret their experiences around the concept of 'technoshamanism'. The DJ is referred to as the shaman/navigator who takes the participants on a journey to the accompaniment of 'mind-bending music', with the help of Ecstasy, where they can enter altered states of consciousness to experience non-mundane worlds. This can also be achieved without the help of drugs, because of the combination of rhythmic drumming, exhaustive, all-night dancing and the flickering lights that are part of the whole scenario. The music itself is said to be enough to take one on flights outside the body and to enable individuals to undergo physical metamorphosis, such as the experience of changing into an eagle or, more often, a caterpillar. Dance as 'flow' through total involvement merges the act with the awareness of the act, producing self-forgetfulness, a loss of self-consciousness, transcendence of individuality and fusion with the world (Csikszentmihalyi 1975: 43). Another one of Scott Hutson's informants said: 'it is through dance that I have found transcendence … my soul is free to soar amongst the heavens … allowing a clearer vision of the world that I am creating'. Some report out-of-body experiences that may involve hallucinations that bring them close to God (Hutson 2000: 39).

Ravers claim to attain a sense of community with others, to the extent that they feel they become one, not only with the other participants, but with 'all that is'. Many emphasize the positive experience of communitas, bondedness and love with other participants, a sense of wholeness and collective unity, as well as a feeling of being outside time. As Hutson writes, 'Dance, as a technique of ecstasy, becomes a portal to transformation' (2000: 44). Some pagan ravers use pagan imagery and view the all-night trance-dances as a rite of passage. Others use symbols and images that are personally evocative. One person relayed how she found herself dancing on a black floor covered in a 22-pointed star reminiscent of the Kabbalistic sephiroth, writhing and shaking wildly in unison with others (Saunders et al. 2000: 171). The skilled DJ might weave a narrative with the sounds selected to play, and so lead the journeyers in certain directions.

Preparations leading up to the actual trance-dance can determine a 'good setting'. One Australian woman explained how the day's activities and environment produced a relaxed feeling among the ravers during the day, and that the love and care put into the preparations enhanced her later experiences of love and communitas during the rave itself. The setting was at an old country house on several acres of land. During the day people enjoyed the benefits of massage, yoga and t'ai chi, or just sat around a swimming pool. The build-up to the evening was carefully orchestrated. At sunset a bonfire was lit, there were fire dancers, fireworks and lasers projected from the house, thus creating 'a trippy wonderland of light, smoke and images'. There were drummers, floral decorations, and a large screen flashing the words 'one love'. People felt a tangible 'connectedness' to everyone else (Saunders et al. 2000: 170).

Some dance parties may be held in obviously religious venues, such as a church or monastery. Nicholas Saunders attended a dance party in a 600-year-old monastery in Normandy, replete with goddess statues, beautiful paintings and hundreds of candles, where the participants were accommodated in cells that used to be occupied by nuns in another era. An altar was the focal point for the trance-dance. As Saunders remarked (2000: 173):

> I felt that the altar and being in a church, provided just what was missing from other dance venues: a worthy focus for our spiritual attention. But the atmosphere also relied on everything being done with love and care, and the fact that we were all together for so long.

Saunders also asked himself whether this occasion in the setting of a church was any more 'spiritual' than the raves he had attended in disused warehouses, and decided that, while it was certainly a 'good setting', it was no more spiritual than other raves in equally good settings.

Although raves infiltrated the night-time underground of Australian capital cities, especially Sydney and Melbourne, from the late 1980s, they were largely clandestine events conducted in empty city warehouses and industrial estates. Because of the mild Australian climate and the vast openness of the country, some decided that they did not like the way raves had become so commercialized and the move was made to hold dance parties out in the bush – usually on large private properties. The rave then became the doof, and in spite of the difficulties of moving sizeable technical equipment long distances, doofers willingly put much time and effort into preparations and driving several hours to an event.

The combination of all-night dancing in a communal setting, the repetitive beat of loud doof music, flashing lights and the ingestion of substances such as hallucinogenic mushrooms or Ecstasy, provides the doofers with easy access to a trance state where many experience a sense of timelessness and oneness with others on the dance floor. While in trance, many have experienced shamanic-like death and rebirth experiences, and being out of their body, as 'Emma' recounts (Soltau 2005: 37):

> My first transcendental experience I was dancing to an intense set, and I noticed that I wasn't in my body any more. I was sitting about four meters above the dance floor, I was everything around me but had chosen a point of perception. I could see the whole dance floor and everyone on it from above. This was not a case of, I thought I experienced this. I *was* above the dance floor looking down.

Many have had encounters with aliens or non-human entities, communication with animals and plants, and awareness of spirits of plants and trees. Another person ('Chris') experienced fractals of colours and shapes: 'I was sucked into a fractal-spinning-spiraling form where everything is spiraling out of this thing, it has a couple of strange geometric, almost hexagonal shapes surrounding it', and looked as if it were 'creating the universe' (Soltau 2005: 39).

A common theme is that of seeing or feeling an energy or force that resides in and around everything, and energy waves and colours that emanate from the people on the dance floor. Some say that the energy is tangible and feels like 'stringy, fuzzy, static, rope' (Soltau 2005: 41). 'Doug' reported seeing light lines that appeared to connect everything in the universe:

> I see light lines that make up the underlying structure of reality ... I see particles of light zip in and out of creation at a consistent pattern. Other times I see a UV spider web that connects all things together, as every light particle forms a relationship with surrounding particles a magnetic force line is generated, that I sometimes come to view as the super strings that make up the manifested world.

Doofers believe that the use of entheogens opens up the individual to the spirit world, that the dance floor is a healing space, and the dance experience can rejuvenate the doofer, especially through the releasing of negative energy and the 'bringing through' of positive energy via the doof experience. They also state that a sense of self-realization comes from the knowledge that everything in the universe is connected.

Des Tramacchi (2000: 209) writes that many young people participating in 'doofs' are aware of the concept of 'set' and 'setting' as determinants of the quality of their subjective experiences. Many regular users of psychedelic substances, he says, believe that 'set' is 'adversely influenced by immoral actions', and 'the regular use of psychedelic drugs can be seen to promote morality and deep self-reflection'. However, while Tramacchi accentuates the positive notions of self-reflection as promoting morality, the obverse situation can also occur – one's 'set' may be such that immorality might be exacerbated in individuals who are confused, fearful and ingesting substances in order to escape themselves.

What Lies Dormant?

According to Shanon, while most people who partake of ayahuasca have positive experiences that can change the way they look at life and other people for the better, it is possible to have severe negative reactions, especially if it is taken with certain foods and with prescription medications. As with any intense psychedelic, it can precipitate short- or long-term changes in personality or catalyse psychotic or neurotic episodes. Shanon cautions that ayahuasca can have disastrous effects, and might have tragic outcomes for people with psychotic tendencies, or those who suffer from any serious psychopathology (Shanon 2002: 329). Consuming the ayahuasca brew can be exhausting and may cause depression. Shanon insists that drinking ayahuasca should only be done in a responsible manner, when one is in a good state of mind and prepared both physically and mentally, and only in a ritual context, when it is administered by someone who knows what they are doing. This sentiment is reiterated strongly by others. Saunders et al. reinforce the element of spiritual intent when taking psychoactives (2000: 51). Shanon advises using them only as a sacrament and incorporating them into a religious ceremony in the company of others who have the same commitment (Shanon 2002: 330). The indigenous use of ayahuasca was taken for a specific cultural purpose in the company of a small group of people. With the spread of ayahuasca, and other entheogens, to different parts of the world, this is often not the context in which it is taken.

Nevertheless, even indigenous people taking ayahuasca in the appropriate cultural settings were not guaranteed a positive experience. For example, the Desana (who we came across earlier) say that a certain yagé vine produces visions of snakes that jump, and although an individual might wake from a trance in a calm state and profoundly satisfied, at other times he will have fleeting and disturbing images that are difficult to interpret. On other occasions the person might be overwhelmed by the nightmare of jaguars' jaws or paralysed by fear at feeling snakes coiling around his extremities (Reichel-Dolmatoff 1969).

While spiritual outcomes might be one result of the ingestion of a psychedelic drug, consciousness-expanding drugs are not for everyone. As Saunders et al. (2000: 13) remark, '... it is the intention with which a psychoactive substance is used that makes all the difference. Drug addicts act out of desperation rather than choice and find themselves lost rather than found through the use of drugs'. Some people are more susceptible to addiction than others, and there is always the possibility that an underlying mental problem is exacerbated by psychoactives, leading to disturbing psychotic episodes. In a person with underlying schizophrenia, for example, the sudden dissolving of the ego can be terrifying and may have long-lasting repercussions. As one person remarked: '... it's the drug that opens the door to what is already resident inside the person' (Saunders et al. 2000: 206). Saunders et al. reiterate this problem (p. 223):

> It is extremely dangerous for people with a history of schizophrenia or severe psychiatric illness to take any of the substances mentioned in this book [*Ultimate High*] unless as part of a highly controlled, medical treatment programme.
>
> Someone who uses psychoactives to escape from a mentally troubled state is more likely to find himself further in trouble, rather than getting relief, since many of the substances intensify the mood the taker finds himself in already.

Psychoactives, say reflective takers, should only be used in a caring and safe atmosphere ('good setting'). If the person is feeling uneasy, depressed, fearful or confused ('bad set'), it is not a good idea to take them. If any drugs are used out of hopelessness or helplessness, poverty and desperation, or as some form of escape ('bad set'), they can ruin lives. In addition, if there is no guidance, or one is not prepared, or badly prepared beforehand, with no integration of the process afterwards, problems can arise. In cultures that have institutionalized the use of entheogens for religious purposes, care is taken as to how they are administered, the dosage and the occasion, and the use of the drug is surrounded with cultural meanings.

While listening to now familiar and repetitive words of caution about drug use, it needs to be said that experiences brought on by the senses without the use of drugs can be just as terrifying and dangerous, as Paul Stoller's sojourn in Nigeria, West Africa, reveals. In an attempt to understand sorcery and healing in Nigeria, Stoller became apprentice to Songhay sorcerers from 1976 to 1984. As an apprentice, he says that he memorized magical incantations and ate the special foods of initiation, and was even indirectly involved in an attack of sorcery on a woman that resulted in her having temporary facial paralysis. He himself was attacked by opposing sorcerers, and that resulted in temporary paralysis of his legs in 1979. Subsequent to that experience, he took all the precautions against sorcery that anyone else in Nigeria would take, but remained in the field. However, when he returned to Nigeria in the summer of 1984, his experiences led him to flee the field, as dread and fear swept over him. Long-term fieldwork, he writes, does not guarantee any profound experience; on the other hand, if a fieldworker pursues the other's reality 'too hotly', they can be brought 'face to face with a violent reality that is no mere epistemological exercise' (Stoller and Olkes 1987: 229). The reality of life among the Songhay impressed upon Stoller that the basic premises of Western science can be challenged by other philosophical traditions and wisdoms, and that there can be profound depths to those traditions.

Spiritual Tourism

Many people in the West are now actively looking to tribal people to provide keys to a spiritual path that seems to elude them in their own cultures. The widespread and increasing interest in alternative medicines, spirituality, spiritual tourism and indigenous religions indicates the pervasive human pursuit of something more than a scientific paradigm can explain. Spiritual tourism has sprung up as a form of travel which promises to provide a holiday with a difference – one that might bring to light knowledge through experience derived from cultures that are less tainted by Western materialism, and more 'authentic'; perhaps even provide a key to life's mysteries. Along with all-inclusive package tours to centres of known mainstream religious importance, or sites of feminist spiritual significance and/or ancient Celtic sites, indigenous sacred knowledge is now a prime target for the spiritual tourist seeking enlightenment.

To the dismay of anthropologists and indigenous people alike, the New Age has heralded an upsurge in this kind of travel. Sacred journeys, promising spiritual retreats and programmes of healing and personal growth, a return to the ancient traditions and purification through indigenous ceremonies, sweat lodges, vision quests and even soul journeys all form part of the bill of fare. Most seekers hope that these ancient practices will provide new spiritual knowledge, and the opportunity to learn something that escapes them in the modern West. Some individuals have reported that they have gained valuable insights on this kind of journey. Bob Hodge (in press), for example, went on his own spiritual tour with his partner Gabriela, and found that postmodern tourism allows knowledge, emotion and spirituality to interact. Their journey took them to sites of religious significance in several parts of the world. The outcome of this journey was, he said, private and personal, but too important a phenomenon to be left out of academic discussion. One visit that was particularly powerful for Hodge was in the Cave of Dicte, on Crete, a place associated with Greek goddesses, which was said to have been the birthplace of Zeus. Personally riveting experiences of researchers are inserting themselves into other academic accounts (see, for example, Blain (2002); Harvey (in press); Letcher (in press); Tramacchi (in press)). Some researchers are even suggesting that we should consider a wider community of 'other-than-human' entities that exist alongside our own human community, world views that are more in line with indigenous ontologies.

Entheotourism

Apart from the familiar and well-trodden pilgrimages to sites of religious signific-ance in Europe (such as Lourdes, Assisi, Stonehenge), the modern Western search for self now leads seekers to more exotic and sometimes difficult-to-access locales, where indigenous people are known to take hallucinogens as part of their religious practices. Entheotourism – spiritual tourism with the addition of psychoactives – has emerged as the most recent adventure journey. Countries such as South America and Mesoamerica, with their ancient civilizations and known shamanic practices, are luring the adventurer who does not mind a bit of discomfort into more intriguing areas to experience rituals, where ayahuasca is administered by local shamans or purported shamans. Having been influenced by the popularization of ayahuasca in books, the media and television documentaries (as well as some anthropological accounts, it must be added; Michael Harner's works contributing in no small way[11]), the entheotourist can look forward to the possibility of an extraordinary sentient experience. An additional incentive to travel to places on or near the Amazon, is the fact that the hallucinogen ayahuasca can be taken legally.[12]

South American shamanic ayahuasca rituals and foreigners' experiences of them are described in *In Search of the Ultimate High* (Saunders et al. 2000: 115–23). Eager tourists are generally provided with accommodation as well as the ayahuasca. After long journeys up the Amazon in the company of other tourists from different parts of the world, they are usually each offered a toilet roll and a vomit bowl, and then assisted in their spiritual journey via the ayahuasca 'sacrament'. Accompanied by shamans singing chants, blowing smoke and camphor into the air, and rattling for most of the night, they invariably experience discomfort, nausea and powerful visions that might change their lives.

One website offers enticing journeys into the Amazonian rainforest that include lessons in ethnobotany, ecology, shamanism and anthropology, with indigenous and non-indigenous teachers offering their experience and knowledge (entheogens not included). At Guaria de Osa, on the Osa Peninsula of Costa Rica, don Pablo Amaringo, a 'once-practicing shaman and healer in the Amazon', holds painting and dream interpretation workshops alongside Western scientists such as ethnobotanist Jonathon S. Miller Weisberger, and anthropologist Jeremy Narby (www.GuariadeOsa. com – accessed 7 June 2006). The exotic tropical setting of the Osa Peninsula is transported to places like Ruby Lake Resort, British Columbia, Canada, via public talks and slide presentations by Weisberger, where audiences can become acquainted with rainforest conservation and cultural heritage projects being conducted in places like the Ecuadorian Amazon (Sentient Experientials: info@GuariaDeOsa.com) This is surely an admirable, environmentally positive and supportive enterprise to promote the case for helping the indigenous people and the rainforests of South America, and may be the only avenue left for halting the destruction of an ecologically fragile environment. Promotion of an indigenous-managed ecological reserve goes hand in hand with ecological tourism, which may or may not be advantageous to the people and environment they so desperately want to protect.

While some indigenous people may not oppose the visits of Westerners seeking sentient experiences in their rainforests (and other areas), and may even view these seekers as potential allies against the destruction of their environment (see the video, *Shamans of the Amazon*[13]), an influx of entheotourists (and there may be a fine line between ecological tourism and entheotourism) may eventually be as harmful to their way of life as the miners and loggers. A large influx of spiritual seekers could just as easily upset a fragile ecological system and demean the religious aspects of indigenous plant sacraments and cultures that sustain them. At an Ayahuasca Conference held in San Francisco in March 2000 (organized by the California Institute for Integral Studies), José Campos reported that, largely due to entheotourism, 'ayahuasca's reputation in Peru is getting worse', and with the increase in the number of tourists, the vine is decreasingly available; 'one has', says Campos, 'to go further and further into the jungle to find it'. He also said that ayahuasca tourism was 'hurting the traditional use' because entheotourists from the USA (and presumably other parts of the world) 'end up doing it in commercial contexts and not in sacred contexts'.[14]

Indigenous use of entheogens is sensitively employed in culturally appropriate and institutionalized ways. South American Indian shamans, of whom Harner (1973), Reichel-Dolmatoff (1971), Classen (1993) and Shanon (2002) write, induce states of consciousness which lead ingestors to make sense of their cosmologies, to heal members of the community and to act in accordance with social norms. The influx of eager entheogenic tourists on a large scale (especially if they introduce hallucinogens that are unknown to a small village community) will change drastically not only the ecological balance, but also the culture and, perhaps, the traditional reasons for taking the entheogens by members of that community. While Western trippers might have their entire world outlook changed by their experiences, the indigenous people they visit briefly might eventually regret the day they came.

In the next and final chapter I revisit the technologies discussed throughout the book, consider the whole notion of what constitutes reality, give some case examples of transpersonal anthropology, touch on the thorny issue of mental illness and altered states, and offer some suggestions for future research.

–8–

An Anatomy of Reality

It is easy to jump to the conclusion that because a psychological explanation is offered for a phenomenon, therefore the phenomenon – such as a myth – cannot, so to say, speak the truth about the invisible world. This conclusion is too facile. For instance a physiologist may be able to explain the workings of the eye, the brain, and the central nervous system, when a perception takes place. In a sense, he 'explains' the perception. But this does not at all show that the perception is true or false. The physiologist simply wants to explain the normal process of sight perception.

Smart, 1969

In the sixth century, Gregory the Great said that holy men, through an inner awareness, could discern which of the voices and images of their visions were illusions and which were revelations.[1] In the twenty-first century, academics are still debating the difference between illusions and revelations; the basic arguments are the same, although the discourse has changed somewhat. Now the major arguments are fundamentally psychological, neurophysiological or phenomenological/experiential; the latter including the religious/spiritual. These different approaches all question the nature of reality, and many conclude that the Western medical model puts an end to any other speculations on experiences that have been referred to variously as metaphysical, other-worldly, praeternatural, supernatural and extraordinary. Others, however, are not content to dismissively reduce such phenomena to materialistic explanations. In this chapter, I take a multidisciplinary approach to the phenomena that Gregory the Great and his contemporaries might have debated during the sixth century, and reiterate that the senses are the media for the phenomena.

Revisiting the Technologies

Throughout this book I have extracted from the literature what I see as universal patterns to sensorial methods that take people through portals. Visual symbols such as mandalas, iconic images or tarot card pictures can act as aids, and mental imaging can be cultivated and intensified by various exercises – such as focusing on the Tattva cards, looking into the centre of a black and white spiral or concentric circles, or training the eye to visualize. If one enhances visual practices through exercises such as looking fixedly at an image, then sustaining the image with closed eyes, and finally projecting the image externally, it is possible to become adept at imaging and to be able to control and concentrate the mind more easily. Active imagination, when properly trained, can mould sense perception and act as an intermediary between the physical and the metaphysical.

Sound is another aid to crossing the threshold. Certain kinds of music are not only uplifting, but can move us into another kind of reality. The Gregorian chant is particularly powerful, as is repetitive drumming, and 'joyful' or emotive singing, which draws and heightens the emotions. Both instrumental music and the human voice can be equally productive, and sometimes it is the sound vibrations and the number of beats per minute that are effective.

If sound is played for several hours and accompanied by rhythmic and repetitive movement, such as dancing and whirling, there is a loss of self and a feeling of bliss, ecstasy and union with the Divine, or an intense sense of communitas and connection with others. When chanting/singing is added, it is even more likely that, through repetition, and over several hours, the individual will move into trance, or a trance-like state, at which time the mundane world is left behind. Additional external technical aids, such as incense, emotional music and full engagement with the activity, can lead to states that diverge from our everyday reality. Sometimes when in trance, the body can become immune to pain, as evidenced in chapter 5, or pain itself can act as a catalyst for the experience. Entheogens are another avenue to altered states, but can cause enormous problems for some, and take away a sense of control over the process.

Each one of the techniques has been highlighted separately in the previous chapters for analytical purposes, but there is usually more than one sensorial mode employed at any one time to move one through the portals, a fact that has been amply demonstrated throughout this book. Cognitive factors are only one aspect of the embodied experiential dimension. The Desana of South America are a good example of the multi-sensorial (indeed synaesthetic) nature of methods of transcendence that incorporate sensory symbolism, involving visuals, colour, temperatures, flavours, odours, sounds and tactilities; a tune, for example, may contain an odour, a gender, a colour, a temperature, as well as vibrations (Reichel-Dolmatoff 1971). Under the careful ministrations and guidance of a Desana shaman, each of the senses is stimulated, together with the taking of hallucinogens, to ensure that the celebrants attain their experience. It is also a group process, not to be undertaken lightly.

The importance of 'set' and 'setting' cannot be emphasized too strongly, especially with the use of drugs, for if care is not taken to control the sensory environment of the person, or if s/he has underlying psychological problems to begin with, the experiences may be a lot more than they bargained for; the drugs may produce or exacerbate an underlying problem, and there may be long-term deleterious effects.

The research of Saunders, Saunders and Pauli (2000: 165) indicates that although it is advantageous, it is not necessary to have an established religious structure in which to explore spirituality using psychoactives, but it is important to have some kind of support network to help to make sense of the experience afterwards, and, of course, to provide assistance should something go wrong. Certain beliefs, especially when strongly held, may shape an experience, but, as one person said, 'faith may help in spiritual experiences, but it is definitely not required. If the spirits find it appropriate, no faith in anything is needed. It was the LSD that opened my eyes, but trees were the ones that taught me about spirituality' (Saunders et al. 2000: 35).

In 1970, psychologist Bernard Aaronson used hypnotic suggestion to produce conditions under which 'quasi-mystical' experiences occurred (Wulff 1997: 18). One of Aaronson's subjects reported being 'transported into an experience of great beauty: sounds, colors, and contours all were enhanced; space seemed almost solid; each object and its placement seemed part of a Divine order' (p. 18). It seems, therefore, that a 'mystical' experience can occur with or without the aid of drugs, within an established religious structure or not, and, on the odd occasion, for no reason at all.

It is clear from all this that the body (at least while it is alive) is the avenue through which our mind (and spirit/soul) works. Motivated by his interest in the possible biological basis of spiritual experience, Rick Strassman, in the School of Medicine at the University of New Mexico, carried out clinical research on brain chemistry and psychedelic drug experimentation, with sixty volunteers using dimethyltryptamine (DMT). He concentrated on DMT because it occurs naturally in our bodies and is also part of the normal make-up of other mammals, marine animals, grasses and peas, toads and frogs, mushrooms and moulds, as well as barks, flowers and roots (Strassman 2001: 4). Strassman discovered that DMT is connected with the pineal gland,[2] a tiny organ situated in the centre of the human brain, and he suggested that naturally occurring altered states of consciousness are brought about by high levels of pineal DMT production. He hypothesizes that the pineal gland is possibly the 'seat of the soul' (p. 56), and that DMT, which is naturally produced by the pineal gland, facilitates the soul's movement in and out of the body and is an integral part of birth and death experiences, meditation and even sexual transcendence. When the volunteers in his research project were injected with DMT, they reported that they felt as if they were 'somewhere else' and that they were perceiving different levels of reality, levels that are 'as real as this one', but that 'we cannot perceive them most of the time' (p. 315). Strassman concluded that DMT was not inherently therapeutic, and that as far as the experiences of the volunteers were concerned, set and setting were equally important (indeed crucial) as the drug itself, reiterating what others have stated in chapter 7. He suggests that further scientifically instigated DMT research might provide important clues to the mystical regions of the human mind and soul.

While Strassman's research is scientifically adventurous and original, it still offers a unidimensional model in terms of analysis. More useful, to my mind, is Geoffrey Samuel's 'multimodal framework' (MMF), which he used to examine his data on Tibetan shamanism.

Basically, the MMF advocates that a more analytically realistic and useful model to understand multiple ways of knowing and to move away from the dichotomies between mind and body is to look at knowledge as a 'patterning of mind and body as a totality' (Samuel 1990: 6). Previous opposing theories, suggests Samuel, can be brought together by employing a new attitude, which he likens to the change in perception that was adopted by physicists on the introduction of relativity theory. A trained physicist himself, Samuel suggests that a new theoretical framework is necessary because the old theoretical frameworks no longer explain the world adequately. What we need, he says, is a framework that is more analogous to the multiply interconnected, and multi-centred, underground network of a rhizome (p. 2), because it offers a scientific approach to understanding cultures that could incorporate an 'otherworld', without denying the possibility of its existence. Samuel's MMF rejects the mind-body dichotomy, instead viewing mind-body as parallel aspects of a total system.

As Samuel points out, rational thought does not have to oppose symbolic thought; he argues for a theoretical framework that embraces informal and non-scientific knowledge and gives equal value to traditional and Western scientific modes of knowing. Following Clifford Geertz's notion of 'webs of significance' (Geertz 1973: 5), Samuel writes (1990: 11):

> Rather than speaking of 'webs of significance', therefore, I suggest that we view the structures of meaning and feeling in which and through which we live as patterns formed by the currents in the course of a vast stream or river. The direction of the stream is the flow of time. Geertz's 'webs' now correspond to semi-permanent currents, or to use William Blake's term, 'vortices', that have become established in the onward flow of the river.

Such a view offers a broad conceptual schema that encompasses a variety of bodies of knowledge without necessarily selecting a single, all-encompassing system that denies non-Western paradigms their rightful place in our understanding of what it is to be human. As a case in point, I cite the Desana, briefly alluded to on several occasions earlier.

The Desana have carefully formulated theories about the structure and function of the brain. Direct observation of brain structure through aeons of hunting and warfare has provided Desana people with much practical knowledge about the brain's anatomy.

They have seen human and animal skulls cracked open to expose the brain, observed that a wounded animal may become paralysed because of brain injury, and noted the similarities between monkey brains and human brains. In addition, they have remarked on the biochemical processes caused by different hallucinogenic drugs, and how they influence behaviour.

Putting a simple explanation on the Desana's detailed and complex understanding of mind and brain does not do it justice; nevertheless, for my argument that other cultural knowledges might be equally worthy of consideration as those of the West (indeed, that in some instances they might be even more sophisticated), I summarize it as follows, from the work of Reichel-Dolmatoff (1981).

The Desana recognize that the brain is comprised of two hemispheres, and that certain areas within these two hemispheres have different but complementary functions. So far, this is not unlike what scientists in the West have to say about the brain. The Desana, however, take many more things into consideration than the physical body in their understandings and explanations. The brain, they say, is compared to a large rock crystal that is divided into small hexagonal prisms, each one containing a sparkling element of colour energy. Another way they describe the brain is that it consists of 'layers of innumerable hexagonal honeycombs' (Reichel-Dolmatoff 1981: 82), or that it is like 'a huge humming beehive' or 'a termites' nest' (p. 83). Sometimes the brain is compared to a geode that is 'lined inside with a multitude of sparkling crystals'. The two hemispheres are said to be essentially symmetrical, and the great fissure between the two is a deep riverbed formed by the cosmic anaconda, or cosmic energy. The convolutions of the physical brain are thought of as compartments and are called *kae*, each one being regarded as a diminutive brain in itself. Each *kae* contains images, colour, odour, a specific quality, and is related to concepts such as honesty, amiability and spirituality, or undesirable personality traits (as well as much more). Thus, 'all sensoria are highly specialized, although inter-related' (p. 82). Although the concept of nerves is not present in this explanation, the Desana speak of 'threads' that convey luminous impulses from one *kae* to another (p. 82).

The totality of *kae* is *ka'i*, what Westerners would call 'mind'. The mind in the brain is thought by the Desana to be the main organ of human cognition and behaviour. All sensorial stimulations are of great interest to the Desana, and while most adults have accumulated a large body of knowledge of the neurological processes by direct observation and discussion, it is the shaman who is recognized as the specialist in brain/mind relationships.

This is a very brief sketch of the Desana's highly complex view of the brain and mind, and I urge the reader to consult Reichel-Dolmatoff's entire article. I mention their views briefly here in order to point out that another culture has, over much time, thought very deeply about the human body, specifically the brain, and how it works in relation to all the senses. What is clear from this glimpse of the Desana's approach to mind/body/senses is that Western science offers but one explanation of the brain's structure and function, among other equally intriguing and deeply considered formulations.

What Is the Nature of Reality?

Peter Berger and Thomas Luckmann, who wrote *The Social Construction of Reality* (1966), defined reality as 'a quality appertaining to phenomena that we recognize as having a being independent of our own volition'; we cannot 'wish them away' (p. 13). They define 'knowledge' as 'the certainty that phenomena are real and that they possess specific characteristics' (p. 13). Knowledge and reality, then, according to Berger and Luckmann, are interlinked concepts.

However, what is real to a Tibetan monk may not be real to an Australian dockside worker, and the knowledge of the criminal differs from the knowledge of the criminologist. So, how is any body of knowledge established as reality? Following on from Alfred Schutz, who focused on the structure of the common-sense world of everyday life as the foundation of knowledge, Berger and Luckmann concluded that knowledge is concerned with the analysis of the social construction of reality. So we are talking here about the nature of reality and the nature of knowledge. Something is real because we know it is real, and we judge other people's sense of reality or non-reality by what they 'know' is 'real'. If their sense of reality is different to my sense of reality, then 'they' are suspect.

The 2001 film, *A Beautiful Mind*, portrayed the life story of American mathematician, John Nash, who had schizophrenia. During the film, the audience was swept along with the thoughts and sense of reality experienced by Nash. We acknowledged his relationships with his friends (both real and imaginary); we were convinced of the reality of his deciphering work with the FBI and of the people who were conspiring against them. But about halfway through the film, there was a moment when we, the audience, experienced a shift in our perceptions. We realized that what we had been acknowledging as real until that moment was only in the mind of John Nash. Until that crucial point, we were partaking in the truth as Nash experienced it. Our reality was altered only because we were provided with other points of view. These different viewpoints alerted us to some conflicting perspectives and demanded that we acknowledge the 'falsity' of our previous perceptions.

Common-sense knowledge is the taken-for-granted knowledge that one shares with others in the routines of everyday life, and this becomes 'paramount reality', or reality that is given a highly privileged position over any other. Language used in everyday life continuously provides us with the consensus of what constitutes paramount reality. It is a world shared easily with others, yet it is constantly being confirmed and renegotiated. Most of us who do not suffer from a severe mental illness are able to negotiate the 'sane' world by reading the signs that we pick up from others. As Ruth Finnegan (2002) deftly demonstrates, humans creatively communicate through an amazing array of sights, sounds, smells, gestures, looks, movements and touches that overlap and intertwine. As she says, linguistically defined rationality 'is not only itself controversial but also arguably a limiting model of humanity' (p. 27). The multiple bodily resources we call on in order to communicate with each other form an often unacknowledged, but important whole of how we transmit and receive information. All these sensory resources contribute to the way we negotiate our daily interactions with others; how we are supposed to act, what others are expecting from us and what is appropriate behaviour. Each of us has only an approximate idea of this consensus, but in spite of this, most of us can function in more or less appropriate ways in group situations by watching and listening. Our conscious mind is picking up on sensations, feelings, thoughts, intentions; we deliberately consider what our senses tell us and respond accordingly. If the 'clues' are not picked up in a suitable fashion, others might say we are strange, bizarre, eccentric or even mad.

Postmodernists have acknowledged that there are a multitude of standpoints, and tales can be told from many different perspectives. In *A Thricefold Tale*, Margery Wolf (1992) clearly demonstrates that there are contested meanings to any event. She relays a particular event in a small village in northern Taiwan, where she did fieldwork in the 1960s, using three different writing genres and approaches: the first was a piece of fiction that she wrote about the event; the second, her unanalysed field notes, consisting of interviews and observations she made at the time; the third, she wrote in the first person, in a style that she thought acceptable to academic readers. All three texts involved the same set of events, yet each one had different 'outcomes'. These three accounts are presented as separate chapters in the book, and each is followed by her own commentary, demonstrating how different approaches to the same data reflect writing genres, perspectives and attitudes. They also show how reality can be perceived differently, and how the telling of any tale can distort data.

A Western physiological approach, as Laughlin, McManus and d'Aquili (1992: 34) point out, is that our nervous system constructs the world of everyday experience, and we normally operate on our *cognized models of reality*. That is to say, we experience our models of reality *as though* they are reality, and then *project* the model into our experience as reality (p. 84). Our subjectively sensed, experienced reality undergoes another step in interpretation as we translate our experience into culturally defined concepts that have been picked up through a process of socialization in concert with the physicality of the senses. When we move from one culture to another, we have to relearn different cultural norms and expectations. Most people are able to do this – some are more easily able to adapt than others (and it is expected that anthropologists will excel at this). How well we understand all these different perspectives has important consequences. As Wolf's *Thricefold Tale* demonstrates, the truth is rather precarious and depends on the teller.

When anthropologists spend long stints of time in other cultures, they become acculturated to other ways of looking at the world. This is expected; but what is not expected is the inexplicable experience that might subsequently challenge their own belief system in ways that had been thought inconceivable, and for which they have no explanation. In the past, anthropological studies of other cultures omitted such experiences from their published accounts. This has not been the case so much in recent years.

Anthropology as a discipline is still extremely reluctant to pursue such matters, and it is the brave anthropologist who reveals, as Edith Turner (1993: 9–13) did, that 'spirits do exist'. With the advent of self-reflexive accounts that include the voice and bodily experiences of the ethnographer, there have been some intriguing admissions, particularly in the area of anomalous experiences: after undergoing physical ordeals that included fasting and lack of sleep, Grindal (1983) saw a dead man rise up and dance in Ghana; Desjarlais (1992) and Peters (1981) both experienced shamanic trance in Nepal; Marton (1994) saw a spirit light while researching Afro-Cuban Santeria; McCarthy Brown (1991) participated in Voudou; Favret-Saada (1980) experienced witchcraft in rural France; Susan Greenwood (2000, 2005) engaged in magic with practitioners of witchcraft in London; and Jenny Blain (2002) interacted with the spirit worlds of Seid-Magic as practised in North European paganism.

At this point, it is worth delving into contemporary magical practices, as researched by ethnographers such as Jenny Blain and Susan Greenwood, to highlight how the senses are employed to move into magical realms. Blain describes her participation in events of the seid-workers (Scandinavian shamans), which involves interaction with the spirit world while in an altered state of consciousness. Describing one event, she says, first there is 'scene-setting', which calls for the protection of non-human entities, and involves chanting the runes and invocation of deities who perform 'spae-working' (foretelling or prophesying). After these preliminaries, there is singing, drumming and guided mediation in order for participants to enter a light trance; all this provides a ritual space that is transformed into a highly charged setting. It is then that the seeress enters 'realms where the others do not follow', in order to seek guidance and answers to questions. The questioning, writes Blain (2002: 10), is couched in the language of Eddic poems. As an example:

> ... through worlds have I wandered,
> seeking the seeress whom now I summon ...
> Cease not seeress, 'till said thou hast,
> Answer the asker 'till all (s)he knows ...

The answers to the journeyer's questions are conveyed through imagery, and may have to be opined by another method of divination, such as consulting the runes. Techniques to engage with spirits in other realms (known as the Nine Worlds) include drumming, chanting and singing to achieve ecstatic communication with the spirits (p. 20). When in these other realms, the journeyer may encounter beings such as ancestors, animal 'allies', spirits of the land or of plants and deities, who act as teachers (p. 21). Preparatory activities may include breathing exercises and guided meditations, in accordance with a Norse cosmological framework. Blain gives a description of the preparations (p. 25), and the following is a truncated version of a journey (pp. 35–6).

After the room is prepared, the seid leader sings or calls to the dwarf-guardians of the four directions (north, south, east, west), sings a song referring to various spirits, evokes an atmosphere in which people align themselves with the cosmology of northern Europe, and spirit or animal allies are asked to assist or lead them. Drumming and singing accompany and facilitate the ecstatic state. The meditative guided visualization takes people through a tunnel of trees, to 'the plain of Midgard and the great tree Yggdrasil', through caverns of earth, or they may spiral through the Nine Worlds, coming to a bridge where the maiden Modgudr guards the gates of Hel's realm, the abode of the dead. While participants wait at that spot, the seer or seeress enters through the gate, 'urged on by further singing and drumming', in order to seek answers to participants' questions. Once questions are answered, the meditation guide helps all to make the return journey, back to normal consciousness.

The meditation is replete with symbols and images from Norse literature and assists practitioners to 'see', feel and sense things that are relevant to this cosmology. Repeated journeys enhance this cultural/cosmological awareness. This is a similar technique to that called 'pathworkings' in other pagan groups.

Multi-sensorial techniques include drumming, dancing, singing, a repetitive pattern of question and answer, different instruments, the setting, with its special costumes, the preparation of the space and, occasionally, the use of 'teacher plants' (entheogens). Blain writes of the central experience of the seid-worker from an insider's point of view (and her own, as a practitioner), and of the need to 'take spirits seriously'. She urges us to move away from the Western way of 'othering' and decontextualizing specific spiritual/magical practices, and to resist the contemporary Western phobic approach to shamanism ('shamanophobia') (Blain 2002: 49), particularly neo-shamanism, which tends to be belittled, because it is new to the West, and open to accusations of being 'New Age' (a term that is almost always used pejoratively).

Susan Greenwood (2000, 2005), has had similar experiences in magical worlds, with very similar trance techniques being used, and also urges us to take these accounts seriously. In *The Nature of Magic* (2005) she explores the pagan approach to magic and the natural world, recounting how practitioners such as witches, druids and shamans seek to relate spiritually and physically with nature through 'magical consciousness', and how magical practices engage the senses. Both nature and humans are often described using similar terms: the rainforest is 'a moist green womb'; places have 'moods' (p. 42). Pagans talk of the interconnectedness of all things, animate and inanimate, and propose that we can extend ourselves to other creatures and 'feel the inner body-sense of amphibians, reptiles and lower mammals' (p. 43).

Scottish shaman, Gordon McLelland, cited extensively throughout Greenwood's (2005) book, talks about the expansive nature of magical consciousness and the way the shaman can move into an awareness of 'a holistic interconnected pattern of energies and forces' (p. 96). Symbols and metaphors used in shamanic work are sometimes seen as 'gateways' into other realities, and Gordon uses these and the avenue of dance to contact spirits. Always there is the Western problem of whether these spirits and other realms are merely a projection of one's own psyche. To most pagans, such a distinction does not matter. One of Greenwood's informants views the 'otherworld' as 'a land of everything out there and in here too' (pointing to herself). It is 'a whisper away', a 'heartbeat away'; the spirits 'speak to you through smell, pressure on your body, through vision, not only eye vision but many different visions'. 'The spirit residing in me merges the otherworld with this world' (Greenwood 2000: 27).

Some neuropsychologists are questioning whether we can use our subjective sense of certainty of the objective reality of our everyday world to establish that *that* world is really real. d'Aquili and Newberg (1998), for example, question whether it is even possible to determine that various hyper-lucid states are less real than consensus reality. They maintain that it is foolish reductionism to state that because various hyper-lucid states of consciousness can be understood in terms of neuropsychological processes, they are therefore derivative from a baseline reality. Indeed, the reverse argument could be made just as well. They conclude that each is real in its own way and for its own adaptive ends. When attempting to understand various cultural explanations about spirit worlds, we should keep this point in mind, especially when endeavouring to explain and reduce into Western academic discourse, concepts that many Westerners fail to comprehend. Some academics are realizing this and plunging into radical participation in order to understand through the direct experience.

Anthropologists who have had such experiences have usually been 'well steeped in the cosmological and mythopoeic framework' of the people they are studying (Young 1994: 173). They therefore have a framework that sets the scene for the experience to be interpreted. Cultural competence and sensitivity to the importance of symbols, imagery and the senses all take time to acquire, and call for being open to different ways of looking at the world.

To fully engage in fieldwork of a religious nature involves the researcher in his or her own intensification of awareness, and this can alter one's perception of self and the world. In a conversation that David Young (1994: 173) had with a Zen monk, he was told that 'spirits are not considered by most Buddhists to be supernatural phenomena, but part of the natural world which has many levels'. When spirits appear, they assume a form that can be understood by the person. That is why an animist might see an animal spirit or a Christian might see an angel. Young tells us briefly of his own visions while in the field, of waking up in his bedroom on two different occasions and seeing someone in the room, then finding that they disappeared when he switched on the light. When Young told others of this, they responded that they had had similar experiences (Young 1994: 168–9).

Young suggests that a useful working model for experiences such as 'visions' – and one that might bridge the gap between the personal experience, those of informants and that of the scientific community – is to regard them as 'manifestations of reality that impart information that could not be accessed in any other way'. He puts forward a 'creative energy model' that considers so-called apparitional figures as a type of energy field which is projected and given form by an individual (1994: 183). He does not suggest that the visions have an ontological reality of their own (though others might argue that they do), but that beneath consciousness there are many 'levels of being' in the unconscious, the core of which Tillich (1951) referred to as the Ground of our Being, or the ultimate reality in which we all participate. Similar to this notion is the Buddhist idea of a level of reality that connects each of us with all other things in the universe (Young 1994: 178).

In order to understand these deeper levels, we anthropomorphize them into a form that we can communicate to others within a particular framework of ideas. Young suggests that 'spirit' is a type of hermeneutic bridge that allows one to dialogue with those levels of one's being which are not normally accessible. Further, rather than considering these phenomena as simple psychological projections, they might be a kind of energy projection that is an aspect of the person and that could assume a semi-independent form and consciousness for a limited period of time (Young 1994: 177). Cultures that acknowledge the possibility of accessing deeper levels of awareness have devised special techniques, such as meditation and trance, for gaining knowledge. Thus, the forms which appear in visions 'should not be ignored, but treated with respect' (p. 187), a comment that has been made by several researchers.

Other Ways of Knowing

The Dene people (or northern Athapaskan) of Canada, of whom Jean-Guy Goulet writes, say that people 'know with the mind'. By this they mean that communication (and therefore knowledge) can occur through ways other than words – through images, waking dreams and sources located outside themselves, such as deceased human beings or spiritual entities living in the 'other world' or 'other land' (Goulet 1994a: 32). A person with religious experience is described as someone who 'knows' (Goulet 1994b: 113–39). The Dene place great importance on knowledge gained from all experiences, especially those that come from these 'other ways'. Knowledge that is gained in a non-experiential or mediated way, such as from books or second-hand accounts, is regarded with doubt; it is, they say, not true knowledge. Only personal experience and personal perception is considered to be true knowledge.

Dene people who develop the ability to travel to and from the 'other land' through dreams and visions are known variously as preacher, prophet or dreamer. Such a person dispenses knowledge on the basis of experiences in the 'other world'. To know is to perceive directly with one's senses or one's mind. Because the Dene consider that religious experience has precedence over explicit religious teachings, a person is told only as much as their experiences convey to the Dene that they also 'know'.

This becomes important if an anthropologist wishes to learn about Dene ways. As Goulet discovered, the ethnographer must be willing to dream and experience visions and to offer accounts of these experiences, thus establishing a relationship of trust and a willingness to learn and understand.

Having imbibed this approach, and after immersing himself fully in Dene culture, Goulet began experiencing dreams while in the field, which he recounted to others. He also participated in rituals and was able to enter into the cognitive and emotional responses of the Dene people, even at a psychic level. Like the Dene, he began experiencing dreams that had a prophetic nature. In one quite startling instance, he saw his own double. While sitting quietly around a fire in a teepee with a group of elders, discussing preparations for a forthcoming ceremony, he saw someone fanning the fire only to realize, with a start, that the person he was watching was 'a detailed life-size image' of himself (Goulet 1994a: 30). On another occasion he saw an apparition of a recently deceased girl (Goulet 1994b: 129).

Although Goulet's experiences gained him knowledge of Dene religious beliefs that he would not otherwise have had, he is reluctant to attribute his experiences to an 'other world' as the Dene do. Nevertheless, he does not wish to deny or ignore the range of phenomena that both they, and he, experienced – phenomena that usually go unacknowledged or are relegated to the category of 'preposterous' in Western systems of knowledge. Instead, Goulet advocates a 'middle way', which accepts the reality of extraordinary experiences, but leaves them open for further investigation.

After Benny Shanon's extensive experiences with ayahuasca in South America, he also 'came to appreciate the conflict between two modes of being in the world, between two modes of knowledge', the intuitive and the analytic. His rational, scientific mind was founded on a distance between knower and known, while his intuitive mind brought him into a direct relationship with things known (Shanon 2002: 356). He realized, he said, how limited the scientific approach is, and that there are realms of knowledge that demand relinquishing all critical, distanced analysis if one is to access such knowledge. Further, that intuited knowledge cannot be passed on to others in an objective manner, but has to be experienced by each person and each generation on their own. In spite of this, however, he regards Western science as the best practical tool at our disposal to 'guard us against the pitfalls of uncritical mystification' (p. 40).

The Autonomous Imagination

Both Gilbert Herdt and Michele Stephen (1989) have considered Mekeo (New Guinea) esoteric knowledge in the light of what they call the 'autonomous imagination', which closely resembles Jung's idea of the collective unconscious. In Stephen's monograph, *A'aisa's Gift*, she describes the autonomous imagination as 'the existence in the mind of a continuous stream of imaginary thought that operates mostly outside consciousness and beyond conscious control' (1995: 99). For the Mekeo, the sense of self centres on the conscious, waking experiences of the physical body, but they are also aware of a 'hidden aspect' to each person that is separable from consciousness and the physical body. This hidden part acts almost like a totally independent entity, and can operate in another mode of existence. It can leave the physical body and even 'thwart the intentions, desires, and interests' of the physical body. This hidden aspect of the self is said to exist partly in 'the shadowy and perilous disembodied realm'. It is the 'hidden self' (p. 135), which exists in the world of dreams.

Although the autonomous imagination is not usually available to consciousness, it can enter consciousness in dreams spontaneously, and sometimes in waking visions, and is experienced as taking place independently of a person's conscious invention or will. With special training, a person may learn to bring the stream of imagery into consciousness. This happens during the controlled trances of shamans, some meditative practices and certain Western psychotherapeutic techniques. The autonomous imagination draws on memories and information unavailable to conscious thought. It is distinguished from ordinary consciousness by being more freely and richly inventive than ordinary thought processes, emerging into consciousness as vivid, hallucinatory imagery, and possessing a different kind of access to memory.

It is also especially sensitive and responsive to external (cultural) environmental cues, enabling communication to and from deeper levels of self without the person's conscious awareness. Stephen's arguments are based on the assumption that a phenomenological world exists independently of the human mind, and that the complexity of such a world is described, interpreted and ordered in different ways by different cultures (1989: 43). Long stints of fieldwork among the Mekeo convinced Stephen of the intrinsic merit of such an assumption.

Through myth, ritual and culturally coded symbols, a culture provides the individual with a means of communication to that part of the mind outside consciousness that is mediated by the autonomous imagination. The notion of autonomous imagination seems to bridge the extremes of a neurophysiological explanation and one that states the existence of spirit worlds. Another similar view is put forward by G. Obeyesekere, based on his research among Sri Lanka ecstatics. He suggests that a special kind of consciousness emerges in ecstasy, trance or dream vision that has a creative capacity to generate subjective imagery and cultural meaning. He calls it 'hypnomantic consciousness' (Obeyesekere 1981: 169).

It may be that 'consciousness' is as close to the notion of 'spirit', and 'levels of consciousness' is as close to the notion of 'different realms of existence', as empiricists are willing to accept. In the end, this may be just a matter of semantics and not important to the essence of what people say they experience. Indeed, if we replace one term for another, we might end up with the same argument. But using one set of terms in preference to another might be advantageous, as it can eliminate immediate bias and renew investigations into areas that have long been abandoned because of the stigma attached to them.

As a case in point, Beverley Scott (1997) suggests that the term 'inner voices' should replace the term 'auditory hallucinations', as it has less pejorative connotations. She also suggests that inner voices may be associated with different layers that comprise consciousness or spirituality, and that the Eastern notion of chakras may offer a more useful way of dealing with the experiences of hearing voices than the Western psychological model.

In yogic teachings, the body's energy system is comprised of three parts: an energy field (aura), energy centres (chakras) and energy pathways (meridians). Fields of light are associated with each chakra, and chakra energy, linked through complex energy pathways, is believed to spring from the points where consciousness and body meet. The seven primary chakras, or centres of consciousness, are spinning energy vortices that correspond to the places where major nerve plexuses and endocrine glands are located. These chakras can be opened to various degrees using certain techniques. Scott suggests that what are perceived as voices may depend upon which chakras are open and at what angles they are open.

Part of Scott's argument focuses on positive, negative or neutral inner-voice experiences. Some positive outcomes from people 'hearing voices' have been noted throughout history. Gandhi's voice inspired him to fight for greater social justice; Martin Luther King felt uplifted and inspired by his inner voice; and Quakers listen to 'the still, small voice within'. Some people report voices that have warned them of impending danger.

Scott compares these positive inner voices with the more negative voices heard by people with mental illnesses, such as schizophrenics. She classifies the former as positive, higher level voices, and the latter as negative, lower order voices. She points out that the voice or voices heard by schizophrenics are often demeaning voices which sometimes counsel suicide, and that they are of a different order, or come from a different level of consciousness, to the uplifting messages heard by people such as Ghandi. Perhaps this is a bit simplistic, especially as she seems to consider inner voices that convey positive messages as being of a spiritual nature and negative voices as not being of a spiritual nature. Nevertheless, Scott points out that Western psychiatry classifies *all* such inner voices as an indication of mental health problems, when some voices may indicate experiences of a spiritual nature. Western society is not a contemplative society, and we are more likely to view inner voices as indicative of mental illness, diagnosing such an experience in terms of psychiatric deviance, when someone may be undergoing a 'spiritual emergency' that might lead to some benefit to the individual (Scott 1997: 56).

Scott suggests that the concept of *spiralling* (her emphasis) layers is the key, with the upper layers being higher states of consciousness. This, she says, is a more useful way of investigating inner voices, as it moves away from the mainstream view of normality and its assumption that there is simply one layer of waking consciousness. However, she does not consider the chakra theory to provide the whole answer. It is merely, she says, a starting point for more research.

Further thoughts on positive experiences that provide knowledge or insights, and negative experiences that leave the individual with feelings of hopelessness, meaninglessness and depression, are taken up by Tobin Hart (1997). Hart uses the term 'inspiration' (being breathed into, filled or inflamed) and its concomitant feelings of enthusiasm, accompanied by some transcendent knowledge, as positive, in opposition to negative feelings that have depression as their emotional centre. When one is inspired, one feels uplifted. Conversely, negative feelings result in feelings of alienation, a sense of the self as separate from others and a view that life is burdensome. Accompanying negative feelings is obsessive mind chatter and a circularity of thought such that the person cannot rise above the negativity. The inspired person, on the other hand, is often accompanied by a feeling of being uplifted, energized, 'connected' and 'opened'; some may feel an all-encompassing empathy, understanding and compassion for everything.

Inspiration, he says, is 'a specific epistemic event, a process of knowing', and that inspiration is one possible way of 'shifting the center of our knowing' (Hart 1997: 49). If we shift the style of our current Western epistemic style, from one of rationality to one that is more intuitive, and pay more attention to sensory awareness and perception, we could then move away from 'a thinking observer, to a connected, aware participant' (p. 53). People who have undergone such an ontic shift sometimes say that it was like lifting a veil, and have likened it to a spiritual epiphany (turning point). With inspiration, says Hart, there is a heightened sense of awareness of the environment one is in, and sometimes a feeling that the self has expanded. Paying attention, letting go and listening allow inspiration to flow. One can also be inspired by hearing a moving piece of music or looking at a thing of great beauty (a sunset, a work of art). Inspiration can be cultivated through acts of kindness and creativity, moving beyond a personal challenge or limitation, as well as through love and meditation. All these things involve the senses.

Mental Illness, Shamans and Spirituality

Comparisons have been made between shamanic, Buddhist, yogic and schizophrenic experiences, in an effort to explore and evaluate altered states of consciousness. In the past, these various experiences were subsumed under a general category of what Walsh (1993: 739) refers to as 'exhibited equifinality' (more or less the same in the long run), which is demonstrated by the following quote from Alexander et al. (1966, cited in Walsh 1993: 740):

> The obvious similarities between schizophrenic regressions and the practices of yoga and Zen merely indicate that the general trend in oriental culture is to withdraw into the self from an overbearingly difficult physical and social reality.

Walsh is adamant that this position is untenable and cites this view as demonstrating Western bias against accepting the reality of states of consciousness that cannot be relegated to waking, sleeping or the pathological. As many researchers in the past have had little or no personal experience of altered states of consciousness, there is a tendency towards 'cognicentrism', with researchers assuming their own state of cognition is optimal.

Walsh insists that shamanic, Buddhist, yogic and schizophrenic states should not be conflated, and suggests a method of 'mapping' these various states using a multidimensional exploration of the available data, incorporating both the subjective and the objective, the emic and etic observations and reports. Employing three main sources in his argument, he draws on descriptions in the available literature (citing the work of researchers such as Eliade, Harner and Noll), and first-hand reports of shamanic altered states of consciousness, from indigenous practitioners (here he uses Balinese and Basque reports) and from Westerners who have undergone at least one year of intensive shamanic apprenticeship in Huichol, Nepalese and South American traditions. Finally, Walsh calls on his own extensive experiences with shamanic journeying, having learned the techniques from Michael Harner.

Walsh's 'map' focuses on the ability to concentrate – whether this is fluid or fixed; the ability to communicate; the level of awareness of the environment and the context of the experience; the degree of arousal/calm; and sensitivity or subtlety of sensory perception, the content of inner experience (visual images that are formless or with form). He makes further subdivisions relating to the modality of the form, organization, intensity and psychological level; whether the experiences are painful or pleasurable, and the sense of identity or self.

Using his 'mapping' model, Walsh tracked similarities and differences across a range of dimensions of experience and the practices that facilitated them. He noted that differences can not only manifest between each tradition, but within each tradition, though there is 'some experiential and functional overlap' between the states (Walsh 1993: 754). Comparing differences in concentration, he noted that in Buddhist insight practice,[3] attention is fluid, while in yogic practice, attention is fixed; concentration in Buddhist and shamanic practices is momentary, in yogic states it is fixed and in schizophrenic states it is drastically impaired.

Training in concentration is a common element in consciousness-altering traditions and relates to the aspect of control (Walsh 1993: 756):

> Closely related to concentration is control. Two different dimensions of control should be distinguished. The first is the ability to enter and leave ASC at will, and the second is the ability to determine the experiential content of the ASC.

In the three spiritual traditions, the practitioner is trained to enhance control; in schizophrenic states, control is severely reduced. In the following excerpt from Richard McLean's (2003: back cover) tragically compelling account of his own schizophrenia, it is clearly the case that he is *not* in control:

I am crouching in an alleyway. They can't see me here, so for the moment I am safe. There must be hundreds of loudspeakers projecting secret messages at me, and umpteen video cameras tracking every move I make. They will tie me up, soak my feet in water and have goats lick my feet down to the bone ...

Comparing the ayahuasca entheogenic inebriation to psychosis, Benny Shanon (2002: 29) writes that, while admittedly some aspects of ayahuasca inebriation 'resemble some aspects of psychosis', the two experiences are fundamentally different. Psychosis, he says, is neither voluntary nor wished for. No one ever enjoys or sincerely wishes to be psychotic. The issues of control and awareness are the most compelling arguments for difference between the two experiences. The ayahuasca drinker has significant control over what is happening to him or her under the intoxication, while this is not true of the psychotic. The most basic psychological themes that occur in ayahuasca visions are concerned with people's understanding of their own personality and life, says Shanon, and one can gain new perspectives on particular life situations through the visions. While ayahuasca does not always evoke beneficence (indeed, it can evoke 'an overall ambience of evil'), Shanon insists that ayahuasca experiences cannot be taken out of context. While some patterns of behaviour might be classified as psychotic by a mental health professional who lacks knowledge of ASCs, a crucial difference is whether the person is 'master' of the non-ordinary experience or 'enslaved' by it. The insane person, he insists, is 'chaotically pushed around by the non-ordinary experience, becomes frightened, and more fear is created'. 'Unlike madness, the ayahuasca experience is usually felt to be structured and meaningful', and the experience can be 'most rewarding, uplifting, and enjoyable' (pp. 263–4). Perhaps the most compelling argument for the difference in the awareness of people in ayahuasca-induced ASCs is that ayahuasca drinkers do not confuse their visions with states of affairs in the ordinary external reality. They conceive their visions as presenting separate realities which cannot be apprehended without ayahuasca.

Neil Douglas-Klotz (1997) surveyed some of the basic attitudes held by the main somatic psychology pioneers, Elsa Gindler, Wilhelm Reich, Gerda Alexander and F.M. Alexander, with regard to the relationship of breath awareness to neuroticism, schizophrenia and visionary states of awareness. One of the questions posed by Douglas-Klotz is: can one distinguish between vision and schizophrenia in a functional way? In attempting to answer this question he refers to Wilhelm Reich, who wrote: 'There is not a single neurotic person who is capable of breathing out deeply and evenly in one breath' (Reich, cited in Douglas-Klotz 1997: 64–75). For Reich, respiration was intimately connected with the natural impulse of an organism to 'expand in pleasure and contract in anxiety' (Reich 1948: 333).

This idea could be investigated by further research, and it seems that many researchers in different disciplines are interested in pursuing similar ideas. As Henry Vyner points out, there is no scientific consensus in the West as to what the defining characteristics of a healthy mind are, and we would do well to look in other directions for fresh views on mind and consciousness (Vyner 2002). Neurobiology, which is the current recourse taken by medical science, is limited. In a documentary entitled *God on the Brain*, initial attempts are made with regard to responding to some of the questions raised by Vyner (below).[4] For example, neurological tests on individuals engaged in deep meditation indicated that the parietal lobes of the brain 'shut down', sending blood to the temporal lobes, and that the temporal lobes are the key to meditative states and perhaps mystical experiences. As the parietal lobes give us a sense of ourselves, this shutdown might contribute to the effect of dissociation, or loss of a sense of self. Newberg, d'Aquili and Rause (2002) found that reduction of activity in brain centres that normally create a feeling of self can also generate out-of-body perceptions. Experimentally stimulating the temporal lobes can produce abnormal activity in the brain and result in religious revelations, or at least the experience of a 'sensed presence' (something that is beyond the self). Electromagnetic fields can affect the brain and induce feelings of such a presence in some people. In experiments by Michael Persinger of Laurentian University in Canada, 80 per cent of those tested experienced the 'sensed presence'. It was suggested that there is a temporal lobe sensitivity continuum, and that highly sensitive individuals are more likely to experience the presence than those who are at the low end of the continuum, which might explain the 20 per cent who did not experience a presence. In similar experiments, meditating monks and Franciscan nuns in deep prayer showed similar decreases in the orientation part of the brain. It was suggested that temporal lobes are the key to neurotheology, (see also Ramachandran and Blakeslee 1998), but other researchers have critiqued some of this work, demonstrating biases in defining religiosity in terms of particular experiences (see Albright 2000). There is a highly complex network of communication in the brain during mystical and trance experience; it is too simplistic to state that 'God' is merely a product of neurology.

Neurological mechanisms, write Newberg et al. (2002), can be 'coaxed into operation' (p. 79) by somatic stimulation such as music, dance and all the senses discussed in this book, and can drive the limbic and autonomic systems, dramatically affecting the borders of the self. Multiple sensory modalities are involved in drumming rhythms in any given performance, affecting individuals in nuanced ways, according to responses evoked by the body's reaction to basal rhythms, a notion with which our clubbers from chapter 7 would no doubt agree. Contributing to the response of the drumming are other factors, such as fasting, hyperventilation and different smells that all affect the body's physiology (Gellhorn and Kiely 1972). Repetitive auditory and visual stimuli drive cortical rhythms and bring about intensely pleasurable or ineffable experiences. When a number of the senses are stimulated simultaneously, with the help of music, visuals, smells or environmental ambiance, individuals can be lifted 'out of their isolated individual sensibilities' (Newberg et al. 2002: 79) and become immersed in something larger than themselves. This might be a sense of merging with God (Christians and Sufis), sensations of oneness with the universe

(Buddhists), merging with the goddess (modern pagans), a sense of communal energy (doofers on earth dance floors in the Australian bush) or ceremonially coming into contact with Ancestral presence (Aboriginal Australians).

Somewhat similar to Geoffrey Samuel's approach, Newberg et al. (2002: 173) argue that science and religion do not have to be incompatible: 'one need not be wrong for the other to be right'; and that the neurophysiology of religious/mystical experiences are but one way of explaining them. The goal of the emerging field of neurotheology, they propose, is 'to understand the connection between biology and spirituality' (p. 175), and this can be done with a more holistic approach. As well as understanding what is occurring in the brain, other factors, such as myth, bodily sensations, emotion, community, and so on, must be taken into consideration alongside the scientific focus on physiology. However, neurotheology, they suggest, is a 'crucial factor' (p. 178).

Some fascinating data are emerging from Western approaches to the study of the brain (the film *What the Bleep* introduced scientific ideas to the general public), and neurobiology scholars are increasingly turning their attention to age-old religious and spiritual traditions for enlightenment. Michael Winkelman calls on a shamanic paradigm that involves 'basic brain processes, neurognostic structures, and innate brain modules', to suggest that the universal principles of shamanism, such as soul flight, animal spirits and death-and-rebirth experiences, reflect 'fundamental brain operations and structures of consciousness' (Winkelman 2004: 193). Indeed, the shamanic paradigm may provide a framework that reconciles both scientific and religious perspectives, by explicating the biological underpinnings of spiritual experiences and practices and providing a basis for an evolutionary theology.

Henry Vyner's enquiries (2002) into consciousness took him to a group of Tibetan Buddhist lamas who have been employing meditation to study empirically the stream of consciousness for more than two thousand years. Vyner proffers that as science is the study of observable phenomena, the phenomena that appear in the stream of consciousness are observable in precisely the same way that phenomena of the material world are observable, and that the investigation of mental phenomena might be done by organizing a new area of research within the field of psychology – that of descriptive psychology. His current research is ongoing and to date has involved interviews with two hundred Tibetan lamas.[5] It is to be hoped that the rich Tibetan point of view will be taken into account alongside that of a Western psychological approach, in order to gain deeper insights into body, brain and experience. In any case, Vyner's ruminations with the Tibetan lamas has led him to raise a number of questions about processes of the mind that could be useful starting points in the field of descriptive psychology, questions such as: what are the defining characteristics of a healthy mind? what are the intrapsychic (as opposed to biological or social) causes of psychopathology? how do various rituals (such as rituals of transformation that might involve trance states) change the structural and dynamic characteristics of the mind? how might such rituals help to cultivate a healthy mind? These are all questions that have been pondered by Tibetan Buddhists for many years, and about which they have developed great insights.

It is now recognized by Western researchers that participating in spiritual behaviours, such as prayer, meditation, ritual and physical exertion, can lower blood pressure, decrease heart rate, lower rates of respiration, reduce levels of the hormone cortisol and create positive changes in immune system function (Newberg et al. 2002: 86). In other words, spiritual activity is good for you! In addition to bodily and chemical stimulation, it seems the cognitive content in which religious ritual is performed is necessary to trigger the emotional states that make a 'successful' ritual, one in which the participant felt that the activity was meaningful for them. In other words, personal meaning is highly important, and a 'good' ritual engages brain, body and ideas; the synthesis of all three is what makes a ritual powerful, turning 'a meaningful idea into a visceral experience' (p. 90). This can also be turned on its head, as evidenced throughout these chapters: the visceral can promote the experience. The body can generate effects and the mind reacts. Also, the mind can set things in motion through thought (which is what occurs in meditation). The body is important, but so is the mind, and when working in concert with one another, they can provoke a powerful experience.

Madman or Mystic?

[M]y depression was, at its core, a spiritual crisis – the sickness of a soul which could not find God.

John[6]

I feel I'm missing out on the mystery of life sometimes when I disregard things as mere delusions. There's a grey area between a true mystical experience and one due to mental illness. Even before I became ill, I used to have experiences of a clairvoyant nature.

Richard McLean[7]

The state of someone's mind and the treatment of people designated by society as 'mad' are highly debatable issues. What is accepted as psychological deviance or psychosis in some societies may not be regarded in this way in others, or another society may have a different, perhaps gentler, way of handling a person who exhibits abnormal behaviour, to that of the Western medical model. Indeed, there is often a very fine line between what some refer to as a 'spiritual experience' and what others refer to as a 'psychotic episode'. I cite Jack Kornfield and his discussion of some spiritual practices as a case in point.

Kornfield (1994) talks about the physical effects of spiritual practice that involves deep concentration and repeated meditation or prayer, or a combination of yoga, concentration and breathing exercises. The key is to practise with undivided attention on some spiritual awareness exercise. Somatic effects can include: a build-up of great energy which can result in vibrations, involuntary bodily movements, chills, feelings of floating in the air, tingling, waves of pleasure, the sensation that insects are crawling all over the skin or that the skin is being pricked with needles. Coloured light/s that turn into a strong golden or white light may be seen, and the body may feel that it is dissolving into the light, or the body may feel extremely heavy. Swirls and patterns may be seen, the shape of the body may feel as if it is changing, and there may be sensations of heat and melting. The body may seem to stretch to a great height or become very small. Hearing may become very acute or the person may hear inner sounds, such as bells, musical notes or, sometimes, voices. The senses of taste and smell may also become profoundly sensitive. Deep concentration, says Kornfield, may evoke visions that are compellingly real and seem to be 'as real as our day-to-day reality' (p. 125). Often there is a release of strong emotions that results in the person feeling that they are on an emotional roller coaster, experiencing a range of feelings, from sorrow and despair to delight and ecstasy. The majority of these visions may be entirely pleasurable, but powerful altered states, if not monitored properly, might open up too rapidly for the novice, who may experience adverse affects, such as (p. 131):

> powerful agitation, loss of sleep, paranoia, disorientation, and even physical experi-
> ences such as painful sounds, fiery temperatures, or temporary blindness ... A further
> manifestation of great difficulty can be experienced as a loss of boundaries, in which the
> sense of oneself and others dissolves to such an overwhelming extent that one feels the
> feelings of others, experiences the movement of traffic as though it were within one's
> own body, and finds it difficult to have any coherent sense of self ... Yet another realm
> of difficulty arises with the upsurging of powerful parts of oneself that are split off from
> our ordinary consciousness. These may manifest as hearing voices, unstoppable visions,
> hallucinations, and repetition of previous 'psychotic' experiences in the case of those
> who have had them in the past.

Kornfield discusses the case of one student who registered for a three-month retreat that he offered. Impatient to have his own experiences, the student, rather than follow the instructions given to him, decided to 'get enlightened' as quickly as possible in his own way. He became disassociated and began to experience all sorts of altered states; after a 24-hour period of sitting in intense concentration without instruction, he got up, filled with 'explosive energy', at which time he became fearful, agitated, moving 'in a wild and manic state, as if he had temporarily gone crazy' and was unable to sleep (Kornfield 1994: 131). Fortunately, Kornfield and his team knew how to cope. They started him on a programme of long-distance running, changed his diet from vegetarian food to meat loaf and hamburgers, got him to take frequent hot baths and showers, had him do heavy digging in the garden, and kept someone with him all the time. After three days he was able to sleep again, at which time he was allowed to meditate slowly and carefully. Kornfield says (p. 131):

> While his experiences may have been valid spiritual and psychic openings, they were not brought about in a natural or balanced way, and there was no way he could integrate them.

I cite Kornfield's work in detail above because the experiences of his young student seem to parallel many of the experiences of people with specific kinds of mental disorders – especially those of a psychotic nature: loss of sleep, paranoia, agitation, disorientation, loss of boundaries, hearing voices, unstoppable visions, hallucinations and repetition of previous 'psychotic' experiences in the case of those who have had them in the past. Chronic schizophrenia is one of the most disturbing mental illnesses and it has shattering effects and outcomes for sufferers and those close to them. As one sufferer said:

> It's very difficult to be sane one day and the next to be hearing voices for the very first time ... You suffer from terrible fear, you think people are after you, and it's very scary... You think the voices are trying to hurt you or kill you...[8]

To return to Jack Kornfield and his student, instead of sending his student immediately to a psychiatric ward to be calmed down through drugs, Kornfield and his team dealt with him as if his experiences were due to intense meditation and not a psychotic episode of a mentally deranged person, even though he displayed symptoms that could have been diagnosed as such. They did not give him drugs; instead, they calmed him down by directing his excessive energy into physical activities. After three days he returned to 'normal'. As Kornfield says, they put the brakes on, slowing down a powerful energetic process to bring him back to a balanced state. In a supportive environment, various physical, non-invasive methods could have been used to do this, in addition to those that Kornfield used: t'ai chi, walking, changing the diet to heavy foods, massage, hiking – anything that might 'ground' the person.

Although people undergoing extremely psychotic episodes may not be able to be handled without the aid of properly administered drugs (and I am not advocating the complete elimination of drugs that have helped people to cope with their mental illness and lead a normal life), perhaps the kinds of methods that Kornfield's team employed could be used with certain episodes of mental illness before the administering of heavy chemicals that can have disastrous side effects. It would certainly be worth investigating.

While earlier anthropological accounts tended to 'lump' shamanism, mental disorders and even mystical experiences into one category, Luhrmann cautions that we can fall into the opposite trap of attributing to 'madness' some sort of romantic freedom. As she points out, most people who end up in a psychiatric hospital are deeply unhappy and seriously disturbed. Many of them lead lives of humiliation and great pain (Luhrmann 2000: 208):

> To try to protect the chronic mentally ill by saying that they are not ill, just different, is a misplaced liberalism of appalling insensitivity to the patients and to the families who struggle so valiantly with the difficulties of their ill family members. Most people who are really schizophrenic are far too ill to serve as religious experts.

Most cultures can recognize the difference between someone who is 'mad' and someone who is a religious specialist such as a shaman (though some shamans may exhibit behaviour that at times seems abnormal to that society). They also recognize that some aspects of behaviour that might occur in trance states may be caused by something else. For example, some trance states that occur in Northern Kenya among the warrior age-grade of the Samburu pastoralists are associated with situations of tension and danger and regarded as a sign of machismo and self-assertion; and among the Abelan tribe of New Guinea, young bachelors sometimes exhibit similar symptoms which are described, not as spiritual intervention, but as 'deafness' (Lewis 2003).

A shaman is someone who is able to go in and out of altered states of consciousness at will. This indicates mental control. Although the regional experience and explanation of illness may vary from one culture to another, there appears to be worldwide acceptance of the major mental illnesses of schizophrenia, manic-depressive disorder, certain anxiety disorders and substance abuse. Although some shamans exhibit behaviour that is different to that considered 'normal' in a particular society, they are not consistently associated with having a mental illness.

Taking a psychobiological approach, James Austin (1999) set out to explore the differences between a schizophrenic episode and the self-transcending state that is experienced in Zen meditation. Devising a table for their comparison according to their observable characteristics, he noted that a Zen meditator in a deep meditative state loses any sense of self-other orientation, perceiving himself to be at one with the universe, while the reverse is the case for a person undergoing a psychotic episode; the self-other dichotomy is concretized and there is no understanding of anything except through the ego. A schizophrenic attack exhibits characteristics that are diametrically opposed to the state of self-transcendence. However, this may not be a good comparison. It might be better to compare a schizophrenic episode with a shamanic trance state or someone who is possessed with a spirit, rather than someone who is seeking a calm, inward-looking state.

Studies carried out by researchers like Saver and Rabin (1997), investigating the differences between culturally accepted religious behaviour and psychotic behaviour such as that displayed by people with schizophrenia, point to the affective result of the experience: mystics almost always describe their experiences as ecstatic and joyful, whereas psychosis sufferers are often confused and terrified by theirs. This is really not a very convincing argument, however, as some mystical experiences might also be frightening. The principal difference seems (to me) to be the way the individual copes in his/her society after the experience. People who are not mentally ill can return to 'normal' and once again function effectively in society, with no long-term ill effects. For the psychotic person, however, withdrawal from normal reality is involuntary and usually highly distressing; they can be very disturbed for many years and sometimes their entire lives; and psychotic states can drive them into progressively deeper states of social isolation. The difference, then, is how they react in society and how the experiences affect their everyday behaviour. Newberg et al. suggest that another difference is that mystical experiences tend to be rich, coherent and 'deeply dimensioned sensory experiences'. In plain terms, they simply *feel* very real.

But is this a sufficiently adequate distinction? I remain unconvinced, and would advocate more research in this area.

Opening the Wrong Doors?

Experimenting with exercises that induce an altered state of consciousness is not without its problems, some of which, instead of ameliorating a mental problem, may serve to exacerbate it. Fred Hanna demonstrates this in his discussion of his own experimentation with opening subliminal doors (Hanna 1997). Hanna began to experiment with self-hypnosis at the age of sixteen, and, realizing that this produced some interesting introspective insights, experimented further with meditation accompanied by repeating the sound mantra 'om'. He continued his lone pursuits without the aid of a teacher, with only advice from books that he serendipitously picked up along the way. He felt, he said, as though he had 'found a secret pathway into the inner caverns of the mind and self' (p. 100). During his meditations he experienced 'intensely vivid scenes ranging from galaxies to elaborate patterns and surreal landscapes' (p. 100), all of which he found most enjoyable. He began, he says, to understand the meaning of Upanishadic phrases such as 'the One without a second' and 'Thou art That', feeling that he had achieved a state of transcendence that revealed to him the core of reality. He felt that he had opened a door that enabled him to 'attain a glimpse of a transcendent reality beyond perception of the world', one that could not be accessed by 'mundane cognitive processes' (p. 101). Subsequent experimentation revealed increasingly interesting insights. He developed an exercise that enabled him to relate empathically to other creatures and to see the world as if through the eyes, ears and feelings of other people and animals such as birds. These experiments, however, were not all pleasurable, and he had 'dramatic mood swings, dark nights, and depths' (p. 103).

He came to realize that even though transcendent knowing can take place, there is still the possibility of a person returning to 'narcissistic, borderline, schizotypal, or histrionic traits which often remain untouched' (Hanna 1997: 104). He cites N. Thera (1964: 107, cited in Hanna 1997: 104) as noting that even the highest meditative attainments 'cannot penetrate deep enough into the recesses of the mind for a removal of moral and intellectual defilements'. A key element, notes Hanna, is whether a person's transcendental experience evokes compassion and empathic knowledge of others, and results in reducing one's egocentric preoccupation. Egocentrism and lack of empathy are common traits among people with certain personality disorders. Although Hanna found that the more he delved into his practices, the more empathic he became, he realized that this does not take place automatically. At times he noted a sense of self-aggrandizement, intense and not necessarily positive emotions, and a 'cognitive reorganization'. He came to the conclusion that the sanity of a person depends on whether these issues are adequately confronted and worked through.

Contemporary thinking acknowledges that psychotherapy and psychopharmacology work hand in hand, the one complementing the other in the case of severe mental illness, especially severe psychosis. So it would be unconscionable to say that we should 'do away with' all psychopharmacological medications for patients who fare better and lead more 'normal' lives with them. As Luhrmann writes (2000: 208): 'For patients with serious symptoms [of psychiatric disorders] psychopharmacological treatment is imperative'. On the other hand, some medications are prescribed on an almost ad hoc basis, with little initial time spent with patients to ascertain properly whether or not heavy drugs are called for each time a patient presents, as American psychiatrist Sydney Walker (1996) reveals. The medical profession on the whole is restricted by time and finances, and it is easy to understand (but not excuse) why someone might be prescribed a drug as an intermediary step for managing time constraints in overfilled hospital or psychiatric wards. However, medications do not always work well, and the dosage differs from one patient to another. There is still quite a bit of experimentation occurring with individual patients before arriving at the most appropriate medication and dosage. In some places (in some Australian states, for example), there is a 'revolving door' policy of treatment in psychiatric units, and the person presenting in an extremely disturbed manner will be highly sedated, kept for one or two days, and then allowed to leave. This does not help the long-term treatment of the patient, but serves only as a temporary Band-Aid.

If psychotherapy and psychopharmacology work more effectively together, as has been demonstrated,[9] perhaps other disciplines, such as sociology, anthropology and comparative religion, could also contribute to our understanding of the mind, and how the body affects the mind and vice versa. Anthropologists who are ready to accept and report their own anomalous experiences while in the field are more likely to gain an appreciation of the religious beliefs of the people they study. Such scholars are also more likely to produce innovative new theories (such as Hufford's experiential source theory, and Edith Turner's spirit hypothesis) and so contribute to ongoing theoretical debate. A multidisciplinary approach to questions of spiritual experience, mystic experience and mental illness is now called for, and team research into these types of experiences would shed more light on all aspects of the mind. This is an interesting area of research that involves the interface of science and religion.

Future Possibilities?

There is already a cautious consideration of this kind of approach, and a clinical paradigm shift could occur if psychiatrists were to pay attention to the potential sources of strength in religion and spirituality. The importance of the previously 'forgotten factor' (religious-spiritual) has important implications in clinical practice (Josephson, Larson and Juthani 2000). Historically, psychiatry has been not only neutral, but sometimes antagonistic toward these factors. The father of psychiatry, Freud, labelled religion as a neurosis and a sign of weakness and helplessness. The psychiatric DSM manual,[10] compiled by the American Psychiatric Association, which is widely used as the basis for diagnosis, has been criticized for religious insensitivity, especially with its frequent use of religion as case examples to illustrate psychopathology.[11] Increasing data are emerging, however, to suggest that religious/ spiritual commitments more frequently seem to offer protection against some medical and psychiatric disorders.

Josephson et al. (2000) note that, on the whole, most people in the general population would welcome a more religious or spiritual approach to mental health care. This grass-roots urge for change in the mental health paradigm has influenced mental health care professionals and the subsequent growing literature on clinical issues of psychotherapy and spirituality. Instead of viewing spirituality as evidence of illness, it is often viewed now as associated with preventing illness and monitoring treatment or illness outcomes (p. 534). Personal assumptions, rather than published research, have often influenced psychiatrists' attitudes toward religion/spirituality in the past. This does not mean that psychiatric illnesses are not found among religious/spiritual individuals, but, when large populations of individuals were studied, the rates of mental disorder seemed to be lower among those who were active in religion. However, serious mental illness can also be associated with religiously inspired harsh parenting and abuse, or the destructive nature of some charismatic-led groups, or excessive reliance on a guru/master figure. When religious beliefs are taken into consideration, a spiritual-religious assessment could help the psychiatrist to explore the patient's world view, as long as the psychiatrist is open to a wide variety of expressions of spirituality and not using his/her own beliefs as a baseline measure of religious beliefs.

The article by Josephson et al. (2000) is useful for its discussion of spiritual approaches in psychiatric practice, especially its emphasis on the psychiatrist's subjective approach to religion/spirituality and its influence on the way s/he carries out treatment of the patient. In fact, religion and spirituality have now entered the domain of some psychiatric practices, and there is more recognition of the need for psychiatrists-in-training to be aware of these factors in both assessment and treatment of patients.

The relation between certain regions of the human brain and incidence of aggressive and violent acts is being discussed in some scientific circles.[12] Given that there are techniques for moving into an altered state of consciousness, might the introduction of such techniques, as well as meditation, help people with mental problems?

Contemplating the notion of inspiration and mental health concerns, Hart ponders the question of whether patients exhibiting depression, anxiety, alienation and confusion are suffering from a lack of inspiration (1997: 63). If this is so, we might take Hart's musing further and ask: might it be possible not only to 'cultivate inspiration', by employing the prelude to inspiration: setting, set and symbols, but also, with the help of psychiatric medicine, to alleviate some especially debilitating mental illnesses. A thorough investigation of the physical, mental and spiritual aspects of each individual might well be considered before contemplating the long-term use of drugs without taking into account other possibilities.

In 2003, the US-based Metanexus Institute on Religion and Science instigated a multidisciplinary, multimillion dollar research programme, The Spiritual Transformation Scientific Research Program, which is investigating diverse spiritual phenomena, with the focus on spiritual transformation. Its principal investigator and president, Solomon H. Katz, states that this innovative project 'provides a fresh model for scholars who are asking questions and seeking answers to explain phenomena that are as old as antiquity and as new as tomorrow', one that is (refreshingly) scientifically rigorous, yet 'freed from the prejudices of the past'.[13] This is truly a multidisciplinary project, with researchers from anthropology, sociology, psychology, psychiatry, pharmacology, neurology, biology, neuroscience and religious studies. The response of 470 qualified letters-of-intent from scholars across the globe and from top international research institutions shows evidence of the important trend towards taking this type of study seriously.

We are now living in very stimulating times with regard to the interface of science and spirituality. New technologies, and more open attitudes to all sorts of possibilities, may provide us with some very exciting discoveries on the mind, the body, the senses, consciousness and age-old questions that humans have pondered for millennia. Further multidisciplinary research into the mind, body and consciousness that involves the medical profession, anthropologists and religious specialists would not only be of great benefit, but, it seems to me, will be imperative in the future. This multidisciplinary team might also include physicists. Scientists are now saying that the universe we live in is not the only one, that there could be an infinite number of universes (a multiverse), each with its own law of physics. In a documentary aired on BBC Radio on 14 February 2002, this new scientific possibility was discussed by several American physicists.[14] The most recent thinking is that there are parallel universes, other spatial dimensions and 'membranes'. Our universe could be 'just one bubble floating in an ocean of other bubbles' (Michio Kaku, City University of New York). What is intriguing in all this is the notion that atomic particles like electrons have the possibility of, in some sense, being in more than one place at one time. It is even possible that the particles do not only exist in our universe, but 'flit into existence in other universes as well', and there are 'an infinite number of these parallel universes, all of them slightly different' (Dilly Barlow, Programme Narrator). Alan Guth, of Massachusetts Institute of Technology, suggests that superimposed on top of the universe that we know is an alternative universe where Elvis Presley could still be alive.

All the matter in the universe is connected to one vast structure: a membrane. Called the membrane theory, or M theory, it is such an enigmatic idea that these scientists refer to the M as standing, not only for membrane, but for the magic, mystery or madness of the universe. Included in M theory is the notion of an eleventh dimension 'where all the rules of common-sense are abandoned' (Dilly Barlow). The eleventh dimension is 'only one trillionth of a millimeter from every point in our 3-dimensional world – closer than the clothes on our bodies' (Paul Steinhardt, Princeton University).

The other universes, adds Michael Duff of the University of Michigan, are parallel to ours, may be quite close to ours, but we will never be aware of them. They may even have different laws of nature operating. The parallel universes move through the eleventh dimension like waves. Michio Kaku of City University of New York, adds, 'some of these universes may look just like ours, except perhaps you're not there'.

These are new and exciting possibilities which undoubtedly will contribute to a merging of science and spirituality in the future. One thing is certain, the body and its senses are at the heart of science and spirituality. We are embodied beings, and although transcendence may be achieved through escaping the body, it still has to escape through the somatic senses. By contemplating such notions and allowing for an infinite number of possibilities, physicists may eventually find a common space with the mystics and madmen of past, present and future – perhaps somewhere in a bubble in the eleventh dimension.

What force governs? My answer at the moment is that there are two worlds, visible and invisible. They tangle with each other in increasingly perceptible ways ... if we have the courage to see.

J.L. Waldron, 1998

Separateness arises from identifying the Self with the body, which is made up of the elements; when this physical identification dissolves, there can be no more separate self. This is what I want to tell you, beloved.

Hindu scripture

Notes

1 Entrances and Exits

1. Entheogens in relation to Alice in Wonderland are discussed in a later chapter.
2. I speak of 'alternate reality' in the singular here, only to point out that it is different to 'ordinary' reality. 'Alternative reality' and 'alternate realities' will be used interchangeably throughout, as there may be many different realities.
3. After Gebhart-Sayer (1985).
4. As this knowledge is only discussed in terms of males, it is unclear whether the same applies to women.
5. Clinical and textual material from various religious traditions and cultures reports a range of such experiences. The *Journal of Transpersonal Psychology* lists a number of these experiences in the preface to each issue.
6. Driving mechanisms may be enhanced by concentration either upon the driver or upon some associated symbolic percept. Modern 'uppers' and 'downers' may also aid in hyper-excitation or hyper-relaxation.
7. See Butler (1970) for exercises using flashing colours to bring about a change in consciousness.

2 Mandalas and Visual Symbols

1. Fechner, cited in James 1982: 50.
2. Thought to be of Hebrew origin, its development through history has incorporated elements from Egyptian, Chaldean, Greek, Persian and Arabian schools of thought, as well as some elements of Christianity.
3. This sounds very similar to the idea of 'thought forms' in Western esotericism. See, for example, Besant and Leadbeater's 1905 book, *Thought Forms*.
4. The initiatic prelude of the Futuhat (I, 51).
5. See sketches on p. 00 of this article.

3 Portals of Sound

1. A Songhay (Nigeria, Africa) sorcerer speaking to Paul Stoller (Stoller and Olkes 1987: 560).

2. Music as part of a mystical technique was represented in ecstatic Kabbalah and is still employed by some Kabbalists today. See Idel (1997).

3. The use of specific sound beats is being used by some therapists to produce a range of beneficial effects, such as improved sleep, stress-reducing relaxation and expanded learning states. F. Holmes Atwater, who is Research Director of the Monroe Institute in the USA, writes that to induce beneficial altered states, a chief method used at the Monroe Institute is to place an individual in an environment of greatly reduced stimulation for short periods, usually less than two hours. Here they may lie on a bed in a dark, soundproofed room or float in a buoyant liquid at skin temperature. During such short periods of restricted sensory impetus, introduced sensory information, such as aroma, colour, music, touch and binaural beating, can lead to alterations in consciousness.

4. Western occultism is based on the Neoplatonic notion that all things, forces and beings find expression in the universe (which is an infinite web of interwoven forces) by means of vibrations.

5. It is easy to see why people who have mental disorders might be attracted to occult groups. However, occultists insist that there is a very big difference between people who hallucinate and hear voices involuntarily, and those who voluntarily project images, sounds, and so on, under the control of the waking self.

6. The poet Tennyson experimented with the repetitive chanting of his own name and found that it enabled him to enter a trance state, and during this state he became aware of some greater aspect of himself. He used this experience as the basis for his poem 'The Ancient Sage'. In this poem the Sage goes on to say that he found himself with a body of a different order, and with a consciousness which far transcended his waking mind.

4 Dance and Movement

1. Body posture is proposed by Felicitas Goodman (1990) to be extremely relevant to experiences in altered states of consciousness cross-culturally. Searching through ethnographic data on postures depicted in art, photos and statuettes, she postulates that a combination of posture, meditation and drumming/rattling can lead to specific trance experiences, and that these experiences can be repeated by others, even those outside the particular culture in which they are found.

2. John 13:14–15 is the biblical passage that forms the basis for the foot-washing ritual: 'If I then, your Lord and Master, have washed your feet; ye also ought to wash one another's feet. For I have given you an example, that ye should do as I have done to you.'

3. Although the two key terms, *!kia* and *n/um* have been translated into English, as trance (*!kia*) and energy (*n/um*), Richard Katz feels that the English terms are inadequate for expressing their full meaning.

5 Tactile Portals: Negotiating the Demands of the Flesh

1. Aristotle Text 20: *On the Soul*, Book II, ch. 2, para. 19, translated by W.D. Ross.
2. Bardon refers specifically to Papunya art, but this notion is found throughout Australia.
3. Interestingly, the term 'shimmering' is used in Temiar (Malaysia) shamanistic discourse. When the interpenetration of human and spirit occurs during Temiar healing ceremonies, it is aesthetically marked by 'shimmering' in the visual, kinetic, tactile and auditory channels. Shimmering things exist at the boundary between the visual and the kinetic. Things that shimmer attract and activate the spirits. See Roseman 2005: 219, 221.
4. Watson challenges art historians not to ignore the sense of touch and sound in their appreciation of Aboriginal art, and its connection with a spirituality that involves the intrinsic interpenetration of humans, land, and spirit.
5. All these authors have commented on a variety of stimuli, including pain, to achieve ASCs in religious experience.
6. The Sun Dance originated around 1700 and spread throughout the North American Plains tribes, reaching its height in the 1800s. The ceremony brought tribes together and was an annual event of both social and religious significance. From anthropological accounts, it seems that tribes in different regions had more or less the same format for the ceremony. See Spencer (1977), *The Native Americans*, for the Teton and the Oglala; Lincoln (1994) for the Lakota; Jilek (1989) for the Sioux. The ceremony was banned by the American Bureau of Indian Affairs in the 1880s, but persisted in secret until the early 1930s, when Sun Dance celebrations were permitted, but not the piercing. It was revived in the early 1960s by various Native American groups, and in 1972 American Indian activists danced and pierced at a Lakota Sun Dance held on the Pine Ridge Reservation. The formerly outlawed practice of self-mortification was included in the revived ceremonies.
7. See Hullet (1981), and also some of the many websites on this festival, for example, http://www.geovision.com.my/malaysia/general/religious/festivals/thaipusam.html (accessed 7 June 2006).
8. The Hindu god of war, and the youngest son of Lord Siva, in his aspect of the six-headed, twelve-armed Murugan, or Karttikeya, Subramaniam is the universal granter of wishes.
9. http://allmalaysia.info/msiaknow/festivals/thaipusam/ (accessed 7 June 2006).
10. Wavell, at www.bmeworld.com/flesh/altered/alterkavadi/kavadiintro.html (accessed 7 June 2006).
11. This paragraph is attributed to Collen Ward, *Ethos*, Winter 1984, at www.bmeworld.com/flesh/altered/alterkavadi/kavadiintro.html (accessed 7 June 2006).

12. http://www.bodyplay.com/fakir/index.htm (accessed 7 June 2006).
13. http://www.bodyplay.com/fakirart/index.htm (accessed 7 June 2006). See also Favazza (1996) and Steele (1996).
14. http://www.bodyplay.com/hooks.htm (accessed 7 June 2006).
15. Ibid.
16. Personal communication with an Indian woman who lives in Australia but makes visits to India once a year.
17. The negative consequences of this force are imposed on women, who have been blamed in some manner, historically and cross-culturally, for its power and its effect on society as a whole.
18. This information is taken from 'Celibacy of the Clergy', Catholic Encyclopedia: http://www.newadvent.org/cathen/03481a.htm (accessed 7 June 2006).
19. See St John of the Cross, *Noche oscura*, I, 9: ii, 5, and *Subida*, III, 2.

6 Olfactory and Gustatory Portals

1. Quoted in Howes (1991b: 129).
2. Perhaps 'odour-denying' is misleading, as the media bombards us with messages that remind us of the presence of undesirable smells, offering products that are designed to smother natural bodily odours and replace them with sweet-smelling perfumes. 'Odour-suppressing' is probably a more appropriate term, as, conscious of 'bad' natural smells, we attempt to conceal them with the use of unnatural cover-ups, from deodorants to mouth washes for our bodies, and cleaning products for our domiciles.
3. No reference is made to women in this account.
4. Sensual contact with a sacred object, whether a sculpted figure, a painting, a mandala, a stupa, a holy man, a tree, a mount, a book or a substance (among other things) is also looked upon as giving hope to believers.
5. The others are: mandala: the diagram which liberates by seeing; mantra: the syllables which liberate by hearing; mudra: which liberates by touching; and consciousness transference: which liberates by thinking. See Tulku (1986: 242, n. 152). In *The Tibetan Book of the Dead*, there is mention of a six-part classification of liberation which includes seeing, hearing, wearing, tasting, touching and remembering (thinking). The latter (remembering/thinking) defines 'ordinary' mental reference to the Enlightened One, Buddhas, Bodhisattvas and also consciousness transference. For more on this, see Mullin (1986).
6. Utterance 269, cited in Nielsen (1986: 9).
7. Prayer of divination priest, cited in Nielsen (1986: 31).
8. For example, Northern Nigeria; Vanuatu, Melanesia.
9. This is the case in the Zar spirit possession cult of Northern Sudan.
10. Zar cult in Northern Sudan.

11. As in the Zar spirit possession cult of Northern Sudan.
12. In ancient Egyptian funerary rites, the corpse was anointed with fragrant oils to ensure the dead person's passage into the underworld (Forty 1999: 68).
13. Aboriginal Australians and the Ongee of the Andaman Islands. In north-east Arnhem Land (Australia), for example, yellow, red or white clay is painted on the body of the living to protect them from spirits during a funeral ceremony. See Morphy (1984). The Ongee walk in single file, stepping over the tracks of the person in front of them so as to mix the odours and thus confuse spirits. When the Ongee want to communicate with the spirits rather than avoid them, they paint a particular design in clay on their bodies, which is said to affect the quality of the smell released by the body and even carries 'a coded message' to their ancestral spirits, who will protect them (see Classen 1993).
14. Inayat Khan (1994: 108). Many of the breathing practices can be found in this source, and on the Sufi website, www.nurmuhammad.com/Meditation/Core/naqshbandimeditationillustration.htm (accessed 7 June 2006).

7 Entheogens as Portals

1. Dan, aged nineteen, cited in Saunders et al. (2000: 187).
2. The earliest set of writings that compose the four Vedas, compiled by priests and poets believed to be associated with the early Indus Valley people, in the geographical area that is now known as greater Punjab, covering parts of Pakistan and north-west India.
3. http://www.erowid.org/ (accessed 7 June 2006).
4. Desana women do not take hallucinogens.
5. These terms are used by Humphrey Osmond, who also proposed the word 'psychedelic' in 1956.
6. To view her art, see Glover (1982).
7. Lysergic acid diethylamide – a synthetic drug, though it is found in ergot, a fungus that grows on grains.
8. A commercial street drug.
9. Nelson uses three dimensions: personality, operation (procedures and activities that directly trigger conditions) and the phenomenological dimension (the form of the experience as reported by the experient).
10. Doofs are non-commercial dance parties that are usually held in a bush setting in Australia. See St. John (2001); Hume (2003); Tramacchi (2000).
11. Harner's books might be the first port of call for information on shamanism, along with publications by Carlos Castaneda and Terence McKenna.
12. Though once banned, in the late 1980s, the Supreme Court of Brazil allowed ayahuasca to be taken for religious purposes.

13. Video, *Shamans of the Amazon* (2003), SBS television, Sydney, NSW, Australia. Originally released by Australian Film Finance Commission (2002). Director: Dean Jefferys.
14. http://www.erowid.org/general/conferences/conferences_ayahuasca1.shtml (accessed 7 June 2006).

8 An Anatomy of Reality

1. Gregory the Great was a sixth-century pope and the author of *Dialogues*, which contained discussions of miracles and visions. *Dialogues of Gregory the Great*, 4:50, cited in Zaleski (1987: 89). See Gregory the Great, *Dialogi*, ed. Umberto Moricca (1924), Rome; and Gregory the Great, *Dialogues*, trans. O.J. Zimmerman (1959), New York.
2. What fascinated Strassman (2001: 61) is that the human pineal gland becomes visible in the developing fetus 49 days after conception, which is the moment when there is the first indication of male or female gender, and that the Tibetan Buddhist Book of the Dead teaches that it takes 49 days for the soul of the recently dead to reincarnate. He admits this is logically shaky, but intuitively appealing.
3. Walsh focused on Vipassana, Buddhist insight meditation (which differs from others such as Anapana-sati), observing the breath and concentration meditation (which is single-pointed) in many of his dimensions for mapping.
4. Australian Broadcasting Commission series, *Compass*, aired on 29 August 2004 in Australia.
5. See Vyner 2002 for more details of the published interviews.
6. 'John', late fifties, cited in Saunders et al. 2000: 60.
7. Richard McLean, writing of himself in his book (2003: 171).
8. Thursday 6 May 2004, 'Smell and Schizophrenia', *Catalyst*, Australian Broadcasting Commission (produced by Steve Salgo). An interesting point that was raised in this programme was research that indicates a connection between smell detection and schizophrenia. According to researchers at the University of Melbourne, people with a low score on a 'scratch and sniff test' were more likely to develop schizophrenia. Early diagnosis of schizophrenia might be possible using the sense of smell as a test. See also Brewer et al. 2003.
9. See Luhrmann (2000: 204) for detailed sources demonstrating this.
10. *Diagnostic and Statistical Manual of Mental Disorders DSM:IV:TR* (2000), Washington, D.C.: American Psychiatric Association.
11. This manual has been criticized by psychiatrist Sydney Walker (1996) for other reasons as well.
12. A useful website is Brain and Emotions Research at the University of Wisconsin-Madison: http://www.news.wisc.edu/packages/emotion (accessed 7 June 2006).

13. The Spiritual Transformation Scientific Research Program, 2004, www. metanexus.net/spiritual_transformation (accessed 7 June 2006).
14. Transcript available at http://www.bbc.co.uk/science/horizon/2001/ parallelunitrans.shtml (accessed on 7 June 2006).

Bibliography

Abram, D. (1997), *The Spell of the Sensuous: Perception and Language in a More-Than-Human World*, New York: Vintage Books.

Albrecht, D. (1999), *Rites in the Spirit: A Ritual Approach to Pentecostal/Charismatic Spirituality*, Sheffield: Sheffield Academic Press.

Albright, C.R. (2000), 'The "God Module" and the Complexifying Brain', *Zygon*, 35(4): 735–44.

Atwater, F.H. (2001), 'Inducing Altered States of Consciousness with Binaural Beat Technology', http://brain.web-us.com/inducing.htm (accessed 7 June 2006).

Austin, J. (1999), *Zen and the Brain: toward an understanding of meditation and consciousness*, Cambridge, MA: MIT Press.

Australian Museum (2000), *Body Art*, Mossman, NSW: Outback Print.

Averbuch, I. (1998), 'Shamanic Dance in Japan: the Choreography of Possession in Kagura', *Asia Folklore Studies*, 57(2): 293–329.

Baklanoff, J.D. (1987), 'The Celebration of a Feast: Music, Dance, and Possession Trance in the Black Primitive Baptist Footwashing Ritual', *Ethnomusicology*, 31(3): 381–94.

Bardon, G. (1979), *Aboriginal Art of the Western Desert*, Adelaide: Rigby.

Becerra, L., Breiter, H.C., Wise, R., Gilberto Gonzalez, R. and Borsook, D. (2001), 'Reward Circuitry Activation by Noxious Thermal Stimuli', *Neuron*, 32(5): 927–46.

Beckert, J. (1997), 'Tantrism, Rasa, and Javanese Gamelan Music', in L. Sullivan (ed.), *Enchanting Powers: Music in the World's Religions*, Cambridge, MA: Harvard University Press.

Bell, R.M. (1985), *Holy Anorexia*, Chicago: University of Chicago Press.

Berger, P. and Luckmann, T. (1966), *The Social Construction of Reality*, New York: Doubleday.

Berndt, R.M. and Berndt, C.H. (1993), *A World that Was: the Yaraldi of the Murray River and the Lakes, South Australia*, Carlton, Vic.: Melbourne University Press.

Besant, A. and Leadbeater, C.W. (1905), *Thought Forms*, London: The Theosophical Publishing Society.

Bhaktivedanta Swami Prabhupada, A.C. (1980), *The Science of Self-Realization*. New York: The Bhaktivedanta Book Trust.

Biocca, F. (1997), *The Cyborg's Dilemma: Progressive Embodiment in Virtual Environments*, Michigan: Michigan State University Press.

Bishop, C. (1996), *Sex and Spirit*, London: Duncan Baird Publishers.

Blain, J. (2002), *Nine Worlds of Seid-Magic: Ecstasy and Neo-shamanism in North European Paganism*, London: Routledge.

Blundell, G. (1998), 'On Neuropsychology in Southern Africa Rock Art Research', *Anthropology of Consciousness*, 9(1): 3–12.

Bohm, D. (1965), *The Special Theory of Relativity*, New York: W.A. Benjamin.

Borchert, B. (1994), *Mysticism*, York Beach, ME: Samuel Weiser.

Bourdieu, P. (1977), *Outline of a Theory of Practice*, trans. R. Nice, Cambridge: Cambridge University Press.

Bourgignon, E. (1972), 'Trance Dance', in J. White (ed.), *The Highest State of Consciousness*, New York: Anchor Books, pp. 331–43.

Bowe, B. (1999), 'Dancing into the Divine: The Hymn of the Dance in the Acts of John', *Journal of Early Christian Studies*, 7(1): 83–104.

Brewer, W., Stephen, J., McGorry, P., Francey, S., Phillips, L., Yung, A., Anderson, V., Copolov, D., Singh, B., Velakoulis, D. and Pantelis, C. (2003), 'Impairment of Olfactory Identification Ability in Individuals at Ultra-High Risk for Psychosis Who Later Develop Schizophrenia', *The American Journal of Psychiatry*, 160: 1790–4.

Buber, M. (1985), *Ecstatic Confessions*, ed. Paul Mendes-Flohr, San Francisco: HarperCollins.

Burnham, S. (1990), *A Book of Angels*, New York: Ballantine Books.

Bush, Nancy Evans (2002), 'Afterward: Making Meaning After a Frightening Near-Death Experience', *Journal of Near-Death Studies*, 21(2): 99–133.

Butler, W.E. (1970) [1959], *The Magician: His Training and Work*. Wellingborough, England: Aquarian Press.

Bynum, C.W. (1987), *Holy Feast and Holy Fast: the religious significance of food to medieval women*, Berkeley: University of California Press.

Bynum, C.W. (1992), 'The Female Body and Religious Practice in the Later Middle Ages', in *Fragmentation and Redemption*, New York: Zone Books, pp. 161–99.

Califia, P. (1988), *The Lesbian S.M. Safety Manual*, Boston, MA: Alyson Publications.

Camporesi, P. (1989), 'The Consecrated Host: A Wondrous Excess', in M. Feher (ed.), *Fragments for a History of the Human Body*, New York: Zone, pp. 221–34.

Carroll, L. (1971), *Through the Looking-Glass: and what Alice found there*, London and New York: Oxford University Press.

Celebi, C., 'Sema, the Universal Movement', www.sufism.org/society/sema1.html (accessed 7 June 2006).

Classen, C. (1993), *Worlds of Sense: Exploring the senses in history and across cultures*, London: Routledge.

Classen, C. (1998), *The Color of Angels: Cosmology, gender and the aesthetic imagination*, London: Routledge.

Classen, C. (2005), 'McLuhan in the Rainforest: The Sensory Worlds of Oral Cultures', in D. Howes (ed.), *Empire of the Senses*, Oxford: Berg, pp. 147–63.

Classen, C., Howes, D. and Synnot, A. (1994), *Aroma: the Cultural History of Smells*, London and New York: Routledge.

Clunies-Ross, M., Donaldson, T. and Wild, S.A. (eds) (1987), *Songs of Aboriginal Australia*, Sydney: University of Sydney.

Comphausen, R. (1997), *Return of the Tribal: A Celebration of Body Adornment, Piercing, Tattooing, Scarification and Body Painting*, Vermont: Park Street Press.

Corbin, A. (1986), *The Foul and the Fragrant: Odor and the French Social Imagination*, Cambridge, MA: Harvard University Press.

Corbin, H. (1969), *Creative Imagination in the Sufism of Ibn 'Arabi*, translated from the French by R. Manheim, Bollingen Series XCI, Princeton, NJ: Princeton University Press.

Crapanzano, V. (1973), *The Hamadsha: A Study in Moroccan Ethnopsychiatry*, Berkeley: University of California Press.

Csikszentmihalyi, M. (1975), 'Play and Intrinsic Rewards: a Neuropsychological Model', *Journal of Humanistic Psychology*, 15: 41–63.

Csikszentmihalyi, M. and Csikszentmihalyi, I. (eds) (1988), *Optimal Experience: psychological studies of flow in consciousness*, Cambridge: Cambridge University Press.

Csordas, T.J. (1994), *The Sacred Self: a cultural phenomenology of charismatic healing*, Berkeley: University of California Press.

Csordas, T.J. (1997), *Language, Charisma, and Creativity: the ritual life of a religious movement*, Berkeley: University of California Press.

d'Aquili, E. and Newberg, A. (1998), 'The Neuropsychological basis of religions, or why God won't go away', *Zygon*, 33(2): 187–201.

Damasio, A. (1994), *Descarte's Error: Emotion, Reason, and the Human Brain*, New York: Avon Books.

Damasio A. (1999), *The Feeling of What Happens: Body and Emotion in the Making of Consciousness*, New York: Harcourt Brace.

De Boer, P.A.H. (1972), 'An Aspect of Sacrifice: II. God's Fragrance', in *Studies in the Religion of Ancient Israel* (VT Suppl. 23), Leiden: E.J. Brill, pp. 37–47.

Deacon, A.B. (1934), 'Geometrical Drawings from Malekula and Other Islands of the New Hebrides', *Journal of the Royal Anthropological Institute* 64: 129–76.

Desjarlais, R. (1992), *Body and Emotion: The Aesthetics of Illness and Healing in the Nepal Himalayas*, Philadelphia: University of Pennsylvania Press.

Devereux, G. (1974), 'Trance and Orgasm in Euripides: Bakchai', in A. Angoff and D. Barth (eds), *Parapsychology and Anthropology*, New York: Parapsychology Foundation.

Dhar, H.L. (1999), 'Research on Meditation', *Original Research Articles*, http://bhj.org/journal/1999_4103_july99/original_505.htm (accessed 7 June 2006).

Doblin, R. (1991), 'Pahnke's "Good Friday Experiment": A long-term follow-up and methodological critique', *The Journal of Transpersonal Psychology*, 23(1): 1–28.

Doore, G. (ed.) (1988), *Shaman's Path: Healing, Personal Growth and Empowerment*, Boston, MA: Shambhala.

Douglas, M. (1975), *Purity and Danger*, London: Routledge and Kegan Paul.

Douglas-Klotz, N. (ed.) (1989), *The Divine Dance*, San Francisco: PeaceWorks Press.

Douglas-Klotz, N. (1993), 'Ruth St. Denis: Sacred Dance Explorations in America', in D. Adams and D. Apostolos-Cappadona (eds), *Dance as Religious Studies*, New York: Crossroad, pp. 109–10.

Douglas-Klotz, N. (1997), 'The natural breath: Towards further dialogue between western somatic and eastern spiritual approaches to the body awareness of breathing', *Religious Studies and Theology*, 16(2): 64–75.

Dronfield, J. (1995), 'Subjective Vision and the Source of Irish Megalithic Art', *Antiquity*, 69: 539–49.

Dronfield, J. (1996), 'Entering Alternative Realities: Cognition, Art and Architecture in Irish Passage-tombs', *Cambridge Archaeological Review*, 6: 37–72.

Drury, N. (1988), *Pan's Daughter: The Strange World of Rosaleen Norton*, Sydney: Collins.

Eck, D.L. (1985), *Darsan: Seeing the Divine Image in India*, Chambersburg, PA: Anima Books.

Ellis, C. (1984), 'Time Consciousness of Aboriginal Performers', in J. Kassler and J. Stubington (eds), *Problems and Solutions: Occasional Essays in Musicology presented to Alice M. Moyle*, Sydney: Hale and Iremonger.

Ellis, C. (1985), *Aboriginal Music: Education for Living: Cross-cultural Experiences from South Australia*, St Lucia: University of Queensland Press.

Ellis, C. (1997), 'Understanding the Profound Structural Knowledge of Central Australian Performers from the Perspective of T.G.H. Strehlow', in D. Hugo (ed.), Strehlow Research Centre Occasional Paper no. 1, Alice Springs: Strehlow Centre Board.

Erlmann, V. (2004), 'But What of the Ethnographic Ear? Anthropology, Sounds, and the Senses', in V. Erlmann (ed.), *Hearing Cultures: Essays on sound, listening and modernity*, Oxford: Berg, pp. 1–20.

Ernst, C.W. and Lawrence, B.B. (2002), *Sufi Martyrs of Love: the Chishti Order in South Asia and Beyond*, New York: Palgrave MacMillan.

Evans, S. (2002), 'The Scent of a Martyr', *Numen*, 49(2): 193–211.

Faivre, A. (1995), 'Introduction', in A. Faivre and J. Needleman (eds), *Modern Esoteric Spirituality*, New York: Crossroad.

Faure, B. (1998), *The Red Thread: Buddhist approaches to sexuality*, Princeton, NJ: Princeton University Press.

Favazza, A.R. (1996), *Bodies under Siege: self-mutilation and body modification in culture and psychiatry*, Baltimore, MD: Johns Hopkins University Press.

Favret-Saada, J. (1980), *Deadly Words: Witchcraft in the Bocage*, Cambridge: Cambridge University Press.

Fazeldean, M. (1987), 'Aboriginal and Christian Healing', in G.W. Trompf (ed.), *The Gospel is Not Western: Black Theologies from the Southwest Pacific*, Maryknoll, NY: Orbis Books.

Feld, S. (1982), *Sound and Sentiment: Birds, Weeping, Poetics, and Song in Kaluli Expression*, Philadelphia: University of Pennsylvania Press.

Feld, S. (1991), 'Sound as a Symbolic System: The Kaluli Drum', in D. Howes (ed.), *The Varieties of Sensory Experience: A Sourcebook in the Anthropology of the Senses*, Toronto: Toronto University Press, pp. 79–99.

Finke, R.A. (1980), 'Levels of equivalence in imagery and perception', *Psychological Review*, 87: 113–32.

Finnegan, R. (2002), *Communicating: the Multiple Modes of Human Interconnection*, London: Routledge.

Flynn, M. (1996), 'The Spiritual Uses of Pain in Spanish Mysticism', *Journal of the American Academy of Religion*, LXIV(2): 257–78.

Foltz, T. (in press), 'Drumming and Re-enchantment: Creating Spiritual Community', in L. Hume and K. McPhillips (eds), *Popular Spiritualities: the politics of contemporary enchantment*, Aldershot: Ashgate.

Forty, J. (1999), *Mythology: A Visual Encyclopedia*, London: PRC Publishing Ltd.

Gaston, A.-M. (1982), *Siva in Dance, Myth and Iconography*, Delhi: Oxford University Press.

Gear, R.W., Aley, K.O. and Levine, J.D. (1999), 'Pain-induced analgesia mediated by mesolimbic reward circuits', *The Journal of Neuroscience*, 19: 7175–81.

Gebhart-Sayer, A. (1985), 'The Geometric Designs of the Shipibo-Conibo in Ritual Context', *Journal of Latin American Lore*, 11(2): 143–75.

Geels, A. (1996), 'A Note on the Psychology of Dhikr: The Halveti-Jerrahi Order of Dervishes in Istanbul', *The International Journal for the Psychology of Religion*, 6(4): 229–51.

Geertz, C. (1973), *The Interpretation of Cultures*, New York: Basic Books.

Gell, A. (1977), 'Magic, Perfume, Dreams', in I.M. Lewis (ed.), *Symbols and Sentiments: cross-cultural studies in symbolism*, London: Academic Press, 25–38.

Gellhorn, E. and Kiely, W.F. (1972), 'Mystical States of Consciousness: Neurophysiological and Clinical Aspects', *Journal of Nervous and Mental Diseases*, 154: 399–405.

Gibson, E.J. (1969), *Principles of Perceptual Learning and Development*, New York: Appleton-Century-Crofts.

Glover, W. (1982), *The Art of Rosaleen Norton*, Sydney: Walter Glover.

Glucklich, A. (1998), 'Sacred Pain and the Phenomenal Self', *Harvard Theological Review*, 9(14): 389–94.

Gombrich, R. and Obeysekere, G. (1988), *Buddhism Transformed: Religious Change in Sri Lanka*, Princeton, NJ: Princeton University Press.

Goodman, F. (1990), *Where Spirits ride the Wind: trance journeys and other ecstatic experiences*, Bloomington: Indiana University Press.

Gouk, P. (2000), 'Introduction', in P. Gouk (ed.), *Musical Healing in Cultural Contexts*, Aldershot: Ashgate.

Gouk, P. (2004), 'Raising Spirits and Restoring Souls: Early Modern Medical Explanations for Music's Effects', in V. Erlmann (ed.), *Hearing Cultures: Essays on sound, listening and modernity*, Oxford: Berg, pp. 87–105.

Goulet, J.-G. (1994a), 'Dreams and Visions in Other Lifeworlds', in D.E. Young and J.-G. Goulet (eds), *Being Changed by Cross-Cultural Encounters*, Peterborough, Ontario: Broadview Press, pp. 16–38.

Goulet, J.-G. (1994b), 'Ways of Knowing: Towards a Narrative Ethnography of Experiences among the Dene Tha', *Journal of Anthropological Research*, 50: 113–39.

Govinda, Llama Anagarika (1973) [1960], *Foundations of Tibetan Mysticism*, London: Rider and Co.

Govindan, S.V. (2005), 'Ayurvedic Medicine and the History of Massage', in C. Classen (ed.), *The Book of Touch*, Oxford: Berg, pp. 365–8.

Greenwood, S. (2000), *Magic, Witchcraft and the Otherworld*, Oxford: Berg.

Greenwood, S. (2005), *The Nature of Magic: An Anthropology of Consciousness*, Oxford: Berg.

Grindal, B. (1983), 'Into the Heart of Sisala Experience: Witnessing Death Divination', *Journal of Anthropological Research*, 39(1): 60–80.

Grossman, K. and Cuthbert, D. (1998), 'Forgetting Redfern: Aboriginality in the New Age', *Meanjin*, 4: 770–88.

Guedon, M.F. (1994), 'Dene Ways and the Ethnographer's Culture', in D.E. Young and J.-G. Goulet (eds), *Being Changed by Cross-Cultural Encounters*, Peterborough, Ontario: Broadview Press, pp. 39–70.

Guenther, H. (1976), *Philosophy and Psychology in the Abhidhamma*, Boston, MA: Shambhala.

Hall, E.T. (1969), *The Hidden Dimension*, New York: Doubleday.

Hamayon, R. (1996), 'Pour en Finir avec la "Transe" et "l'Extase" dans l'Etude du Chamanisme', in M.I. Beffa and D. Even (eds), *Variations Chamaniques*, vol. 2, Paris: University of Paris.

Hanna, F.J. (1997), 'Revolution at Centerpoint: Divesting the Mind, dismantling the Self', in T. Hart, P.L. Nelson and K. Puhakka (eds), *Spiritual Knowing: alternative epistemic perspectives*, Carrollton, GA: State University of West Georgia, pp. 98–123.

Harner, M. (1973), 'Introduction', in M. Harner (ed.), *Hallucinogens and Shamanism*, New York: Oxford University Press.

Harner, M. (1990) [1982, 1980], *The Way of the Shaman: A Guide to Power and Healing*, San Francisco, CA: Harper and Row.

Hart, T. (1997), 'Inspiration', in T. Hart, P.L. Nelson and K. Puhakka (eds), *Spiritual Knowing: alternative epistemic perspectives*, Carrollton, GA: State University of West Georgia, pp. 49–67.

Harvey, E. (2002), *Sensible Flesh: On Touch in Early Modern Culture*, Philadelphia: University of Pennsylvania Press.

Harvey, G. (in press), 'Discworld and Otherworld: The Imaginative Use of Fantasy Literature among Pagans', in L. Hume and K. McPhillips (eds), *Popular Spiritualities: the politics of contemporary enchantment*, Aldershot: Ashgate.

Harvey, S.A. (1998), 'St. Ephrem on the scent of salvation', *Journal of Theological Studies*, April, 49(1): 109–29.

Helminski, C., 'Sema, the Turning of the Soul', www.sufism.org/society/articles/sema_camille.html (accessed 7 June 2006).

Herdt, G. and Stephen, M. (1989), *The Religious Imagination in New Guinea*, New Brunswick, NJ: Rutgers University Press.

Hodge, B. (in press), 'The Goddess Tour: Spiritual Tourism/Postmodern Pilgrimage in Search of Atlantis', in L. Hume and K. McPhillips (eds), *Popular Spiritualities: the politics of contemporary enchantment*, Aldershot: Ashgate.

Howell, J. (1989), 'The Social Sciences and Mystical Experience', in G. Zollschan, J. Schumaker and G. Walsh (eds), *Exploring the Paranormal*, Dorset: Prism Press, pp. 77–94.

Howes, D. (1987), 'Olfaction and Transition: an essay on the ritual uses of smell', *Canadian Review of Anthropology and Sociology*, 24(3): 398–416.

Howes, D. (1991a), 'To Summon All the Senses', in D. Howes (ed.), *The Varieties of Sensory Experience: A Sourcebook in the Anthropology of the Senses*, Toronto: Toronto University Press, pp. 161–72.

Howes, D. (1991b), 'Olfaction and Transition', in D. Howes (ed.), *The Varieties of Sensory Experience: A Sourcebook in the Anthropology of the Senses*, Toronto: University of Toronto Press, pp. 128–47.

Howes, D. (ed.) (2005a), *Empire of the Senses: the Sensual Culture Reader*, Oxford: Berg.

Howes, D. (2005b), 'Skinscapes: Embodiment, Culture, and Environment', in C. Classen (ed.), *The Book of Touch*, Oxford: Berg, pp. 27–39.

Hugh-Jones, S. (1996), 'Coca, Beer, Cigars and Yagé', in J. Goodman, P. Lovejoy and A. Sherratt (eds), *Consuming Habits: Drugs in History and Anthropology*, London: Routledge, pp. 47–66.

Hullet, A. (1981), 'Thaipusam', *Geo Australasia's Geographical Magazine*, December–February, pp. 70–97.

Hume, L. (1995), 'Mental Imagery: the Witch's Doorway to the Cosmos', *Zeitschrift für Religionswissenschaft*, 1: 81–90.

Hume, L. (1997), *Witchcraft and Paganism in Australia*, Melbourne: Melbourne University Press.

Hume, L. (2002), *Ancestral Power: The Dreaming, Consciousness and Aboriginal Australians*, Melbourne: Melbourne University Press.

Hume, L. (2003), 'Doofs and Raves in Australia', in C. Partridge (ed.), *Encyclopedia of New Religions: new religious movements, sects and alternative spiritualities*, Oxford: Lion Publishing.

Hume, L. and Mulcock, J. (2004), *Anthropologists in the Field: Cases in Participant Observation*, New York: Columbia University Press.

Hunt, S. (1998), 'Magical Moments: An Intellectualist Approach to the Neo-Pentecostal Faith Ministries', *Religion*, 28: 271–80.

Hutson, S.R. (2000), 'The Rave: Spiritual healing in modern western subcultures', *Anthropological Quarterly*, 73(1): 35–49.

Huxley, A. (1971) [1954], *The Doors of Perception and Heaven and Hell*, Harmondsworth: Penguin Books.

Idel, M. (1997), 'Conceptualizations of Music in Jewish Mysticism', in L.E. Sullivan (ed.), *Enchanting Powers*, Cambridge, MA: Harvard University Press, pp. 159–88.

Inayat Khan, Hazrat (1991), *Sufi Teachings: The Art of Being*, vol. VIII (*Sufi Message*), Shaftesbury: Element Books.

Inayat Khan, Hidayat (1994), *Sufi Teachings: Lectures from Lake O'Hara*, Victoria: Ekstasis Editions.

Irwin, H.J. (1985), 'Parapsychological Phenomena and the Absorption Domain', *The Journal of the American Society for Psychical Research*, 79: 1–11.

Isherwood, C. (1965), *Ramakrishna and His Disciples*, New York: Simon & Schuster.

Jackson, P. (2004), *Inside Clubbing: Sensual Experiments in the Art of Being Human*, Oxford: Berg.

James, W. (1982) [1902], *The Varieties of Religious Experience*, New York: Penguin Books.

Janzen, J.M. (2000), 'Theories of music in African *ngoma* healing', in P. Gouk (ed.), *Musical Healing in Cultural Contexts*, Aldershot: Ashgate, pp. 44–66.

Jilek, W.G. (1989), 'Therapeutic Use of Altered States of Consciousness in Contemporary North American Indian Dance Ceremonials', in C.A. Ward (ed.), *Altered States of Consciousness and Mental Health: a cross-cultural perspective*, London: Sage, pp. 167–85.

Josephson, A., Larson, D. and Juthani, N. (2000), 'What's Happening in Psychiatry Regarding Spirituality?', *Psychiatric Annals*, 30(8): 533–41.

Katz, R. (1976), 'Education for Transcendence: !Kia-Healing with the Kalahari !Kung', in R. Lee and I. De Vore (eds), *Kalahari Hunter-Gatherers: Studies of the !Kung San and their Neighbours*, Cambridge, MA: Harvard University Press.

Katz, R. (1989), 'Healing and Transformation: Perspectives on Development, Education, and Community', in C.A. Ward (ed.), *Altered States of Consciousness and Mental Health: a cross-cultural perspective*, London: Sage, pp. 207–27.

Kornfield, J. (1994), *A Path with Heart: A guide through the perils and promises of spiritual life*, London: Rider.

Larsen, S. (1976), *The Shaman's Doorway: Opening the Mythic Imagination to Contemporary Consciousness*, New York: Harper and Row.

Laski, M. (1961), *Ecstasy: A Study of some Secular and Religious Experiences*, London: Cresset Press.

Laughlin, C.D. (1994), 'Psychic Energy and Transpersonal Experience: A biogenetic structural account of the Tibetan Dumo Yoga Practice', in D.E. Young and J.-G. Goulet (eds), *Being Changed by Cross-Cultural Encounters*, Peterborough, Ontario: Broadview Press, pp. 99–134.

Laughlin, C.D., McManus, J. and d'Aquili, E.G. (1992), *Brain, Symbol and Experience: toward a neurophenomenology of human consciousness*, New York: Columbia University Press.

Leavitt, J. (1996), 'Meaning and Feeling in the Anthropology of Emotions', *American Ethnologist*, 23: 514–39.

Lee, S.O. and McCurdy, J.C. (1985), *Zen Dance – Meditation in Movement*, Seoul, Korea: Seoul International Publishing House.

Leeuw, Gerardus van der (1963), *Sacred and Profane Beauty: the Holy in Art*, New York: Rhinehart and Winston.

Lester, R. (1995), 'Embodied Voices: Women's Food Asceticism and the Negotiation of Identity', *Ethos*, 23(2): 187–222.

Letcher, A. (in press), 'There's Bulldozers in the Fairy Garden: Re-enchantment Narratives within British Eco-Paganism', in L. Hume and K. McPhillips (eds), *Popular Spiritualities: the politics of contemporary enchantment*, Aldershot: Ashgate.

Levenson, M. and Hayy Khilwati, A. (1999), 'Mystical Self-Annihilation: Method and Meaning', *The International Journal for the Psychology of Religion*, 9(4): 251–8.

Levine, D. (1991),'Reclaiming the Power of Sacred Dance', *The Christian Century*, 108: 334–5.

Levi-Strauss, C. (1970) [1964], *The Raw and the Cooked*, London: Jonathan Cape.

Lewis, I.M. (1989), *Ecstatic Religion*, London: Routledge.

Lewis, I.M. (2003), 'Trance Possession, Shamanism and Sex', *Anthropology of Consciousness*, 14(1): 20–39.

Lewis, T. (1990), *The Medicine Men: Oglala Sioux Ceremony and Healing*, Lincoln: University of Nebraska Press.

Lewis-Williams, D.J. (2002), *The Mind in the Cave: Consciousness, and the Origins of Art*, London: Thames and Hudson.

Lewis-Williams, D.J. and Clottes, J. (1998), 'The Mind in the Cave – the Cave in the Mind: Altered Consciousness in the Upper Paleolithic', *Anthropology of Consciousness*, 9(1): 13–21.

Lewis-Williams, D.J. and Dowson, T.A. (1988), 'Signs of All Times: Entoptic Phenomena in Upper Palaeolithic Art', *Current Anthropology*, 29: 201–45.

Lewis-Williams, D.J. and Dowson, T.A. (1993), 'On Vision and Power in the Neolithic: evidence from the decorated monuments, *Current Anthropology*, 34: 55–65.

Lincoln, B. (1994), 'A Lakota Sun Dance and the Problematics of Sociocosmic Reunion', *History of Religions*, 34(1): 1–14.

Longridge, W.H. (commentator) (1919), *The Spiritual Exercises of Saint Ignatius of Loyola* (trans. from Spanish), London: Robert Scott Roxburghe House Paternoster Rows, EC.

Lonsdale, S.H. (1993), *Dance and Ritual Play in Greek Religion*, Baltimore, MD and London: Johns Hopkins University Press.

Luhrmann, T. (1989), *Persuasions of the Witch's Craft: Ritual Magic and Witchcraft in Present-day England*, Oxford: Basil Blackwell.

Luhrmann, T.M. (2000), *Of Two Minds: the growing disorder in American psychiatry*, New York: Alfred A. Knopf.

MacDonald, G.F., Cove, J.L., Laughlin, Jr, C.D. and McManus, J. (1989), 'Mirrors, Portals, and Multiple Realities', *Zygon*, 24(1): 39–64.

Mackinlay, E. (2000), 'Blurring boundaries between restricted and unrestricted performance: A case study of the mermaid song of Yanyuwa women in Borroloola', *Perfect Beat*, 4(4): 73–84.

Mackinlay, E. and Bradley, J. (2003), 'Of Mermaids and spirit men: complexities in the categorization of two Aboriginal dance performances at Borrolooa, N.T.', *The Asia Pacific Journal of Anthropology*, 41(2): 2–24.

Mains, G. (1984), *Urban Aboriginals: A Celebration of Leather Sexuality*, San Francisco, CA: Gay Sunshine Press.

Marcus, J. (1991), 'The Journey Out to the Centre: The Cultural Appropriation of Ayers Rock', in A. Rutherford (ed.), *Aboriginal Culture Today*, Sydney: Dangaroo Press-Kunapipi, pp. 254–74.

Marton, Y. (1994), 'The Experiential Approach to Anthropology', in D.E. Young and J.-G. Goulet (eds), *Being Changed by Cross-Cultural Encounters*, Peterborough, Ontario: Broadview Press, pp. 273–97.

Maslow, A.H. (1962), 'Lessons from the peak-experiences', *Journal of Humanistic Psychology*, 2: 9–18.

Mastromattei, R. (1988), *La Terra Reale*, Rome: Valerio Levi.

Mazzoni, C. (1996), *Saint Hysteria: Neurosis, Mysticism, and Gender in European Culture*, Ithaca, NY: Cornell University Press.

McCarthy Brown, K. (1991), *Mama Lola: A Voudou Priestess in Brooklyn*, Berkeley: University of California Press.

McDonald, K. (1990) [1984], *How to Meditate: A Practical Guide*, London: Wisdom.

McLean, R. (2003), *Recovered, not cured: a journey through schizophrenia*, Crows Nest, NSW: Allen and Unwin.

Melxack, R. and Wall, P. (1991), *The Challenge of Pain*, London: Penguin.

Merkur. D. (1990), 'Metaphysical Idealism in Inuit Shamanism', in C. Vecsey (ed.), *Religion in Native North America*, Moscow: University of Idaho Press.

Miller, T.R. (1999), 'Mannequins and Spirits: Representations and Resistance of Siberian Shamans', *Anthropology of Consciousness*, 10(4): 69–80.

Milton, K. and Svasek, M. (eds) (2005), *Mixed Emotions: anthropological studies of feeling*, Oxford: Berg.

Moncrieff, R.W. (1967), *The Chemical Senses*, London: L. Hill.

Montaigne, Michel de (1958), *The Complete Works of Montaigne: essays, travel, journal, letters*, trans. D.M. Frame, London: Hamilton.

Morphy, H. (1984), *Madarrpa funeral at Gurka'wuy*, Canberra: Australian Institute of Aboriginal Studies.

Morphy, H. (1989), 'From Dull to Brilliant: the Aesthetics of Spiritual Power among the Yolngu', *Man* (New Series), 24(1): 21–40.

Morphy, H. (1991), *Ancestral Connections*, Chicago: University of Chicago Press.

Morphy, H. (1998), *Aboriginal Art*, London: Phaidon Press.

Moyle, R. (1986), *Alyawarra Music: Songs and Society in a Central Australian Community*, Canberra: Australian Institute of Aboriginal Studies.

Mullin, G.H. (1986), *Death and Dying: The Tibetan Tradition*, Boston, MA: Arkana.

Murphy, M. (1992), *The Future of the Body: Explorations into the Further Evolution of Human Nature*, Los Angeles: J.P. Tarcher.

Nelson, P. (1991), 'Personality Attributes as Discriminating Factors in distinguishing religio-mystical from paranormal experients', *Imagination, Cognition and Personality*, 11(4): 389–405.

Netton, I.R. (2000), *Sufi Ritual: the parallel universe*, Richmond, Surrey: Curzon Press.

Newberg, A., d'Aquili, E. and Rause, V. (2002), *Why God Won't Go Away: Brain, Science and the Biology of Belief*, New York: Ballantine Books.

Nielsen, K. (1986), *Incense in Ancient Israel*, Leiden: E.J. Brill.

Noll, R. (1985), 'Mental Imagery Cultivation as a Cultural Phenomenon: the Role of Visions in Shamanism', *Current Anthropology*, 26(4): 443–61.

Nyanaponika, Thera (1998), *Abhidhamma Studies*, Boston, MA: Wisdom Publications.

Nygren, A. (1932), *Agape and Eros: a study of the Christian idea of love*, trans. A.G. Hebert, London: Society for Promoting Christian Knowledge, and New York: Macmillan.

Obeyesekere, G. (1981), *Medusa's Hair*, Chicago: University of Chicago Press.

Olsen, C. (1994), 'Eroticism, Violence, and Sacrifice: A postmodern theory of religion and ritual', *Method and Theory in the Study of Religion*, 6(3): 231–50.

Orr, D. (2005), 'India in a twist as West "steals" yoga positions', www.hvk.org/articles/0905/129.html (accessed 7 June 2006).

Pagels, E. (1979), *The Gnostic Gospels*, London: Penguin.

Pahnke, W.N. and William, A.R. (1966), 'Implications of LSD and Experimental Mysticism', in C. Tart (ed.), *Altered States of Consciousness*, New York: John Wiley and Sons.

Patterson, C. (1998), 'Seeking Power at Willow Creek Cave, Northern California', *Anthropology of Consciousness*, 9(1): 38–49.

Payne, H. (1993), 'The Presence of the Possessed: A Parameter in the Performance Practice of the Music of Australian Aboriginal Women', in K. Marshall (ed.), *Rediscovering the Muses: Women's Musical Traditions*, Boston, MA: Northeastern University Press.

Percy, K. (2005), 'Adventure and Atrophy in a Charismatic Movement: Returning to the "Toronto Blessing"', *Journal of Contemporary Religion*, 20(1): 71–90.

Peters, L.G. (1981), *Ecstasy and Healing in Nepal: An Ethnopsychiatric Study of Tamang Shamanism*, Malibu, CA: Undene Publications.

Peters, L.G. (1982), 'Trance, initiation, and psychotherapy in Tamang shamanism', *American Ethnologist*, 9: 21–46.

Piaget, J. and Inhelder, B. (1969), *The Psychology of the Child*, New York: Basic Books.

Pink, S. (2000), 'Informants who come "Home"', in V. Amit (ed.), *Constructing the Field: Ethnographic Fieldwork in the Contemporary World*, London: Routledge, pp. 96–119.

Polhemus, T. (1996), *The Customized Body*, London: Serpent's Tail Press.

Prattis, I.J. (1997), *Anthropology at the Edge: Essays on Culture, Symbol, and Consciousness*, New York: University Press of America.

Puccini, V. (1970), 'The Life of Suor Maria Maddalena de Patsi, 1619', in D.M. Roger (ed.), *English Recusant Literature 1558–1640*, Yorkshire, England: Scolar.

Ramachandran, V.S. and Blakeslee, S. (1998), *Phantoms in the Brain*, New York: William Morrow.

Rasmussen, K. (1908), *The People of the Polar North*, London: Kegan Paul.

Rasmussen, K. (1927), *Across Arctic America*, New York: G.P. Putnam and Sons.

Rasmussen, S. (1999), 'Making better "scents" in anthropology: Aroma in Tuareg sociocultural systems and the shaping of ethnography', *Anthropological Quarterly*, 72(2): 55–73.

Reader, August L. III (1995), 'The Internal Mystery Plays: the role and physiology of the visual system in contemplative practices', *Alternative Therapies*, 1(4): 54–63, reprinted from *ReVision*, Summer 1994, 17(1).

Regardie, I. (1979), *Foundations of Practical Magic: An Introduction to Qabalistic, Magical and Meditative Techniques*, Wellingborough, England: Aquarian Press.

Reich, W. (1948), *The Function of the Orgasm*, New York: Simon & Schuster.

Reichel-Dolmatoff, G. (1969), 'El contexto cultural de un alucinógeno aborigin: Banisteriopsis Caapi', *Revista de la Academia Columbiana de Ciencias Exactas, Físicas y Naturales*, 136(51): 327–45, Bogota.

Reichel-Dolmatoff, G. (1971), *Amazonian Cosmos: The Sexual and Religious Symbolism of the Tukano Indians*, Chicago: University of Chicago Press.

Reichel-Dolmatoff, G. (1981), 'Brain and Mind in Desana Shamanism', *Journal of Latin American Lore*, 7(1): 73–98.

Richerson, G.B. and Bekkers, J.M. (2004), 'Learning to take a deep breath – with BDNF', *Nature Medicine*, 10: 25–6.

Ricoeur, P. (1994), 'Wonder, Eroticism, and Enigma', in James B. Nelson and Sandra P. Longfellow (eds), *Sexuality and the Sacred: sources for theological reflection*, Louisville, KY: Westminster/John Knox Press, pp. 80–4.

Ritchie, I.D. (2000), 'The Nose Knows: Bodily Knowing in Isaiah 11.3', *Journal for the Study of the Old Testament*, 87: 59–73.

Roseman, M. (2005), 'Engaging the Spirits of Modernity: Temiar Songs for a Changing World', in D. Howes (ed.), *Empire of the Senses*, Oxford: Berg, pp. 212–23.

Ross, E. (1993), 'She Wept and Cried Right Loud for Sorrow and for Pain', in U. Wiethaus (ed.), *Maps of Flesh and Light: The Religious Experience of Medieval Women Mystics*, Syracuse, NY: Syracuse University Press.

Roth, B. and Creaser, T. (1997), 'Mindfulness meditation based stress reduction experience with a bilingual inner-city program', *Nurse Practitioner*, 22(5): 2151.

Rountree, K. (2004), *Embracing the Witch and the Goddess*, London: Routledge.

Ryan, P. and Ryan, P.J. (1992), 'A Sense of Touch', *America*, 166(13): 31.

Samuel, G. (1990), *Mind, Body and Culture: anthropology and the biological interface*, Cambridge: Cambridge University Press.

Samuel, G. (2004), *Tantric Revisionings: New Understandings of Tibetan Buddhism and Indian Religion*, Aldershot: Ashgate.

Saunders, N., Saunders, A. and Pauli, M. (2000), *In Search of the Ultimate High: spiritual experiences through psychoactives*, London: Rider.

Saver, J. and Rabin, J. (1997), 'The neural substrates of religious experience', *Journal of Neuropsychiatry and Clinical Neurosciences*, 9: 498–510.

Scott, B.J. (1997), 'Inner Spiritual Voices or Auditory Hallucinations?', *Journal of Religion and Health*, 36(1): 53–63.

Shanon, B. (2002), *The Antipodes of the Mind: charting the phenomenology of the ayahuasca experience*, Oxford: Oxford University Press.

Skevington, S.M. (1995), *Psychology of Pain*, New York: John Wiley and Sons.

Smart, N. (1969), *The Religious Experience of Mankind*, New York: Charles Scribner's Sons.

Smart, N. (1989), *The World's Religions*, Cambridge: Cambridge University Press.

Smith, H. (2000), *Cleansing the Doors of Perception: the Religious Significance of Entheogenic Plants and Chemicals*, New York: J.P. Tarcher/Putnam.

Soltau, M. (2005), 'Spontaneous Shamanism: Shamanic Experience at Psychedelic Dance Parties', unpublished Honours thesis, School of History, Philosophy, Religion and Classics, The University of Queensland, Brisbane, Australia.

Spencer, R.F. (1977), *The Native Americans: ethnology and backgrounds of the North American Indians*, New York: Harper and Row.

St. Denis, R. (1939), *An Unfinished Life*, New York: Harper and Brothers.

St. John, G. (ed.) (2001), *Free NRG: Notes from the Edge of the Dance Floor*, Alton, Vic.: Common Ground.

Staal, F. (2001), 'How a psychoactive substance becomes a ritual: The case of Soma', *Social Research*, 68(3): 745–78.

Stafford, P. (1992), *Psychedelics Encyclopedia*, Berkeley, CA: Ronin Publishing.

Steele, V. (1996), *Fetish: fashion, sex and power*, New York: Oxford University Press.

Stephen, M. (1989), 'Self, the Sacred Other and Autonomous Imagination', in *The Religious Imagination*, pp. 41–64.

Stephen, M. (1995), *A'aisa's Gifts: A Study of Magic and the Self*, Berkeley: University of California Press.

Stirrat, R.L. (1977), 'Demonic Possession in Roman Catholic Sri Lanka', *Journal of Anthropological Research*, 33: 2133–57.

Stoller, P. (1989), *The Taste of Ethnographic Things: The Senses in Anthropology*, Philadelphia: University of Pennsylvania Press.

Stoller, P. (1995), *Embodying Colonial Memories: Spirit Possession, Power and the Hauka in West Africa*, New York: Routledge.

Stoller, P. (1997), *Sensuous Scholarship*, Philadelphia: University of Pennsylvania Press.

Stoller, P. and Olkes, C. (1987), *In Sorcery's Shadow*, Chicago: University of Chicago Press.

Stowe, D.W. (2004), *How Sweet the Sounds: Music in the Spiritual Lives of Americans*, Cambridge, MA: Harvard University Press.

Strassman, R. (2001), *DMT: The Spirit Molecule*, Rochester, VT: Park Street Press.

Streng, F. (1985) [1969], *Understanding Religious Life*, Belmont, CA: Wadsworth Publishing.

Sullivan, L.E. (1997), 'Enchanting Powers: An Introduction', in L. Sullivan (ed.), *Enchanting Powers: Music in the World's Religions*, Cambridge, MA: Harvard University Press.

Suskind, P. (1986), *Perfume: The Story of a Murderer*, trans. J.E. Woods, New York: Alfred A. Knopf.

Swain, T. (1993), *A Place for Strangers*, Cambridge: Cambridge University Press.

Taussig, M. (1993), *Mimesis and Alterity: A Particular History of the Senses*, New York: Routledge.

Thera, N. (1964), *The Smile of the Cloth and the Discourse on Effacement: Two Discourses of the Buddha*, Kandy, Sri Lanka: Buddhist Publication Society (Wheel Series N. 61/62).

Thera, N.M. (1975), *A Manual of Abhidhamma*, Kandy, Sri Lanka: Buddhist Publication Society.

Tigunait, Pandit Rajmani (1999), *Tantra Unveiled: Seducing the Forces of Matter and Spirit*, Honesdale, PA: Himalayan Institute Press.

Tillich, P. (1951), *Systematic Theology*, vol. I, Chicago: University of Chicago Press.

Tokarska-Bakir, J. (2000), 'Naïve Sensualism, Docta Ignorantia, Tibetan Liberation through the Senses', *Numen*, 47(1): 69–112.

Tonkin, E. (2005), 'Being There: Emotion and Imagination in Anthropologists' Encounters', in K. Milton and M. Svasek (eds), *Mixed Emotions: anthropological studies of feeling*, Oxford: Berg, pp. 55–70.

Tramacchi, D. (2000), 'Field Tripping: Psychedelic Communitas and Ritual in the Australian Bush', *Journal of Contemporary Religion*, 15(2): 201–13.

Tramacchi, D. (in press), 'Entheogens, Elves and Other Entities: Encountering the Spirits of Shamanic Plants and Substances', in L. Hume and K. McPhillips (eds), *Popular Spiritualities: the politics of contemporary enchantment*, Aldershot: Ashgate.

Trompf, G. (1991), *Melanesian Religion*, Cambridge: Cambridge University Press.

Tulku, Thondup (1986), *Hidden Teachings of Tibet: An Explanation of the Terma Tradition of Nyingma School of Buddhism*, Boston, MA: Wisdom Publications.

Turner, D. (1997), *After Life Before Genesis,* New York: Peter Lang.

Turner, E. (1993), 'The Reality of Spirits: A Tabooed or Permitted Field of Study?', *Anthropology of Consciousness*, 4(1): 9–13.

Turner, E. (1994), 'A Visible Spirit Form in Zambia', in D.E. Young and J.-G. Goulet (eds), *Being Changed by Cross-Cultural Encounters*, Peterborough, Ontario: Broadview Press, pp. 71–95.

Turner, E. (1996), *The Hands Feel It: Healing and Spirit Presence among a Northern Alaskan People*, De Kalb: Northern Illinois University Press.

Turner, V. (1968), *The Drums of Affliction: A Study of Religious Processes Among the Ndembu of Zambia*, Oxford: Clarendon Press.

Van der Leeuw, G. (1973), *Sacred and Profane Beauty: The Holy in Art*, New York: Holt, Rinehart and Winston.

Vauchez, A. (1977), *Sainthood in the Later Middle Ages*, trans. Jean Birrel, Cambridge: Cambridge University Press.

Von Sturmer, J. (1987), 'Aboriginal Singing and Notions of Power', in M. Clunies-Ross, T. Donaldson and S. Wild (eds), *Songs of Aboriginal Australia*, Oceania monograph 32, Sydney: Sydney University Press, pp. 63–76.

Vyner, H. (2002), 'The Descriptive Mind Science of Tibetan Buddhist Psychology', *Anthropology of Consciousness*, 13(2): 1–25.

Waldron, J.L. (1998), 'The Life Impact of Transcendent Experiences with a Pronounced Quality of Noesis', *The Journal of Transpersonal Psychology*, 30(2): 103–34.

Walker, B. (1983), *The Women's Encyclopedia of Myths and Secrets*, London: Pandora.

Walker, S. (1996), *A Dose of Sanity*, New York: John Wiley and Sons.

Walsh, R. (1993), 'Phenomenological Mapping and Comparisons of Shamanic, Buddhist, Yogic, and Schizophrenic Experiences', *Journal of the American Academy of Religion*, LXI(4): 739–69.

Walsh, R. and Vaughan, F. (1980), *Beyond Ego: Transpersonal Dimensions in Psychology*, Los Angeles, CA: J.P. Tarcher.

Ward, C.A. (ed.) (1989), *Altered States of Consciousness and Mental Health: a cross-cultural perspective*, London: Sage.

Watson, C. (2003), *Piercing the Ground: Balgo women's image making and relationship to country*, Fremantle, WA: Fremantle Arts Centre Press.

Watson, G. and J.-G. Goulet (1992), 'Gold in; gold out: the objectification of Dene Tha accounts of dreams and visions', *Journal of Anthropological Research*, 48(3): 215–30.

Wavell, S. (1967), *Trances*, New York: E.P. Dutton & Co.

Weil, S. (1952), *Gravity and Grace*, New York: Putnam.

Whitley, D.S. (1998), 'Cognitive Neuroscience, Shamanism and the Rock Art of Native California', *Anthropology of Consciousness*, 9(1): 22–37.

Wikan, U. (1992), 'Beyond the Word: The Power of Resonance', *American Ethnologist*, 3: 460–82.

Wilson, S.C. and Barber, T.X. (1982), 'The fantasy-prone personality: implications for understanding imagery, hypnosis, and parapsychological phenomena', in A. Sheikh (ed.), *Imagery: Current theory, research, and applications*, New York: John Wiley and Sons.

Winkelman, M. (1997), 'Altered States of Consciousness and Religious Behavior' in S. Glazier (ed.), *Anthropology of Religion*, Connecticut: Greenwood Press, pp. 393–428.

Winkelman, M. (2000), *Shamanism: The Neural Ecology of Consciousness and Healing*, Westport, CT: Bergin and Garvey.

Winkelman, M. (2004), 'Shamanism as the original neurotheology', *Zygon*, 39(1): 193–217.

Wolf, M. (1992), *A Thricefold Tale: Feminism, Postmodernism, and Ethnographic Responsibility*, Stanford, CA: Stanford University Press.

Wulff, D.M. (1997), *Psychology of Religion: classic and contemporary*, New York: John Wiley and Sons.

Young, D. (1994), 'Visitors in the Night', in D.E. Young and J.-G. Goulet (eds), *Being Changed by Cross-Cultural Encounters*, Peterborough, Ontario: Broadview Press.

Young, D.E. and J.-G. Goulet (eds) (1994), *Being Changed by Cross-cultural Encounters*, Peterborough, Ontario: Broadview Press.

Zaleski, C. (1987), *Otherworld Journeys: accounts of near-death experiences in medieval and modern times*, New York: Oxford.

Zolla, E. (1986), *L'amante Invisible: l'Erotica Sciamanica*, Venice: Marsilio Editori.

Zussman, M. (1998), 'Shifts of Consciousness in Consensual S/M, Bondage, and Fetish Play', *Anthropology of Consciousness*, 9(4): 15–38.

Index

Abelan, 101, 159
abode of the dead, 145
Aboriginal Australians, 39, 54, 80, 155, 169
abstention, 94, 99
active imagination, 18–21, 32–3, 138
alchemy, 20–1
Alice in Wonderland, 1
alienation, 151, 163
aliens, 97, 130
alterations in consciousness, 11, 14, 166
Ancestral Beings, 27, 81–2
Ancestral presence, 80–2, 155
angels, 4, 40, 111
anxiety, 116, 123, 153, 159, 163
aromatherapy, 103
autonomic nervous system, 13–14, 40–1, 59
autonomous imagination, 148–9
axis mundi, 87
ayahuasca, 118–20, 123–4, 131–5, 148, 153

balance, 14, 31, 59, 69, 75, 123, 136, 158
binaural beat, 55–6, 166
binding, 47, 65, 93
brain, 1, 13–14, 27, 41, 56, 59, 100–1, 109, 115, 121, 137–9, 140–1, 154–6, 163
breath, 12, 32, 51–3, 62–3, 66, 69, 108, 113–18, 153
Buddhism, 11, 13, 28, 40, 69, 78, 104, 106
Butler, W.E., 6, 20–3, 29, 30–1, 56–8

Carroll, Lewis, vi, 1
cave art, 8
Cave of the Dead, 8
cave/s, 7–9, 37, 58, 68, 134, 145, 160
central nervous system, 12, 100, 137
ceremonial performance, 49, 52, 54
chakras, 19, 150
charismatic healing, 47
Christian
    hymn of the dance, 63, 68

mystery, 78
theology, 16
Christianity, 20, 23, 43, 106, 165
circles, 9, 16, 37, 118, 137, 163
Classen, Constance, 4, 103–12, 121, 135, 169
clever man, 26
clubbing, 127–8
communitas, 128–9, 138
compassion, 19, 28, 151, 161
corporal punishment, 84
correspondences, 21, 29, 33
creative imagination, 19, 21
crystal, 26, 121, 141
cultural
    appropriation, 91–2
    immersion, 15

Damasio, Antonio, 126
death, 8–9, 14, 26, 39, 41, 44–5, 50, 54–5, 63, 81, 83, 87–90, 104, 108, 110–15, 139
    and rebirth, 7, 9, 130, 155
delusions, 156
demons, 43, 58, 106
Dene, 147–8
depression, 131, 151, 156, 163
deprivation, 12, 14, 59, 84–5, 90, 94, 99, 100, 128
Desana, 120–1, 132, 138, 140–1, 169
devils, 47, 86
devotion, 19, 28, 37, 46, 58, 77, 83, 88, 94–6, 101, 104
didjeridu, 49, 52–4
dissociation, 11, 22, 75, 154
divine love, 67–8
diviner, 105, 111
DMT, 139
Doofs, 74, 127–8, 131, 169
doors of perception, 6, 23
dopamine, 101
Douglas, Mary, 61, 110

Made in the USA
Columbia, SC
27 July 2020

14882389R00115